Political Bias Distortion, Based on Philosophical Agendas

Ernest Lawson Jr.

Order this book online at www.trafford.com
or email orders@trafford.com

Most Trafford titles are also available at major online book retailers.

Print information available on the last page.

ISBN: 978-1-4669-2903-6 (sc)
ISBN: 978-1-4669-2902-9 (hc)
ISBN: 978-1-4669-2904-3 (e)

Library of Congress Control Number: 2012906493

Trafford rev. 04/01/2015

 www.trafford.com

North America & international
toll-free: 1 888 232 4444 (USA & Canada)
fax: 812 355 4082

This book is written in an effort to reveal miscellaneous bias distorted renditions of political and personal philosophical attainments related to segmented incompetency pertaining to hypocrisy to achieve satisfaction of agendas.

To succeed in life may be attained through intellect, moral values and capitalizing on individual merit pertaining to gainful employment, and the ability to communicate with dignity. Also, the other choice is through ambiguous bias, distorted lies with malice; that is what makes the United States of America so unique and great; individual choice. Meaning inevitable consequences are not based on presupposed assumptions dictated by others.

God created mankind in His image, which means God had a brain that He passed on to humans for thinking; and for control of the body there are cells within the brain to control every facet of the body. But, the most important brain cell is the one that controls intellectual moral values. If one is aware of this unique ability, and if appropriately utilized, based on heritage is the difference between functional and dysfunctional, related to incompetency. Which in essence a majority voting constituents in two thousand eight, made a miscalculating, dysfunctional, alienating error by electing Barack Hussein Obama as president. Not because he is African American, but because, unfortunately, of his philosophical bias agenda of disdain for the fundamentals that have stabilized our nation, the United States of America. For over two hundred years, and that is our constitution, ratified September 17, 1787 with forty signatures to include President George Washington which declares and stipulates in Article VII of the Constitution which emphatically stipulates: the ratification of the conventions of nine states shall be sufficient for the establishment of this Constitution between the states so ratifying the same. Done in convention, by the unanimous consent of all the states present, the seventeenth day of September in the year of our Lord one thousand seven hundred and eighty seven, and of independence of the United States of America, the twelfth in witness whereof we have hereunto subscribed out names.

I try not to make statements unless there are circumstances to substantiate my analysis. This book is not written to vilify, only to comment on the facts of reality that is politically contrived to desecrate out nation. I choose to expound and dictate in my first book *Political Self Destruction of Most African Americans* published in June of 2010 prior to the primary between he and Clinton, that is he (Barack Hussein Obama) became president, he would politically self-destruct and demoralize the Democrat party almost to extinction; regards to political extortion. What happened on November 2, 2010; even he tucked his tail like a heel hound and chose to lie about his diplomatic cohesions of wanting to empathize with house control Republicans. That is why he chose to extend the tax regard to the wealthy. And if you believe that, you are dysfunctional, also incompetent. He had no choice because Nancy Pelosi was no longer the speaker representative of the house. However, there are his news media alimentary canal licks rallying to his aide; claiming what an accomplishment; comparing him to President Ronald Reagan.

I came along during the time of President Franklin D. Roosevelt. I read about others, and there's none that you can compare Barack Hussein Obama to. It is my opinion that he is the most narcissistic, militant, averse, deceitful, and incompetent ever elected. And this is because of his philosophical behavioral traits of attempting to lure loyal citizens of America into an extorted dictatorship. However the Democrats, with their double standards (particularly for blacks) have misjudged American society based on catering to an incompetent black man to become president. It is an established fact there is nothing wrong with an African American being president. During 1870, Republican Hiram Rhodes Revels from North Carolina became the first black U. S. Senator. Also, Republican Blanche K. Bruce became the first black to serve a full term in the U. S. Senate from Louisiana. Elected 1874 Hiram Rhodes Revels completed the term of Jefferson Davis for one year.

In essence they were American citizens born here. However, when I reference double standards, former Governor Sarah Palin is not expressing willingness to run for any political office as of to date: February 20, 2011. The media has checked the kind of gown that she will retire in and has constantly humiliated her and her family with foolish incompetent derogatory remarks. Yet the Democrats have elected a president of the United States of America; Barack Hussein Obama. Prior to his election, according to the media, was an affiliate of a home grown terrorist who also attended a church for approximately twenty years being advised by his minister that God damned America; that it is controlled by rich white men and their chickens are come home to roost. Also that nine eleven was an inevitable wake up call.

Not to mention Article II, Section 1 of our Constitution specifically stipulates: no person except a natural born citizen or a citizen of the United States at the time of this adoption of this constitution shall be eligible to the office of president. Is it possible we have a violation of this order; by the way if this is not a double standard, I am a jumbo jet pilot?

CHAPTER 2

The Democrats are marred in a political quagmire pertaining to their renditions of distortion and is totally estranged to the circumstances that exist; because of most African Americans philosophical traits. Because approximately ninety five percent of blacks are hostile to the Constitution, and President Barack Hussein Obama is no exception, most blacks assumed when he was elected to become president he was going to impound the wealth of whites and disburse to less fortunate African Americans which is a rendition of reparation simply because they are not familiar with the Constitution. Also, a vast segment of whites are in the identical category. Unfortunately this is a tradition in most black societies. However most Democrats are in utter chaos; stunned with frustration and beginning to act un-socially with malice like a child that has lost a bottle nipple. For instance there are supposedly fourteen Wisconsin State Senators hiding out in another state rebelling to avoid negotiating on Republican newly elected Governor Scott Walker guide lines supported by a majority Republican state senate. To disregard serving their constituency is appalling. In essence, this act of narcissistic incompetency is a disconnection from reality; also morality which is caused by ineptness of adhering to our Constitution which is taught in grade schools that majority rule.

The Democratic administration lead by Barack Hussein Obama is trying to nullify, I am not advocating that everyone should be a constitutional enthusiast, but at least remain loyal to the importance, it is not perfect, but it is all we have as a cohesive nation to rely on regards to morality. Under the guidance of President Barack Hussein Obama, the Democrat party is in attentive disarray, and the worse is yet to come. Older, loyal Americans to the constitution have grown impatient with this emblematic, socialistic, rebellious, narcissistic; Nat Turner clone of a dictator Barack Hussein Obama. This is not the first political Democratic chaos; during the election of 1860, the Southern Democratic delegates departed the convention in Charleston, West Virginia, and the party segmented into three divisions and nominated a candidate for each Democratic division. In essence, there would be three different presidents serving under the same philosophical banner. However, the Republican Party chose one presidential candidate; President Abraham Lincoln opposed to three individual Democratic Party nominees. The Baltimore Democratic sector chose Stephen A. Douglas. The southern Democratic sector chose John C. Breckinridge. The Democratic union party chose John Bell.

Unfortunately there was another deceitful Democratic hoax fiasco, related to African Americans. During nineteen thirty six President Franklin Delano Roosevelt bribed African Americans from the Republican Party that President Lincoln had inspired their loyalty for over seventy years. By authorizing schools to be built through the southern states in order that blacks could educate their children to become an intricate part of society, regards to independence. After the War Between the States, he chose to draft a document authorizing every African American family to be given forty acres of southern plantation's owner's land, and a government mule; unfortunately he was assassinated. His vice president was a Democrat from Tennessee; Andrew Johnson. Once he became president, he rescinded the order and gave the land back to the plantation owners.

President Franklin Delano Roosevelt deliberately bribed African American from the Republican party in nineteen thirty six by authorizing a research team; sent them to the northern states to investigate black voting philosophy. When they returned they advised that blacks voted in a block cohesive. And is influenced by collaborated efforts to other affluent blacks, and they would flock to their success. So he promoted military Colonel Benjamin C. Davis to General and William Hastie to Staff War Secretary; and gave all farmers a relief check due to drought and of course the New Deal; social security. However this was a blunder for him because all southern blacks of the appropriate age received social security and had never paid into it because most were share croppers. Also most did not have a certificate of birth so the government consulted with the oldest white person in an effort to verify. Many of these whites were senile; so in essence there were many blacks receiving social security at age fifty to fifty five years old. So southern whites became truculent and switched to the Republican Party and that is why most southern states are Republican today. Incidentally, these occurrences were over seventy years ago and ninety five percent of African Americans are still alimentary canal licks for the Democrat Party. As of to date, they are spread over every airway possible defending their succulent ideology of radical bias distortion.

Chapter 3

February 15, 2011. First solo news conference of the year: President Barack Hussein Obama.

I watched this phony imposter rhetoric of answers to questions imposed from the news media to President Obama. There was reluctant stammering and gibberish in an effort to distort the guide lines of his budget. He was attempting to pacify regards to congressional modification ad-libbing his assessment what it should be; not what it is. This president is out of touch with the founding principles of our nation; also the existing majority of the population of people. Each time I watch this president, I get the feeling that he is grasping for straws related to disappointing surprises. That is inevitable in his profession which he hasn't the morality to determine. However for this to occur there is a definite explanation and it is intellectually defined with one word; incompetent, which is clarified with this definition:

Incompetent:

(1) Without adequate ability, knowledge, fitness, etc.; failing to meet requirements; incapable; unskillful.
(2) Not legally qualified.
(3) Lacking strength and sufficient flexibility to transmit pressure thus breaking or flowing under stress; said of rock structure and incompetent people etc.; one who is mentally deficient.

In essence, President Obama chose fourteen recipients for the Freedom Medal Ward; which included our former President George H. Bush. I am of the opinion this was orchestrated to humiliate. The award is quite unique and impressive; also honorable. However, my mind is still boggled as to why our former president George H. W. Bush was chosen dead last of the other thirteen recipients, including the chancellor from Germany. During the presentation of the award to President Bush, he joked about him choosing to parachute from air planes at eighty years old. As I recall never once mentioning that he selected the second and only African American serving on the U. S. Supreme Court today; Justice Clarence Thomas.

As a youngster growing up on our farm in Alabama that my great grandfather purchased in 1883, with assigned chores by my parents; to milk cows, slop hogs, plow, chop and pick cotton. My parents and most relatives were not highly educated people; but, utilized common knowledge to appropriately successfully succeed. I recall statements such as to be first in anything you choose to participate in to denote as a success. However to be last is considered to be a failure; and the choices made in life determine which category one belongs when one survives by independent thinking, honest and tasks, but most of all understand your lawful rights based on morality.

I recall very vividly when I became of age to own a bicycle our farm was several miles from town and we were there ginning cotton for profit. I had worked all year, so I requested a bicycle be purchased for me. My mother said fine, but next year. I was completely puzzled because there were funds from the cotton; more than enough to purchase a bicycle. When I was growing up, you never questioned your parent's opinions. If you did it would be open season on your rump. When we arrived back to the farm, after I had cared for the animals, watering and feeding the mules, my mother walked me out back and pointed to over an acre of land and said that belongs to you. You are old enough to plow, chop and pick the cotton. Whatever you earn belongs to you totally. That year after school and weekends, I worked effortlessly and raised a bale of five hundred pounds of cotton. At that time it was worth approximately four to five hundred dollars. She and I went to the Western Auto Store. I chose and purchased one of the most expensive bikes there, which was a Road Master. I rode the bike home; which was several miles away. I was so proud I cried; just to know I earned the right to have and own that bicycle of my choice. These are some of the teachings that are eternally embedded in your heart, brain and mind as long as you are alive. Over time

I began to coordinate the essence of reality based on intellect, morality, dignity, principle, dignity, patriotism, faith, and individual merit which is consistent with our constitution; which many people disregard; which was ratified September seventeenth seventeen eighty seven. Subscribed with forty one signatures, with present and deputy from Virginia, George Washington, being first (not last) which set the political standards for our great nation, the United States of America; which is a precedent globally related to every nomenclature in human society.

President Barack Hussein Obama chose to eradicate this unique tradition when he chose to award former President of the United States of American Republican George H. Bush, to be the final awardable person for the unique Medal of Freedom; indicating that his general consensual for American philosophical traditions are questionable and he is adhering to traits of Marxism. He has militancy for Republicans and it does not matter if you are a former president of the United States. Your place is in the back; as he referred to it at one of his lame radical sadistic speeches.

This insidious deranged child, President Barack Hussein Obama, is a replica of past lunatics; such as an African named Jemmy; year 1739; from Central Africa, South Carolina; organized a rebellious movement of blacks raiding and murdering white people in an attempt to over throw the government and claim America as their own and change to a replica of Africa.

During the year of 1775, a gathering of black terrorists led by William Hunt Captain Jones and General Tye, followed by over approximately nine hundred blacks, entitled the King of England Soldiers terrorized and murdered white citizens for over fifty years.

During the year 1811, a black named Charles Deslondes formed a group of rebellious blacks, over four or five hundred, and began murdering white citizens and burning plantations in the area of New Orleans.

Unfortunately, the most horrendous rebellion was staged by a black named Nat Turner; year 1831. Nat Turner and his band of black rebellious followers staged one of the most historical, horrendous, devastating murdering atrocities of southern whites in American history; around the area of Southampton County, Virginia.

During the year 1800, an African American named Gabriel and his brothers: Solomon and Martin planned a government revolution around Richmond, Virginia. Their plan was to capture the Governor James Monroe, and exterminate all whites. They had recruited over a thousand blacks to their horrible, horrible mission with every weapon available. Fortunately, another black revealed sick covert insurrection. The governor authorized their arrest. They were tried and found to be guilty of conspiracy. Gabriel and his brothers, along with more than twenty five others, were lynched.

During the year 1820, an African American named Denmark Vesey convinced some other black that they were chosen by God preferable to other people and planned a revelation against whites. His plot was discovered and over thirty five along with Vesey were found to be guilty and lynched. Their remains were dissected for public view as a deterrent to others.

None of these rebellious radical leaders, and their followers, were Harvard graduates with law degrees. In essence there were many moral, ethical African Americans; approximately two hundred and seventy two years ago. Unfortunately some allowed themselves to be scammed by rebellious revolutionists such as Nat Turner, Denmark Vesey, utilizing God as their accomplish; especially Nat Turner in 1831 and during recent times; November 18, 1978 it was Jim Jones; the Jamestown human massacre. April 19, 1993; Waco, Texas; David Koresh, leader of a Branch Davidian religious sect; many people lost their lives. Nat Turner of 1831; convinced his followers he saw blood on corn stalks, the thunder roared, the rivers ran red with the blood of whites and that God had chosen him to deliver this catastrophe.

Most appointed and self-appointed leaders use God in an effort to convince. Regards to erroneous deceptions, it is terribly sad and repulsive that after two hundred and seventy odd years some blacks and whites are still obsessed with dysfunctional demagoguery which illustrate vile incompetence. The list of names provided are: Jemmy, William Hunt, Jones, Charles Deslondes, Nat Turner, Gabriel and his brothers, Denmark Vesey and David Walker which were brutal dictators with intentions of exterminating white society in America and change the nation to a replica of the Congo in Africa. Incidentally there was a rebellious group of blacks in the state of Massachusetts called the General Colored Association during 1829. Their representative spokesman was a black militant named David Walker. His demands were not one of us will relent one inch or foot; the white man will have to come and beat us from our America. It is our country more than the white man; which spearheaded the attack on southern whites by Nat Turner in 1831. This resulted in grave consequences for thousands of innocent blacks through the southern states; particularly Virginia, North Carolina, South Carolina, Georgia and New Orleans. The majority of African Americans across the nation deemed Nat Turner to be a hero; for slaughtering whites and symbolized his credibility as equal to President George Washington.

Notably today those identical characteristic sentiments are being suggested for our current president Barack Hussein Obama as a replica of former President Abraham Lincoln and Ronald Regan. However, in essence, the criteria of violence for insurrection for control of others has been abolished in the United States of America; negated by our constitution, adhered to by congress, law enforcement and a major two part system that consists of Democrat and Republican that is under the jurisdiction of "WE THE PEOPLE" at the polling centers throughout America. However there is a unique tradition embedded in American history; that radical socialists never adhered to because of incompetency; such as Nat Turner and others participated in two hundred and seventy odd years ago. There were severe dire consequences including unique demise. The southern militia removed Nat Turner's skin from his body with surgeons and manufactured shoes and purses; and mantle ornaments from his bones.

CHAPTER 4

There were numerous violent incidents that have occurred in past years mostly due to gullibility, related to illiteracy pertaining to whites and blacks. Many utilized violence in an effort to establish notoriety among their peers that were intellectual in regards to individual trade and common knowledge which they were taught to perform with their hands, pertaining to physical traits; mostly during the Iron Age. Most relied on ministers to advise morality, and advice to adlibbed based on assumptions. There were no African Americans Harvard graduates with law degrees; their skills were minimum, related to farming.

Most African Americans, and a huge segment of whites, today are totally unaware of the sequences that are responsible for our nation being the greatest country on God's earth. In essence it has to do with intellectual brilliancy and determination related to morality and understanding the concepts of the founding fathers related to our constitution. There is a large segment of whites and approximately ninety five percent of blacks alienate themselves from which is engraved with the word incompetency; because to ignore something that you are embedded in without choice, which inevitably controls your motivated agendas. This has been the culprit for millions of people for hundreds of years in the United States of America.

During the year of 1957, former F. B. I. Director J. Edgar Hoover indicated that he thought blacks brains were twenty percent smaller than whites; which is totally incorrect and absurd. The brain is structured with billions of neurons that consist of trillions of support cells that control every phase of the human body related to genetic heritage. This is established from your place of origin for instance; African Americans origin began in Africa; so the concept of that genetic heritage is inevitable, which I suspect the majority of people are totally unaware of this unique origin of genetic transparency that dictates behavioral traits based on ethnics.

In an effort to substantiate my accuracy pertaining to genetic controllability I will focus on Africa where my heritage originated. For years I have read, researched and observed documentaries pertaining to traditional African culture simply because I am a heritage of that faction. To understand factions pertaining to genetic controllability, offer the capabilities to alter philosophical traits, regards to agendas, related to moral compromise based on reality; not bias cynicism.

Africa is the second oldest densely populated continent on God's globe that established servitude and owning people for wholesale distribution around the universe for trinkets, blankets, spoons, knives, etc. The refinement of their intellectual artistic taste was to own people which was considered to be an honor; also respected as a sacred privilege regards to assets. This lucrative tradition continued for approximately one thousand years. This barbaric criteria exemplifies crude incompetency; as the worst prolonged improvised agenda ever imposed on people. Unfortunately the southern Democrats adopted that identical aspiration of an agenda. Some became millionaires; such as Nathan Bedford Forrest. Fortunately the U. S. Congress abolished slave trading in the year of eighteen hundred eight. In essence, after being brought to America and introduced to a civilized culture; year sixteen nineteen most blacks practiced their African culture for over two hundred years completely ignoring the ratification of civilization that was in existence prior to their introduction. Three hundred ninety two years later those identical sentiments still exist. Ninety five percent of African Americans do not adhere to our constitution that is the stability of the United States of America. In essence most African Americans are endowed with a heritage, through no fault of their own, that was originated from Africa and passed on through genetic controllability that most blacks are totally unaware of. Those traits that cause a traumatizing culpability in society based on most not being capable of resolving complex conditions regarding their comprehending. They are stubborn to relent for compromise, based on incompetency and once it is proven without a doubt they are incorrect or have been duped with distortion. Their rebellious contempt normally lasts for an eternity with malice and will constantly consult with others in a distorting effort to compensate for lack of intellect. This is a traditional formality with most African Americans to distort reality in an effort to justify for incompetency. They will outright lie to appease for credibility with no regrets in order to accomplish bias philosophical agendas.

The United States of America consists of a diverse society more than any other nation in the universe. Most African Americans are the only ethic that constantly complains about equality. Simply because of a heritage tradition established in Africa approximately one thousand years ago that is congregating around a tribal chief that dictated their philosophical agendas. African Americans are embedded with that genetic controllability that dictates traits. For instance: there were constant tribal conflicts; either to eradicate the tribal chief or the entire tribe because of opposing philosophy regards to traits. Many times the larger tribes would completely eradicate the smaller tribes. This custom was applied mostly in remote areas; larger population dictators resulted to outright genocide. This is not to insinuate that Africa is the only nation that is controlled by segmented brutal dictators that have engaged in hideous persecutions. There are countries that prohibit free speech and if one does not obey could be given life in incarceration or even death.

However this book is not about brutal crimes. It is about genetic heritage controllability embedded in all humans that dictates their philosophical behavioral agendas which a large segment of people are not aware of. Genetic heritage traits are eternal and if one is aware of this unique trait you can make the necessary adjustments to conform relative to moral realty, not bias radical distorted lies. One must be familiar with the country origin of their heritage. For instance, I am an American with African heritage. Throughout this book I am going to relate and equate parallels to centuries of African traditions that are applicable to African Americans today: February 27, 2011; which most blacks will attempt to distort. Beginning with statements quoted during the eighteen sixties by southern Democratic plantation owners: blacks were illiterate, stupid, incompetent and should never be involved in any politics due to their ineptness, regards to candidate and should remain loyal to servitude. During nineteen fifty seven former FBI Director J. Edgar Hoover, stated he believed blacks brains were twenty percent smaller than whites. I pondered these statements because there had to be a reason and there could be two; either racism or reality. I am going to allow the reader to determine based on my analysis.

Let's begin with the eighteen sixties when Africans were brought to America they were hostile, confused and immensely illiterate, totally unfamiliar with speaking English. White began to teach them English, reading and writing. This was a prolonged period of time. During that time they evaluated intellectual comprehension based on their cultural forte and determined most of these people have a dysfunctional trait that is incompetent. In essence that is how their responsibilities were chosen: slave drivers, field workers, home custodies, and animal care takers. There were times they would have sex with the animals.

During nineteen fifty seven, Republican President Dwight David Eisenhower commissioned former FBI Director J. Edgar Hoover to infiltrate the Ku Klux Klan in an effort to demoralize their lynching of blacks. He accomplished this mission and President Dwight David Eisenhower, a Republican, wrote the first civil rights affidavit for southern blacks in eighty five years. Unfortunately, the Democrats were in control of the congress and rejected the bill. However, with the assistance of the military, President Eisenhower integrated schools in Little Rock, Arkansas. FBI Director Hoover became incensed when he learned that blacks were at the Democratic convention in Philadelphia because they could vote in the northern states but not in the south. They were at the convention for Democrats whooping it up while the southern Democratic established Ku Klux Klan where lynching their relatives in the south. Blacks were busy voting Democrat back into office. That is why F. B. I. Director Hoover made that small brain statement. So you be the judge pertaining to this folklore incompetent deficiency.

CHAPTER 5

For approximately four hundred years most blacks in America have survived in an incompetent state of phantasy because most have assumed they are God's chosen people and that the black man will be in control of the universe one day. It is extremely difficult for most blacks to relate to reality because most of their concepts are assumptions based on bias distorted phantasies related to reality. Most are on the opinion that reality should be dissected as a myth and conformed to their satisfaction, related to advantage because they are black and the white man is responsible for their destitution because they do not have civil rights which are incited by Jessie Jackson and Al Sharpton who are surrogates of Congo tribal chiefs ruling in Africa hundreds of years ago.

Let's consider and evaluate the traditions. There were several African leaders in past centuries that planned insurrections to eradicate the stability of our government along with the extermination of all whites instigated by Nat Turner. There were others, but his revolt was the worst in history perpetrated by blacks in American during eighteen thirty one. Can one imagine, according to history, Columbus discovered America in fourteen ninety two civilization was an established culture. Prior to Africans being introduced, in sixteen nineteen, one hundred twenty seven years later, with no American skills, hostile and completely illiterate. By the eighteen sixties, the population of blacks had grown to approximately five hundred thousand in America. During the eighteen hundreds, they began to insert and establish their African genetic traits, regards to identity by the names that they chose related to organizations and institutions. Such as: The African Union Society, The Free African Society, The African Church of St. Thomas, Bethel African Methodist Episcopal, The African Home Society, African Society, The African Masonic Lodge, the African Free School. This indicated more compassion for Africa than America. Our constitution allowed them to organize these organizations and institutions based on liberty and capitalism. In essence most African Americans memoirs to identify with Africa are inevitable which indicates bias distinctions related to Africans and African Americans affiliated with obsessed initiatives for notoriety which is related to bias distorted incompetency.

This is still in existence today. For instance: there was a Miss Black America, a U. S. Congressional Black Caucus that is improvised in some state's government, and let's not forget Black History Month during February, and now our nation has been duped into electing a black president: Barack Hussein Obama; who is supposedly a graduate of Harvard University with a law degree that was a factor enabling him to politically dupe the American citizens into thinking he is an American patriot. He is nothing more than a monolithic surrogate of those rebellious blacks who plotted insurrection atrocities against our nation centuries ago. Only he is attempting to utilize philosophical, diplomatic covert traits in order to attain his ideological renditions of attempted insurrections against America; a sophisticated version emulating past centuries of Nat Turner; in an effort to eradicate our constitution, along with our standards of civil capitalistic liberties, and render our great America into a replica of Africa. Trust me. I have studied the philosophical characteristics of the American people, practically all of my adult life. Particularly African Americans, because most are some of the most bias, distorting, emulating, manipulating, incompetent, liars related to human society. President Barack Hussein Obama is truly politically inept to the fundamental concepts of the constitution that most of the citizens of our nation adhere to.

In essence this book is not written to illustrate demoralization, but to offer an explicit explanation pertaining to reality; related to bias distorted incompetency. For instance: A vast segment of whites in America deserve the Medal of Freedom for inherent political stupidity and vile incompetency for allowing Barack Hussein Obama to seduce them with his tempered speeches simply because he is black and noting he is a Harvard graduate with a law degree. So, inherently a segment of whites began lapping his alimentary canal, weak dizzy and fainting over his political south side of Chicago con deceitful, arranged adaptable speeches, polished for seductive adherence, latent with blatant lies. There is no way this arrogant, narcissistic, incompetent should be president of the most intellectual, moralistic, liberty nation on the Universe. Particularly when he, Barack Hussein Obama, has incited anguish through his speeches by apologizing abroad, instigating that America has something to repent for. His contempt for America is disdaining and compatible to the Iranian regime. This president is in such denial it is very possible he hasn't the slightest inkling of why he was elected president. His charismatic speech deliveries are times deduced with phony rhetoric, but not enough to award him the presidency of the United States of America.

I will attempt an explanation on how he was elected the Democratic primary between him and Hillary Clinton. He being black and Clinton being a white female is one of the most unique parities in the history of America. Many older whites, particularly southerners, would never vote for a woman or a black. Many people had become alienated with the Clintons because of his adultery while being president and she providing defensive excuses; injecting right wing conspiracy engineered by Republicans, as if they gave him the cigar to soak with liquid. In essence, the team of Mike Huckabee and John McCain sabotaged Mitt Romney's chances by complaining about his wealth and he being a Mormon did not help; because of the exploitation publically. This gave McCain the advantage to succeed. Southern voters like Huckabee so they rebelled after the McCain win. For years, McCain had been considered to be a rhino Republican in name only. Not only that, he was still in the Iron Age with the horse and buggy. Millions of older whites were glued to their couches and did not vote. There are approximately thirty seven million blacks in America. Of this population, approximately ninety eight percent supported Obama because he is black. Not only that, for seventy five years they have supported the Democratic Party by a margin of ninety five percent. Of course Hispanics, American population approximately thirty nine million, who vote approximately forty percent Democratic. The combination of blacks, Hispanics and a substantial segment of young; politically inept small dysfunctional brain, incompetent, drug abuse whites is why we have a replica of Nat Turner elected president of the most remarkable nation in the universe; the United States of America.

Suddenly, the noble older whites realize they have a black ass Moslem; most likely born in Indonesia, sitting in the White House that has disdain for America compatible to the Iranian Regime. This president, Barack Hussein Obama, hasn't the remotest idea of how he was elected president.

He has assumed it was his coordinated charismatic benevolent distorting polish rhetoric. Not so!!! He has driven the automobile into the ditch and the tea parties, which are loyal citizens of America that adhere to our constitution will die and go to hell before they allow him to continue driving. Most African Americans are so politically incompetent they assume the tea party consists of all Republicans. Most blacks do not understand the philosophical traits of whites. They assume it is a replica of theirs, which is one of the incompetent, smallest dysfunctional brains globally.

As I have reiterated, Columbus discovered America during fourteen ninety two. Africans were introduced to America during sixteen nineteen, which is a hundred twenty seven years later, uncivilized. Southern whites taught a small segment civility and to read and write. Republican President Dwight David Eisenhower insisted southern educational institutions be integrated; which a tiny segment was three hundred thirty eight years later. Most blacks rejected the idea of attending school with whites. The political and capitalistic control will eternally be established and ratified by whites. Unfortunately for hundreds of years, blacks have not acknowledged this reality. For generations they have, and are still trying the year two thousand eleven; obsessed with uniting an all-black United States of America under their control. They have never attempted to ascertain the heritage of whites and their philosophical traits, other than march and scream with bias incompetent radical racism innuendos. American whites are some of the most intellectual ethnic of people that will adhere to fundamentals related to cohesive arranging. They will determine a serious political problem or personal; ponder and utilize elegance to resolve based on moral reality, not assumptions. Essentially, most whites are loyal to the established principles embedded within our constitution, opposed to blacks. There are more illiterate, incompetent bias white than blacks in our society. There are segments of whites who are militant devious and adhere to radical racism. But, they are not attempting to pursue blacks for some kind of vindictive vengeance because they are black. It is the blacks who are constantly seeking revengeful reparation, regards to vindictiveness based on bias, distorted, incompetent, radical assumptions.

Unfortunately, there is a vast difference related to most black's and white's intellectual perceptions pertaining to the fundamentals of grasping. In essence: related to personnel hiring. A white can apply for employment. Personnel describe his responsible tasks. He will listen intently and is ready for duty because he fully understands what was proposed. A black can subscribe to the same agency for employment, with the same format. He will question the personnel manager constantly about job responsibility and if there is any better job because he is black, proud and a Harvard graduate he should have something a little more to his liking. The personnel manager advises him he will keep his application on file and when something becomes available to his liking he will call him. Over a period of time, then he is not contacted he will turn to bias distorted lies that the company is racist and did not hire him because he is black because they hired a white before him the same day. Unfortunately, this is typical traditional bias traits of most African Americans distorted philosophy.

Whenever there are comprehendible dialogue pertaining to most blacks and you do not allow them to con and distort your abilities to discern; either you are a stupid ass racist white or a black ass nigger trying to be white. Opposed to blacks most whites are a cohesive ethnic of people. They will determine a consequence, political or personal, and ponder what is in the best interest for all who are involved. Pertaining to their discretion; primarily based on moral comprehension of ratified justice of law related to the constitution that is in the best interests for all the people who are citizens of the United States of America.

CHAPTER 6

Unfortunately, a black president has been elected and his bias distorting philosophical traits of an agenda are what is in the best interest for us; meaning blacks demoralizing whites through intimidation. By constantly referring to civil rights and the consequences of slavery which the southern Democrats founded during eighteen sixty six in Pulaski, Tennessee; especially to demoralize, harass and lynch blacks in the southern states. So in essence African Americans reward them today for this tragedy by voting ninety five percent for them to remain in political office. Supposedly, approximately seventeen black were lynched by the Democrats Ku Klux Klan annually for eight years in the southern states during president Franklin Delano Roosevelt's political regime.

Most blacks are a synchronizing genetic ethnic of people who are obsessed with dominance. Unfortunately most are stigmatized with a genetic heritage from Africa; laden with dire incompetence which was brought to America along with the original twenty during year sixteen nineteen. Over three hundred ninety two years later, most have not changed their philosophical agenda of traits. Most adhered to and practiced African traditions for over two hundred years here in the United States of America. As of to date, this genetic controllability, faddish devotion still exist and will never cease. In fact, it has been encouraged with malice to sabotage the United States of America along with our moral values and capitalistic liberty. Slavery never would have existed if blacks had not become so rebellious, violent and belligerent. Whites had no other choice other than retaliate with brute force, not because they were black, but to prevent anarchy.

Most citizens of America, black and white, are totally inept to the traditions of blacks in America attempting to sabotage America and claim as their own. Beginning in seventeen thirty nine through eighteen thirty one, they organized rebellious armies of blacks, antagonizing and murdering white; raiding plantations for over fifty years with the intent of eradicating all whites and organizing their own form of Congo ideology style of control in the southern states. One of the first rebellions began during the year of seventeen thirty nine instituted along the Stone River in South Carolina, incited by former African Congolese soldiers brought from Africa to America. They implemented military ranks, flying African color flags. The South Carolina governor implemented the colonial militia and they were defeated. After the South Carolina fiasco, harsh penalties for blacks were implemented; such as it was considered to be a misdemeanor for white to eradicate blacks and any black caught inciting a revolt was lynched.

Chronological records of significant events in regards to history are invaluable. History is repetitious pertaining to people; although time has generated a different scenario pertaining to agendas. However, the philosophical traits that surrogates adhere to are an identical rendition; unfortunately the same intent is inevitable. Over time they have trained themselves to be extremely covert culprits because of their intellectual abilities to decipher the incompetency of others; utilizing amiable deceitful diplomacy. Even to the events of change in dialect; to synchronize with body language in an effort to impress they are qualified. When it is nothing more than a formulated act of dissertations to accomplish a mission, regards to desecrating the moral fabric of the United States of America.

To implement revolutionist doctrines, regards to dictating standards opposed to our constitution; meaning blacks demoralizing whites in an effort for socialistic black control of America. This is President Barack Hussein Obama's obsessed agenda. Trust me; unfortunately he has a small bias dysfunctional brain that is embedded with incompetency. I suspect he has assumed the combination of blacks, Hispanics and a segment of political incompetent whites elected him to the presidency. Unfortunately he has assumed this is his opportunity to get revenge at the rich whites who control this country and bring their chickens home to roost by eradicating the moral principles America was established on; meaning our constitution and the Declaration of Independence ratified with fifty six signatures July

04, 1776. The Constitution's forty signatures ratified September 17, 1787. These are some of the most precious standards on God's earth and will never be abolished for a narcissistic, radical imposter, lying, incompetent, socialistic dictator who is the president of America today Barack Hussein Obama.

Genetic controllability dictates your philosophical traits, relative to agenda. Obama is a direct heritage of Africa, relative to his father that consists of dominant tribal philosophy. I am of the opinion he hasn't the slightest idea that his heritage is dictating his philosophical agenda. There is a genetic characteristic heritage embedded in all ethics of people. Most haven't the remotest of what dictates their philosophical traits of an agenda, regards to motivations. Most whites are an articulate, compromising, cohesive, ethnic people who are acclimated to sustain based on merit and will often determine serious problems on basis and attempt to resolve with diplomacy. Politically or personal, normally based on morality that is consistent with procedures of laws provided by the constitution. Most whites will never rebel against the constitution because it is embedded in the fundamental philosophy that stabilizes the United States of America. The greatest nation in the universe that consists of a major two party system, Democrat and Republican; each formulated with a senate and house of representatives which maintain the balance in political structured power that is in the best interest for the people.

Through a process of elections by "WE THE PEOPLE" most have accessed this radical president Barack Hussein Obama as a fraud; ratified on November 03, 2010. He has blatantly accused the Republicans of driving the car into the ditch and now they want the keys back. When the car is out of the ditch they must sit in the back. Someone needs to inform this idiotic, psychopathic, incompetent, president, Barack Hussein Obama the Republicans have taken the keys from him through the American process and left the car in the ditch stuck in the mud with him sitting in the back seat. While he is sitting there a total of ninety seven dignitaries, fifty six ratified the Declaration of Independence. Forty one ratified the Constitution. They were some of the most intellectual, brilliant legislators in the history of the universe because approximately two hundred thirty five years later the slogan that adorns the beginning of the Constitution: "WE THE PEOPLE" is going to politically leave Mr. Barack Hussein Obama sitting in the back seat of that automobile that he claims Republicans drove into the ditch. Unfortunately for him it is possible he could sweat the die from his hair. However in essence there is absolutely nothing the bias political distorting incompetent, alimentary canal licking news media can do to resurrect his political stability; regards to he being elected a second term in two thousand twelve. Because he has politically self-destructed based on bias political distorting innuendo; related to incompetency.

Quoting the southern Democrats during eighteen sixty eight that blacks were not suitable for political aspirations in America because they were ignorant and incompetent, and should maintain traditions of serving others. This statement occurred over a hundred forty three years ago and as of to date two thousand eleven, President Barack Hussein Obama has established the truth of these predictions by southern Democrats and proven they are historian geniuses. This is a stigmatization that is embedded in the traditional genetic culture of most blacks in America. Most have never adhered to the general fundamental beliefs of American traditions and most have never attempted transitions in order to become an intricate part of any formulated organization other than church. It is mandatory you explore and exert your intellect with compassion and adhere to the guide lines that America has prevailed on. Most blacks rebel against the traditions of America. Their forte has always been and still is the hell with the white man constitution. It is for him anyway. We know what is best for us; this ideology translates into rebellious incompetency. A child inherits his parent's genetic controllability and his environment is subject to dictate his future. If not taught the appropriate mannerism pertaining to the fundamentals of morality and reality; these are the philosophical traits that are voided with in most African Americans that reside in the United States of America; also a segment of whites. If a child grows up in a hostile, rebellious environment they become addicted to the philosophical traits. Once they enter into young adults they are estranger to change even if they graduate from college with honors, because most blacks are adverse to change. Most whites are not because there is a difference in personality and perception. Most blacks herd behind self-appointed black leaders that distort reality with bias innuendo, such as they are being denied their civil rights. Based on white racism the system is against blacks because of their color and is consistently planning to keep them in poverty. It is those old rich racist Republicans that are causing their problems. So, they rebel assuming that standards will be adjusted to their comprehension. That is why the ghettos in large cities are packed like sardines with blacks waiting for Jessie Jackson and Al Sharpton to get them their civil rights. With most whites there is a total different scenario. They will enter into the work force and expect any kind of employment although they are college graduates and rely on their communicable individual traits based on merit to excel. They do not have self-appointed white leaders that distort reality based on bogus bias lies in an effort to compensate for ingenuity. In essence, most blacks have chosen President Barack Hussein Obama as their Congo Chief to eradicate white capitalistic dominance in America. However, he being tremendously bias and incompetent; was not capable of realizing there is a constitution embedded with laws that are adhered to by a major two party system; Democrat and Republican. Each controlled by a senate and a house of representatives dominated with white superiority. The vast majority of people in the United States of America are white. The Constitution begins with "WE THE PEOPLE" ratified by all whites. Whites were conciliatory enough to elect a black president Barack Hussein Obama. He has betrayed their trust by attempting to eradicate the Constitution which sustains morality, civil rights, equality, and liberty for all Americans. Most blacks live in a fantasy, bias alienating flux of isolation from humanity dictating assumed standards pertaining to society.

Whenever there are comprehendible dialogues pertaining to the reality of diplomacy, you can have researched any claim pertaining to validity and have a dialogue with most blacks concerning the reality of an issue. Most will have prematurely assumed their own assessment opposed to the discernible reality without any research. Most blacks will base their opinion on something they heard or were told from others. If you do not allow them to con and distort your research abilities, either you are a stupid ass red neck white racist or a black ass nigger trying to be white. This is a monolithic solidarity pertaining to most black, educated or not. Unfortunately this is an embedded syndrome related to genetic heritage controllability.

President Barack Hussein Obama is no exclusion. Most African Americans are temperamental and rebellious; regards to being proven inadequate and will never apologize for their incompetency, but will congregate and distort with bias lies and back track in an effort to stabilize their assumptions for erroneous credibility by impugning the integrity of others about what a stupid person you are. But you were not smart enough to communicate with them appropriately so it is your fault because they were wrong in their analogy regard to the subject. This is an old trite phrase utilized by people particularly blacks for hundreds of years and is more prevalent to date than ever before in the history of our nation.

Because of a transformation in accordance with times, people have become more intellectual and are utilizing deviousness to sustain related to bias distorting radical incompetency injected with intimidation to deprive moral lawful legitimacy for personal compensation enhancement related to control of others. Our president, Barack Hussein Obama, is at the top of the list. He and his regime forcedly imposed health care on the nation, not because it was in the best interest for the people, but a carefully plotted agenda by a narcissistic bias philosopher related to black legacy. He was the first and only president to accomplish that agenda of health care. More importantly, he assumed he could destroy the moral fabric of America liberties in order to desecrate the Constitution in an effort to implement Congo socialism under his control which is a surrogate of the late Nat Turner of eighteen thirty one, also the current Mum mar Qaddafi.

CHAPTER 7

We are confronted with one of the most asinine, perplexing implementations to ever develop in the history of the free world, and most like in all civilized society. To elect a president to the most prestigious, intellectual and moralist nation in the universe, meaning Barack Hussein Obama. This was reckless dysfunctional and beyond incompetency; to elect a man because he speaks fluent English and is black. This was one of the most insane concoctions in civilized society, surviving on God's earth. This imposter of a president, Obama, has secluded all personal aspects pertaining to his college documents, including his certificate of birth, also a member of a church congregation for approximately twenty years; reportedly where the minister adhered to doctrines of God damn America. Controlled by rich whites, in the interim their chickens are coming home to roost. He also implied nine eleven was an American condemning; not mentioning his communicable relations with a home-grown terrorist.

I am of the opinion that a segment of whites, especially the young ones, have caught that small dysfunctional brain disease that the late FBI Director J. Edgar Hoover, during nineteen fifty seven, accused blacks of having. I never thought it would be contagious. Unfortunately, it is prevalent among many whites. For instance, I watched a segment of IMUS in the morning on Fox Business; March 11, 2011. He was having a dialogue with one of the small brains, Imogene Webber. This woman knows as much about the fundamental heritage that America was established on as I know about flying a jumbo jet plane. Unfortunately there are millions of whites like her that have united with blacks and a large segment of Hispanics, because their small brains are in unison, pertaining to radical bias distortion. However when the bombs begin to explode around their incompetent asses, they will be yelling that someone should have known through investigating, and should have deterred these tragedies from occurring. Then they begin the incompetent panic mode; accusing Republicans of being negligent and responsible as they did to President George Bush for the nine eleven tragedy; even suggesting he was the orchestrator.

This is an extreme warning, now that you older people are witnessing an attempt to sabotage our liberties; especially whites, because ninety five percent blacks still have that small brain that FBI Director J. Edgar Hoover accused them of for Democrats. President Barack Hussein Obama could be hand carrying a bag of explosives into a crowded building and blacks will continue to vote for him because he is black. I love the United States of America from the bottom of my heart because of the moral integrity that exists, ratified in accordance with our Constitution; awarding liberty and morality related to capitalism. I am pleading; please get off the couch, even if you have to crawl, to the polling station and vote this radical, narcissistic socialist, bias black bigot out of office that has intentions of sabotaging America along with our liberties. Over many years we have had political problems in America, but never of this magnitude with any president, to the degree of this black bias socialistic suspected hideous Moslem that is hoarding his personal documents.

As a nation we know absolutely nothing about this possible traitor. Please vote. I was shopping at a Wal-Mart where two older white women were shopping. There was a product on a top shelf they could not reach. I reached and gave it to them. We had a brief conversation. I lured them into politics; incidentally most whites are skeptical of blacks because they are aware that ninety five percent of blacks are alimentary canal slurps for Democrats. They trusted me and informed me they were staunch Democrats all their lives. I might add, if an opossum was running against President Obama; they are going to vote for the opossum. In reality an opossum is classified as one of the most stupid animals on the globe. A pack of hounds can be chasing him, hot on his trail, and there is a forty foot oak tree sitting next to a corn stalk. The opossum will choose to climb the corn stalk. These are sentiments we as a nation are embroiled in today, parallel to the thinking of an opossum, coordinated by this current Democratic administration reign.

In an effort to authenticate my suspicion, New York Senator Charles Ellis Schumer, elected to the Congress House of Representatives in nineteen eighty one, served seventeen years; elected to the Senate nineteen ninety eight. He has served twelve years there, which is approximately twenty nine years in Congress. He is totally inept; to the ratified established protocol of our Constitution. He is also a Harvard graduate with a law degree. When he emphatically rearranged Article I and Section 1 of our Constitution by indicating they are two separate entities when it specifically read: all legislative powers herein granted shall be vested in a Congress of the United States which shall consist of a Senate and House of Representatives.

Unfortunately this is the density of the current administration controlled by Democrats. Our nation is in peril and all other nations are aware of this incompetent fiasco that is occurring in our great country, the United States of America. There is still hope, but we must extricate the opossums at the ballot box. It might appear I have some kind of bias vindictiveness against President Barack Hussein Obama and his administration. Absolutely not; it is just America is like a female family member to me, that I am loyal to, and President Obama has come along and molested her for no apparent reason other than narcissistic incompetency. There are habitual complainers; basically practically all you ever hear from most black and a segment of whites are that they are being abused by the system, regard to progress in America. Most haven't the slightest idea on how the system was formulated and established. It is fairly simple, the Constitution authorizes your basic liberties to perform on your own individual merit and capitalize on your thinking; regards to attributes to perform, related to intellect. Meaning if you are qualified to drive a truck, the finesse of your brain through genetic controllability has dictated your future. However do not have bias malice for the person that is a school teacher. Incidentally every individual on God's earth has genetic embedded intellectual limitations that are predominantly dictated through heritage controllability; meaning your intellectual expertise factions are limited. There are people that have utilized inappropriate tactics to succeed beyond their intellectual capacity. Unfortunately it creates hesitant mentality, regards to stress, including failure during the philosophical process.

The ability to succeed in life is by choice. In choosing one has to be aware of their qualifications; because qualifications in life are inevitable based on the process of individual traits because it is other people who determine your intellectual capabilities. There are millions of people who dedicate their entire lives assuming and blaming others for their failure to accomplish their priorities, regard to successful endeavors. Most people who utilize this bogus deficiency are extremely vocal with summarized bias distortion. In an effort to disguise their incompetency, related to substance, there are millions of people who adhere to and are captivated with this philosophical trait, regard to an agenda. This is becoming more prevalent in the United States of America than ever before. If it is not quelled, we will become a lost society in America, succumbed to our own ineptness, related to political bias distortions, based on philosophical instigated socialistic entrapment instigated by liberals.

I am a news fanatic. I listen to the news. Liberals are constantly fantasizing and distorting reality based on bias radical political incompetency. In an effort to succeed in sabotaging our liberties most liberals are a unique segment of people motivated by destroying the enthusiasm of others to implement their philosophical agenda of miscellaneous destructive tactics for imminent control of community life. This is in dire opposition to our Constitution. Fortunately they are doomed to fail because this is nothing more than bias distorted philosophical incompetency exploited by those who do not understand who they are and absolutely nothing about the fundamentals of the greatest nation on God's earth, the United States of America.

There were demonstrations in the south perpetrated by Dr. Martin Luther King for the southern Democrats to relinquish the civil and voting rights strangle hold on southern blacks which the Republican congress had specifically ratified for blacks within the fourteenth amendment of the Constitution ratified on July 19, 1868. Many black Republicans in the southern states excelled in the political arena; such as Oscar J. Dunn who became the Lieutenant Governor of Louisiana; Hiram Rhodes Revels who became the first black Republican U. S. Senator from Mississippi in eighteen seventy; Blanche K. Bruce who was the first black elected to the U. S. Senate to serve a full term, also a Republican; Jonathan Gibbs who served as Florida's secretary of state also during eighteen eighty four he served as superintendent of education for the state; Egbert Sammis was elected to the state senate of Florida; Francis Lewis Cardozo served as South Carolina's secretary of state from eighteen sixty eight until eighteen seventy two and was also appointed to the treasury department in Washington, D. C.; Pinckney Benton Stewart Pinchback became the first African American governor of Louisiana; Robert Smalls became a member of the South Carolina Beaufort County School Board.

The Freedmen's Bureau was established and more than five thousand schools were available to black and white students. Previously there were none. Robert Smalls dedicated his professional talents to educating black and white students. Republican African Americans made substantial gains in the political arena. Blacks were engaged in state conventions that organized new state constitutions that gave blacks the right to vote in southern states. Their votes established the foundation for the Republican Party in the southern states during reconstruction after the Civil War in the south. Black and white Republicans, even some white Democrats, worked in unison to rebuild the south. There were approximately six or seven hundred African Americans serving in state legislatures; over twenty were elected to the U. S. House of Representatives, all Republicans. Unfortunately, this moralistic incredible, political and educational progress for white and black Republicans would soon be eliminated because five confederate soldiers established the Ku Klux Klan; organized by southern Democrats to literally exterminate black and white Republicans. Wade Hampton, a Democrat who served as governor and U. S. Senator from South Carolina, instructed Democrats that all violent acts were acceptable; including murder, carried out in the name of white supremacy.

In Vicksburg, Mississippi white Democratic Ku Klux Klan terrorists slaughtered over three hundred blacks to dissuade their support for Republicans. Finally they succeeded in eradicating all Republican whites and blacks from the southern states. Blacks could not afford to leave the south and were violently forced to join the Democrat Party. They are still there today based on ineptness regard to chronological records of significant horrible events.

It is amazing, stunning, and condescending that most blacks are traditionally constantly assuming and never rely on research to substantiate accuracy. There are some who consider themselves commentators pertaining to the political arena who are constantly prevalent on practically every communicable airway available grinning like Jack asses eating thorny briers, assuming and distorting reality; based on their bias, radical, racist, innuendo philosophy such as Al Sharpton; and especially Eugene Robinson. MSNBC utilizes him like a pimp uses whores; constantly on their news station, stammering, grinning and speaking gibberish. Also misleading the general public, especially blacks, with assumptions; he was on Morning Joe, February 18, 2011 munching on briars and scolding the governor of Mississippi, Haley Barbour in regards to license plates in honor of Nathan Bedford Forrest claiming Nathan Bedford Forrest founded the Ku Klux Klan, which is totally incorrect; based on bias distorted lies and racist incompetency. In an unwarranted effort to acclaim notoriety, Nathan Bedford Forrest was born July 18, 1821 along with a twin sister in Bedford County, Tennessee. He lost his father at age seventeen, utilized his God given talents to assist in supporting his family with a very small amount of education. He utilized his common sense abilities, regards to owning slaves and selling them for profit, which was legal because the Africans founded slavery and owning people was an African lucrative legacy. Nathan Bedford Forrest became an expert and very wealthy in the United States of America. He also was a military person who held the rank of General in the southern Confederate Military. He was accused of being a grand wizard in the Ku Klux Klan. However, he never endorsed lynching blacks. He was subpoenaed to testify before Congress during eighteen seventy one and denied being a Klan member. The Congress did not have circumstantial evidence that he was. He was invited to give a speech at the Independent Order of Pole Bearers Association; which was his last public appearance in eighteen seventy five and accepted flowers from a black woman. Forrest City, Arkansas is named in his honor.

Nathan Bedford Forrest was a person who made the necessary adjustments during his life. Without formal education, he utilized the advantages within his talents, based on commodities that Africa established hundreds of years prior to being introduced to America which became a lucrative asset; established by southern Democrats, which politically blacks are their most loyal supporters today with votes of ninety five percent. Blacks should be proud to have license plates fabricated in honor of Nathan Bedford Forrest because he was considered to be a martyr within the southern Democratic Ku Klux Klan which blacks have politically supported for seventy five years or more. I am of the opinion most blacks have a total misconception of the fundamental nature that is responsible for the philosophical renditions that American was established on. Their assumptions have been detrimental to functions, related to their intellectual skills to decipher best interest; pertaining to political party affiliations. Most are enormously committed to the political alimentary canal smooching of the Democrat party regime. The authenticity among the ethnic of most blacks, based on reality, is dismal and virtually non-existence. Most have lived in a fantasy world for hundreds of years; thinking they can organize their own individual code of controlling ethnics; opposed to the Constitution and whites. The thirteenth amendment of the Constitution abolished slavery. The fourteenth amendment guaranteed all African Americans rights to citizenship. The fifteenth amendment established voting rights, which race could not be a factor. Most blacks assumed they could formulate their own country within the United States of America. I recall very vividly some black incompetent idiot requesting the state of Texas be given to all blacks. The political party that most blacks are loyal to, the Democrats, gave them the opportunity in eighteen ninety six, when they revoked their civil rights with the implementation of separate but equal; Jim Crow Rule through the U. S. Supreme Court. That is why southern blacks had to sit in the back of public transportation, including myself and relatives; also in the balconies of theaters and segregated water fountains for sixty nine years. Realistically, the majority of African Americans who reside in the United States of America haven't the remotest idea of why certain restrictions were imposed on our ancestors by Democrats. It had absolutely nothing to do with being black. Without question it is embedded in genetic controllability with an infiltration of philosophical, bias incompetent, assuming, agendas for supremacy to dominate and dictate to others. As practiced in Africa by tribal chiefs while living in Congo destitution. Meaning: Africa is the second oldest nation on the continent. With appropriate recourses and citizens of America has gathered materials for their aid regard to survival. This is potentially what President Barack Hussein Obama has in store for our great nation, the United States of America. However, any statement made is not intended to be derogatory; but, specifically adhering to reality. From the tribes of Africa you have never witnessed men and women scuttling off to work with a lunch bucket. They survive freely off the land; predominately minas schooling in many segments located throughout Africa. Unfortunately, that is a stigmatic genetic heritage that is embedded in most African Americans; they are totally unaware of that has resided in the United States of America for hundreds of years; not realizing they are profiled genetically with African heritage eternally. However, if one is aware of these unique traits, it will enable them to compromise their traits; regard to communicable psychological agendas; this criteria is applicable to all segmented ethnics of people; that are surviving on the universe of God's earth.

CHAPTER 8

Blacks are a unique ethic of people. Their African genetic heritage consists of congregated herding; to instinctively follow self-appointed leaders; based on their being black and are capable of distorting issues; based on bias assumptions. Once their assumptions are solidified in unison, God could catapult down from the heavens and not change their opinion. This has been the traditional trait for Africans and African Americans for approximately nine hundred years. More prevalent in the United States of America today more than ever; because a black elected president, Barack Hussein Obama and his attorney general, Eric Holder. Trust me. Education is not a factor; this is congenital and will never cease to exist because of bias racist lust for contempt; regard to whites. Being an American with African heritage, I have traveled immensely throughout the United States of America conversing with most ethnic people. I am convinced approximately eight five percent of blacks detest most whites. If you ask them why, they stare you down and blurt out hell he white, ain't he? In reality, they really do not know why, other than sheer bias indoctrinated incompetency because we, as a nation of civility deservedly, have respect for all people who have potential characteristic endeavors to communicate with others; related to traits and dignity, based on reality; not assumptions.

Unfortunately, over sixty five million of voting constituents rallied around assumptions when they elected President Barack Hussein Obama because he is black and supposedly a Harvard graduate with a law degree;

listening to Al Sharpton, Jessie Jackson and other bias black misfits constantly dwelling on the same old tiresome subject: equality and racism against blacks. Young political incompetent whites and some older ones became compassionate. While alienating themselves with disdain from President George W. Bush, and based on frustration decided to cast their vote for a communistic, incompetent traitor; regards to the moral fabric of America. Most dignified young whites and some older, know absolutely nothing about the philosophical personified traits of an agenda; regards to most blacks. They assumed Barack Hussein Obama was qualified to be president based on his political distorted persuasive lies; regards to his covert philosophical planned agenda to sabotage the United States of America with malice.

It has taken two years for many to realize, even many Democrats who voted for him, one of the most terrible mistakes in the history of the free world has been made. I am still optimistic, because of my old faithful ratifying of chronological significant events; related to moral justice, pertaining to liberties and capitalism for all people. There is no other political party in the history of the United States of America that has done more than the Republican Party to assist African Americans, and all people; regards to civil liberties and human justice. Now, they are destine to extricate this black Democratic Ku Klux Klansman that has revised the traditions of the southern white Democrats and intend to utilize these tactics on all.

American People: in the name of black power; there is circumstantial evidence of when his attorney general, of all the people in America, rescinded the case brought against blacks, for voting intimidating; when in essence the perpetrators insisted all whites should be exterminated; including their babies. When questioned about the occurrence, U. S. Attorney General Eric Holder's (who represents all people in America) response was: my people have had enough. There was no response from the White House, because he reports to Barack Hussein Obama.

Recently one of the most despicable black bias racism events occurred in Dayton, Ohio. Barack Hussein Obama and Eric Holder, the U. S. Attorney General, demanded the test scores for law enforcement be lowered in order for blacks to pass. This is pure racist insanity. Let's suppose you had a health occurring problem that was serious; you learned your physician's test scores had been altered in order for him to get his license. Unfortunately, this is a formidable tradition; regards to most blacks in America. It does not matter if he can't qualify for a position; give it to him anyway, he is black. Ladies and Gentlemen in America; we are losing our sweet home of dignity and morality. It is being taken over and replaced with nonsensical bias, illiterate racist incompetency, infiltrated and authorized by none other than President Barack Hussein Obama.

It is extremely amazing there is an ethnic of people within the United States of America since sixteen nineteen three hundred and ninety two years, and most cannot distinguish the ultimate criteria pertaining to deciphering and distinguishing the reality of the major difference between the two political parties established in the United States of America; predominately Democrat and Republican. Most African Americans are totally inept to the fact that Republicans have been genuinely faithful since eighteen sixty five when Republican President Abraham Lincoln abolished servitude during eighteen sixty five. The Republican Party began their assistance immediately after by an overwhelming segment of Republicans, black and white, going to the southern states to teach former slaves to read and write in an effort to assist with their independent, economic prosperity to succeed based on intellectual merit of traits. Republican African Americans began to make successful politically endeavors during the eighteen sixties. Then along came the Democratic established Ku Klux Klan and implied that all blacks were stupid, illiterate and incompetent people attempting to rise above their naturally subservient place in human white society. They should and never would be any part of the Constitution. The Republican congress responded to dispel this theory by ratifying the thirteenth, fourteenth, and fifteenth amendment to the Constitution, especially for southern blacks. In an effort that blacks could become an intricate intellectual ethnic of people to improve on their abilities to succeed in a diverse society of people based on their own merit. You guessed it. The Democratic established southern Ku Klux Klan improvised a plan to revoke privileges for southern black civil and voting rights which occurred in eighteen ninety six through the U. S. Supreme Court when they approved the Jim Crow Rule during the court case of Plessey versus Ferguson. Ratifying that separate, but equal was constitutional as long as each race had their own compatible resources. This was nothing more than Democratic devised scheme of deceit. In essence, the southern Democrats knew more about African American traits than they knew about themselves. They knew blacks would swallow this deceit, hook line and sinker. They did. The southern blacks exploded with glee shouting, Mr. Booker T. Washington, he is the president of Tuskegee Institute. He knows what is best for us. We are going to run and control us own stuff. The white man ain't going to tell us what to do no more. We going to get our own country. In essence, they were so damn illiterate, stupid and incompetent they did not realize what the meaning of separate but equal indicated. They are still obsessed with that idea today. Having no resources other than what is accumulated from private industry which is owned by whites. That is the reason southern blacks had no other choice than sit in the rear of public transportation, drink from separate water fountains, not allowed service at white public restaurants. All white public facilities were segregated for over seventy years until Dr. Martin Luther King resulted to demonstrations in an effort to restore civil and voting rights that the Republicans had initially granted in eighteen sixty eight. In essence, that was the only reason nothing more or nothing less. Fortunately it did occur during nineteen sixty four and five. Civil and voting rights were restored for southern blacks; but not without a protest from Democrats. Southern Democrat U. S. Senator Robert Byrd, a former Ku Klux Klansman, filibustered for approximately seventeen hours; which is the longest record to date. The Republican congress came to the defense of blacks once again as a unified personnel and defeated Senator Byrd's longevity filibuster. African Americans civil and voting rights were restored that the Republican congress had ratified in eighteen sixty eight. Incidentally, Senator Robert Byrd has the longest record of being elected to the Senate and as an admitted former Ku Klux Klan. I am certain blacks voted for him to remain in office as a U. S. Senator until his demise. He never was a confederate general and there was no city named in his honor. In essence, blacks voted for him to serve as a U. S. Senator longer than any other. Yet, Al Sharpton and others are complaining about Nathan Bedford Forrest being honored with his name on Mississippi license plates. It was never proven he was a Ku Klux Klansman. In my opinion, this is political bias distortion based on philosophical incompetent agenda in an effort to establish credibility related to collaborated notoriety; which is a tradition embedded in the majority of African Americans in an effort to impress; based on bias prehistoric philosophical agenda to demoralize this; regard to guilt. This is one of the main reasons we have an egotistical narcissistic imposter elected president of our great nation today, Barack Hussein Obama.

Over the years, blacks have established and utilized bias tactics of guilt on whites to compensate for inadequacy by constantly referring to slavery. They are flooding the airways and demonstrating constantly in an effort to intimidate whites; regards to guilt. For no apparent reason, other than seeking superiority in an effort to dominate; and is sabotaging our nation with incompetency. If you do not believe me, check the White House in Washington, D. C.

CHAPTER 9

In an effort to engage within the intricacy that motivates most African Americans is to understand their basic genetic heritage doctrine. Pertaining to their philosophical genetic taught traits; they are taught mostly by some ministers; they are God's chosen people and will eventually control the universe. Most have adhered to this theory. They blame others, especially whites, for impeding their accomplishments. In essence, many affluent blacks have chosen to constantly harass whites in America with updated prehistoric issues related to slavery and the southern Democratic Jim Crow Rule, separate but equal, in an effort to docile whites with guilt; especially young whites who are inept and totally out of touch with reality; regards to the history of blacks in America. Unfortunately, blacks have potentially succeeded with this calculated incompetent, clever plan of maneuvering. The top law enforcing attorney general for the United States of America, Eric Holder, implied that Americans were cowards. Then he related to race not being openly discussed. Trust me. He was referring to whites; simply because most blacks heard in their philosophical thinking, and solidify behind Jessie Jackson and Al Sharpton and other prominent blacks are utilizing the media in an attempt to accomplish their bias radical innuendo that they are being denied their civil rights; regards to racism being exploited by whites against them. There is a large segment of whites who are assuming this to be accurate and are placing inferior partially illiterate, incompetent blacks in positions they are not qualified for to succeed at a professional standard. Our U. S. Attorney General Eric Holder recently substantiated the validity of my accusation by ordering the city of Dayton, Ohio to alter by lowering their test scores for blacks only; in an effort for blacks to get a passing score to become a police officer for the city.

There are approximately three hundred million people who reside in America, or more; and African Americans are approximately thirty six million, which is twelve to thirteen percent. There is not a single position in the private enterprise, state or federal government, that blacks are not involved. Yet, most elite blacks are still screaming racism; many whites were duped with this insanity guilt and elected a black president hoping this would dispel these radical bias racist remarks. But, what most other ethnic people who reside in the United States of America do not understand; it is not about racism; it is about dominant superiority for control. This is an embedded genetic controllability of heritage established from African philosophical traits; it is inevitable; also eternal; once others, especially whites, begin to understand this black sensation of a phenomenon to control others. Most can't pass a civil documented test, according to U. S. Attorney General Eric Holder and President Barack Hussein Obama. This president is typical of what he is advocating for blacks in America. He trained himself to speak in a manner that would be noticeable, through practice. He knew this would arouse people coming from a black man. Unfortunately, sixty five million Americans were gullible for this self-trained factitious act of deceit. However, there are dire consequences in America for this kind of deception because most certainly, he mislead the American people and was elected to a responsibility that he is not qualified for. The only thing that concerns him is exposure; virtually each and every speech he engages in he has to remind the American people he is their president, commander and chief as if they are so inept they do not know.

The hounds are on the opossum's trail. As reported sixty four U. S. Senators, thirty two Democrats and thirty two Republicans have forwarded a document to his attention insisting he personally engage in long term deficit reduction. This reminded me of nineteen fifty seven when Republican president Dwight David Eisenhower formulated the first civil rights bill for southern African Americans in eighty nine years and forwarded it to the congress for approval. The Senate was controlled by Democrats, led by U. S. Senator Lyndon Banes Johnson. The Democrats did not have the votes to reject the bill to restore civil rights for blacks. Twelve Republicans defected that enabled the defeat. Does this remind you of anything that is beginning to transpire to date? President Barack

Hussein Obama is the joke of the universe. He is like a kitten playing with a ball of twine; all over the place. He was on national television and emphatically stated that the dictator Mum mar Qaddafi must go. Later he was back implying that if Qaddafi complied with the imposed guide lines by the U. N. the necessity of that would be respected.

Each time President Barack Hussein Obama appears on television he reminds me of a jackass with large ears; however, not any more. Since Charlie Sheen charades, which remind me jackasses don't smoke crack. These two black political bias distorting racist incompetent men; Obama and Holder, and this statement is predicated to their Dayton, Ohio debacle; where they lowered test scores for only blacks to pass in an effort to become police officers. This is the United States of America; one of the most diverse nations in the universe that was established on intellectual competitiveness; regards to all individuals based on merit, not some bozo bias partial vindictive radical racist tactic only to assist blacks.

This is an astounding radical incompetent illustration perpetrated by these supposedly United States leaders which are in precise contextual agreement that was predicted by the Democratic southern Ku Klux Klan during eighteen sixty eight when it stated that blacks were illiterate, stupid and incompetent trying to rise above their natural place of servitude in society. The late F. B. I. Director J. Edgar Hoover, during nineteen fifty seven, stated that in his opinion blacks brains were twenty percent smaller than whites. These two misfits, Obama and Holder, are blessed with each of those predictions. It is predicted that history is repetitive. Approximately one hundred forty three years later, these two verify those statements were correct for some African Americans. By ordering test scores lowered for only blacks in order for them to excel is setting an incompetent trend for young blacks all over the nation; that they are special and really do not have to apply themselves intellectually. Blacks already have the highest rate of high school drop outs to date. This decision by Obama and Holder to assist blacks by lowering test scores only compounds the issue. Most blacks herd and congregate behind affluent blacks to lead them as they did with Booker T. Washington during eighteen ninety six and had to sit on the back of the bus for almost seventy years. Most blacks are ideologues of we got one of us in the White House. He is going to take care of us; as Attorney General Eric Holder is leading them to believe when he references my people. This president is so narcissistic and incompetent he is acting like a dictator; as if he is going to be pretending in that office forever. This president Barack Hussein Obama has no respect for the established guide lines that our nation was founded on or the people who reside here; related to any compassion. He is obsessed with narcissistic bias racist control, especially over whites. It might appear rather ridiculous for me to make a statement of this caliber; but it is the sincere truth: there is a large segment of African Americans throughout the nation, especially older ones, who are assuming President Barack Hussein Obama is God sent in an effort for blacks to control America. They taught their children that a savior was coming to make atone for what the whites did to them. This tradition was passed on to their grandchildren and great grandchildren. When President Obama came on the scene; he is it; their God sent savior; just for them. This is a philosophical incompetent traditional agenda, when in essence; he doesn't care about anyone but himself. However, he is aware of this assumption because the area in Chicago where he was a community organizer is filled with older blacks. He is quite familiar with their traits which he normally utilizes to politically indoctrinate others. Of course, he is not to overly concerned about blacks, because they are his political servitudes and are totally obscure that there is another major political party in America other than Democrats.

This president is so narcissistic and incompetent until he is acting like a Democratic dictator as if he is going to be pretending in the office for ever. He doesn't care about anyone or anything other than political accommodating dialogues in an effort to maintain credibility based on deceitful bias distortions; related to Republicans. African Americans would not be as successful today if it wasn't for the Republicans; abolishing servitude, ratifying three amendments to the Constitution for their freedom; thirteenth, fourteenth and fifteenth: desegregating southern schools; responsible for the civil and voting rights act being passed in nineteen sixty four and five; responsible for the ratification of affirmative action. Of course, the southern Democratic Ku Klux Klan ratified something; blow torches and ropes with nooses on the end. Most blacks who reside in America are adverse to change unless it is compatible to their solidified traits of one size fits all; meaning emphatically agreeing with their philosophical agenda; and, if not; either you think you are more than they are, or you are a white man nigger trying to be white; and if you are white you are characterized as being a red neck racist cracker that hates blacks.

However, in essence the simple fact is; that most blacks have not the intellectual ability to decipher reality; based on genetic heritage indoctrination, that most are inevitably disarranged with psychoanalysis tendencies which are an embedded tradition; to dispel reality and distort with assumptions until it is suitable for their criteria, which is contrary to existing facts of reality. There is a vast segment of whites synchronized with this bias dysfunctional formality of incompetency; especially the Democratic U. S. chosen elected Senator Harry Reid when he is publicly making statements based on assumptions that the American bona fide citizens, who are compassionate about losing our liberties in the United States of America. Some are eradicating with their philosophical agenda of saving our nation from disparaging socialistic sabotage. My only evaluation of the assumed synopses is that apparently Charlie Sheen is soliciting participants to join him in his endeavors.

Begin at the White House with leading spokesman for the U. S. Senate Harry Reid and President Barack Hussein Obama because he authorized reduction in test scores in the city of Dayton, Ohio for blacks only in assistance for them to pass the written test to become police officers of law. The American citizens are some of the most gracious people on God's earth, but once they analytically determine they have been politically castigated with phony imposter rhetoric; related to bias hypocrisy your ass is grass and they are the lawn mower at the polls for future elections. I make these statements because I am a realist who loves my country and have utilized most of my life attempting to analyze all people in regards to their philosophical agendas; pertaining to life in general, because it is absolutely essential to understand the ethnics of all people. There is not a single day in an individual's life when they are not in contact with others. It can create an adaptable scenario of trust or mistrust based on dignity and morality; which is consistent with the guide lines established by our Constitution; to have numerous collaborative dialogues, enabling one to evaluate philosophical traits pertaining to agendas.

Let's elaborate on the marching during the Dr. Martin Luther King era with thousands of blacks and a segment of whites. Most blacks then, and now, were inept as to why there is a vast difference between equal rights and capitalistic success. Whites have always had their equal and civil rights and a large segment are more destitute than blacks. Life consists of knowing who you are as an individual regardless to ethnic and have the intellect to theoretically diagnose your abilities. Based on human genetic infrastructure, related to capability and adhere to that honest philosophy. That is why the United States is the greatest nation on God's earth; because one is not limited to obtain success. This is something many people, black and white, have never understood. If you do not understand something it is obvious you are assuming, and assuming can be detrimental. This occurred to most blacks during the restoration of their civil and voting rights during nineteen sixty four and five. Most never understood the philosophical revelations then and now because Jessie Jackson, Al Sharpton and other blacks are screaming it never occurred. Based on their perceiver assumptions, most blacks assumed that it indicated sharing wealth to misfits that others had accumulated; especially whites, based on intellectual morality and merit. The ability to communicate with dignity and character and to also understand the unique complex principles that our nation was established on; to admire and adhere to our Constitution and have dignified respect for all people and race will never be a consequence of deterrent.

The demographics of America have changed, for the best interest of "WE THE PEOPLE"; the leading Democrats are adverse to change, which is a tradition of hundreds of years to indoctrinate opposed to adhering to reality. During the election of eighteen sixty, the Democrats in the south walked out of the convention held in Charleston and elected three potential presidents: Stephen A. Douglas, John C. Breckinridge and John Bell; which neither was successful in winning. Republican Abraham Lincoln was the winner. He was assassinated by John Wilkes Booth a Democrat, for abolishing slavery for blacks that was imposed on them by southern Democrats. I might add, during those times all blacks supported the Republican Party.

I mention this fiasco with the Democrats walking out of the convention during eighteen sixty as it happened to be an embedded tradition with Democrats because a hundred and fifty two years later they are still at it. In the state of Wisconsin, fourteen Democrats walked out of the Republican controlled house and senate when a bill had been legally passed for the governor to sign into law which required at least one Democrat to be present. All fourteen congressional Democrats chose to leave the state of Wisconsin and hide out in Illinois. Their intent was to block the bill from being signed into law by Wisconsin Republican governor. There were huge crowds of demonstrators of angry Democrats threatening violence simply because people of the state of Wisconsin voted in a Republican governor and a congress that has the majority and legally passed laws that the Democrats opposed. They also utilized strong intimidation in an effort to quell this law without merit. Most Democrats adhere to Mafia tactics; if you have something they want, and you do not yield to their demands;

they will sabotage you. To substantiate my accusations, during eighteen sixty, the southern Democrats organized militant terrorist groups such as: the Knights of the White Camilla, the Pale Face Brotherhood (in eighteen sixty six they changed their name to the Ku Klux Klan). These groups were specifically to exterminate white and black Republicans during eighteen sixty six. They invaded a Republican hall in Memphis, Tennessee that was filled with Republican voting constituents, black and white, and insisted they all must die; which they slaughtered all that were inside. A minister named Dr. Horton pleaded for his survival and they shot him dead and chased others, who had escaped through the windows, down and slaughtered them also simply because they were Republicans having a political gathering. I am certain readers are going to question; where was law enforcement during this era. The Ku Klux Klan was the most powerful Democratic organization in the south. Their extension reached the state of Indiana; their tactic was to infiltrate city police departments and many of those officers were a Ku Klux Klan participant.

Present Barack Hussein Obama duped and pulled a fast one on the upper echelon of Democrats. Trust me. They are terribly angry; and not just angry; they are ready to assault. It is fairly simple; most Democrats are obsessed with political power in regards to dominative supremacy and will eradicate people in an effort to retain control. They controlled congress for forty years by initiating political bias distorted philosophical concocted lies; eradicating and demonizing Republicans. Trust me. There is none better; their violet record speaks for itself.

They never had a black elected president leading their party and most blacks do not understand themselves and sure as hell not many others do; especially whites. There are many people throughout the nation, television and radio, and other news outlets expressing they do not understand this president, Barack Hussein Obama. Let's analytically resolve the issue. Beginning with most blacks like the ability to think in depth and it does not matter if they are a graduate of Harvard, Yale or Princeton. Most never research the validity of anything. Their genetic heritage dictates assuming simply because the tribes of Africa never had to utilize technical skills for anything. This stigmatic derivative from their late ancestors from Africa is embedded in all African Americans based on genetic controllability eternally. Most blacks are totally unaware of this unique trait that dictates philosophical agendas. Native genetic heritage is inevitable in all ethnic of people, not just blacks. The original nation of ancestry origin dictates philosophical traits in all ethnic of people. If they relocate to another nation, it is absolutely necessary to confine themselves to the established guidelines that prevail.

There are numerous times genetic embedded heritage from their derivative nation can, and will, dictate their philosophical traits; either to adhere or rebel against founding principles which has been devastating for most African Americans. Most refused to deviate from African traditions. For approximately two hundred years, most isolated themselves; either by choice or prevention by southern Democrats. Most never conformed to adherence related to the established principles which are standardized in the United States of America. Most chose to rebel and make bias and distorted racist accusations which white Republicans are responsible for their destitution; which is nothing more than political bias distortion based on philosophical agendas perpetrated by sheer black incompetency. The southern Democrats are guilty of, by violently eradicating the Republican Party of African Americans which President Abraham Lincoln established; to ensure blacks could integrate intellectual into a diverse society with moral dignity related to the established standards that America has to offer. Unfortunately, the southern Democratic Ku Klux Klan deprived blacks in the southern states of this miraculous opportunity to engage their abilities competitively based on their own individual merit to succeed or fail. This is the fundamental standards which our great nation, the United States of America was established on and still is.

As I write this chapter, I am sorrowfully emotional because minus the destructive violence instituted by southern Ku Klux Klan during the eighteen sixties, a replica of this scenario is developing in segments of our nation today. Some are instigating violence in an effort to repeal against elected Republicans to save our nation from sabotage by the Democrats; which could be ten times worse than when they eradicated liberty for southern blacks. Our entire nation is subject to moral and capitalistic extinction. I suggest emphatically: the only resolve we can rely on is God and the Republican Party. I am not suggesting how you should cast your vote, I am relying on you reading this book and come to your own conclusion. In essence I will explicitly outline the premise of my accusations. There are numerous ethic people who have miscellaneous genetic traditions which are synchronized within their nationality; it could be any number of things. However, most blacks are accredited with one which is quite unique, and unfortunately is con scheming. They are the most crafty on the universe with this technique because the validation is sitting in the White House; meaning President Barack Hussein Obama.

Hustler is a philosophical, genetic trait which the terminology is mostly applicable to blacks. It is a derivative of African tribal chiefs; swindling each other in regards to trading animals for humans; such as cattle and pigs. This is not a derogatory remark. Secretary of State Hillary Clinton is a witness because she was some place in Africa and she was accosted by an African to trade for her daughter; regard to animals. This book is not about fiction or assumptions; it is the facts of reality pertaining to human life.

Africans, hundreds of years ago and even today, are our heritage congregated in tribes; with nothing to participate in other than survival off the land and swindle each other and wage tribal war. African Americans carry this genetic controllability, which is eternal; that most blacks are totally unaware of; also ethnics from other genetic lines of descent. Genetic heritage can dissipate some based on the involvement in interracial marriage, or other, which accumulate each line of ancestor which can dictate a split personality for good or worse. Most people spend their entire lives not realizing their philosophical traits are being dictated by heritage back hundreds of years ago. Each nationality of people has genetic embedded traits which dictate philosophical trends; especially African Americans. Most have a unique persona which is predominately caused by African tribal denial of free intervention and choice of opinions. Meaning the tribal chief docile; all under his tribal jurisdiction adhere to his philosophical agenda; which is a genetic heritage brought to America initially during the year of sixteen nineteen. Once they were introduced to a contrary free society of people and were taught some of the prevailing trends, such as to read and write, they began intermixing African and American traits. Unfortunately being a native from Africa, their genetic controllability dictated their philosophical agendas. This is why blacks in America choose to adhere to African traditions for over two hundred years. Most Africans are narcissistic with arrogant violent temperaments; which is reason for constant tribal wars against each other; for tribal dominance and superiority. Most African Americans are embedded with heritage, genetic, philosophical traits eternally which are distinguishable in many ways in the United States of America society today; political bias distortion based on philosophical agendas to impede the established fundamentals of our Constitution in regards to individual liberty for all American citizens and replace with a replica of Africa traditions; where a tribal chief decides obligations and dictates futures and fates.

Once African Americans were taught to read and write they began to decipher individual independence in an effort to control others, to dictate bias ideology based on assumptions related to African tribal genetic instincts pertaining to superiority dominance. Their intent is more prevalent today than ever. For instance, once an individual(s) are introduced to something they see and like; and (he, she, they) do not have the intellectual skills for motivations to acquire or accomplish, they rebel with their assumptions of radical and distorted bias philosophical agendas of accusing others for their inability to accomplish due to incompetency. Most will resolve to political cunning and diplomatic deception utilizing a method of diction to influence in an effort to disguise inadequacy. President Barack Hussein Obama trained himself to instigate this deceptive agenda which is why he is president of the United States of America today; minus qualifications. His intellectual persona of tentative amnesiac, relative to back tracking to deceive the American people with bias, philosophical incompetent rhetoric which is a typical tradition for most blacks; to utilize redundant verbiage for attentive glorification having absolutely nothing to do with the essential part of a subject; regards to an appropriate resolving. It is all about them; hey mama look at me, I am in charge. Approximately sixty five million American voting constituents were lured into Barack Hussein Obama's deceitful doctrine. Most affluent blacks are narcissistic because they want everyone to know of their superiority. Most have minimum status to substantiate the validity of their profound intellectual qualifications because it is an American tradition; minimum skills and black are compatible. To appropriately access this bias, racist and incompetent matter, you need not go any further than President Barack Hussein Obama and his Attorney General Eric Holder. They authorized as a rule of law for the city of Dayton, Ohio to lower the standards for test pertaining to blacks only in order for them to become police officers of city law enforcement. This sent a message to young African Americans: it is not necessary you prepare your intellectual skills to compete; we are going to lower standards to your philosophical, bias, racist and incompetent ratio. This was the change I spoke about when I was running for the presidency to assist blacks in their effort to control America; regard to black power. Most affluent blacks are narcissistic because they want everyone to be aware of their superiority. Most have little idiosyncrasies to verify their status regarding their success.

Let's evaluate President Barack Hussein Obama utilizing his traits of dominance to alert others of his superiority. First, he alerted everyone he had won the presidency. Then he insisted Republicans must sit in the back. In practically every speech he gave he referenced he is the president and your commander in chief. The most conspicuous is with his hands; noticeably with his hands; each and every dignitary he publically appears with he tends to caress and fondle their shoulders or arms; which signifies dominance and superiority. This was a trait of Democratic southern plantation owners to caress the heads of blacks in an effort to insinuate superiority. President Barack Hussein Obama is utilizing this chronologic event on dignitaries who he publicly appears with. It might sound trivia, but it is the significance of dominate superiority over others which is kindergarten childish and incompetent. Unfortunately this is the most vindictive, asinine, incompetent United States president to ever be elected in the history of our nation. All because of political inept, coward, alimentary canal kissing by whites for a political incompetent black; assuming his philosophical thinking traits are equivalent to other ethic people who adhere to the Constitution. In essence blacks have attempted to abolish the established government of America for approximately one hundred eighty five years, beginning in eighteen twenty nine with David Walker through eighteen thirty one with Nat Turner; more prevalent today than ever: because of the election of Barack Hussein Obama.

All through our nation there are approximately thirty six million blacks. Of this number, approximately eighty five percent have disdain for whites. Most whites know absolutely nothing about the philosophical demeanor of African Americans who are some of the most conceited, deceitful, conniving, rebellious, radical, racist, herding people in God's universe. They are constantly inducing for insidious prosperity and will victimize anyone, and will never concede to immorality and most are non-forgiving. Most will carry a grudge eternally based on someone who is intellectually capable of accomplishing something they cannot. If you disavow them the luxury of swindling you, you are a black ass nigger trying to be like those stupid ass, red neck, white folks. They will literally quit speaking to you. If someone should question why they do not speak to you their answer is: he thinks he is a smart ass; thinks he knows more than anybody else. Unfortunately, these are some of the philosophical, genetic thinking traits of most African Americans; that is: bias, inept and incompetent; also self-conceited.

Most blacks have no respect for anyone they deem is more knowledgeable than they are; pertaining to substance. These are just a few of the embedded genetic sum of African American personal convictions which is related to incompetent, idiosyncrasies which caused complete state of abnormality in reference to any other ethnic nationalities. Most haven't the remotest definition between conservatism and liberalism. They tend to solidify all whites philosophical genetic traits as they are against blacks. This may sound as something contrived; but, it is the mere facts of reality because chronological records of significant events are quite revealing. Unfortunately it has been distorted with bias, philosophical favoritism. The actual truth has never been revealed. For instance, you can listen to all news and read newspapers and you will never hear testimony to the actual fact it was the southern Democratic established Ku Klux Klan who persecuted blacks in the southern states; not Republicans. The fundamental proof is documented in the Constitution. Unfortunately, most blacks know absolutely nothing about the Constitution; and more whites are just as guilty. Most whites do except the fact that it is the controlling factor; regards to all residing American citizens. Most blacks have chosen to ignore the Constitution and deem it was written by white folks for white folks and does not pertain to them. Direfully and unfortunately, political incompetent and inept whites unfamiliar with the genetic cultural embedded traditions of most African Americans choose to assist in electing a president: Barack Hussein Obama, who is philosophically embedded with these identical attributed traits.

This president has been candid only once with the American people during his campaigning to become president. He constantly reminded the American people he was going to bring change to the United States of America. I knew the meaning of this statement. Unfortunately, you politically, small, dysfunctional, inept, brain washed whites did not. His change emphatically meant to sabotage the principles American was established on: extract from the wealthy and distribute to persons who have poorly adjusted to our environment of civility; pertaining to intellect and morality. If any individual has not adjusted to the moral fabrics of our Constitution which gives all the right to choose their own destiny; regards to survival. It is solely based on individual choice; choices are dictated from the brain cells which are captivated through genetic heritage controllability. If this heritage is consumed with philosophical incompetent traits your future will consist of disconsolate, accusing others for your inability to attain the necessities of stabilities to appropriately sustain in life. I recall very vividly, during the early forties as a child in grade school, initiated by the State of Alabama; other children would be absent for weeks. When they did return, the teacher would inquire about the reason for their absence. Their reply would be: mama and papa said we do not need education because it is for white folks. Because we live on Mr. Whitfield's plantation, he said we don't need to be educated because he has taken care of mama and papa and he is going to take care of us.

After servitude was abolished during eighteen sixty five, by Republican President Abraham Lincoln, Democratic plantation owners devised a strategy to dictate indoctrinations to blacks. Because blacks were being freed from bondage by Republican President Abraham Lincoln, the only strategy was to prevent blacks from being educated. This was a tradition throughout the southern states, adopted by all plantation owners. They claimed if they can't read or write they will remain on the plantation to cater to demands.

CHAPTER 10

Chronological records of significant events are repetitious; pertaining to political involvements simply because the ethic people are so prevalent, with emulative, philosophical agendas based on genetic heritage. Inevitably, American life is like a carousal. Time dictates and imposes different standards related to miscellaneous scenarios; but the philosophical intent are equal based on the circumstances; related to chronological past events. During the year eighteen fifty seven, there was a court case decided by the U. S. Supreme Court which involved an African American: Dred Scott and his servitude owner: Sanford. In essence, it was legal to own blacks because the nation of Africa founded slavery; owning and selling people for profit. It was a universal commodity for hundreds of years. Dred Scott's owner Sanford had taken him to such states as Wisconsin and Illinois where blacks were free. Dred Scott did not want to return to the state of Missouri where owning blacks was legal. He sued for his freedom from Sanford in order to attain his liberties from the southern Democratic Ku Klux Klan. They adopted the African Congo guide lines: owning people and selling them for profit were lucrative and honorable traditions. The Dred Scott case was decided by the U. S. Supreme Court which set a precedent during that time. He lost his case for freedom from his master by a margin of seven to two; with Chief Justice Roger B. Taney, who was a Democrat slave owner from the south, reading the opinion. Reading his opinion he demoralized all African Americans; deeming they were not and never had been and never would be an American citizen because they had no rights under the Constitution of the United States of America.

The newly formed Republican Party had a strong feeling of displeasure and deemed those statements to be despicable; coming from a U. S. Supreme Court Chief Justice; in essence, vindictively promised to quell servitude which the Republican congress succeeded in keeping their promise; beginning on December 6, 1865; July 9, 1868 and February 3, 1870. These were the thirteenth, fourteenth and fifteenth amendments to the Constitution; ratified especially for African American's liberties so they could have control of their individual lives; to think and choose for themselves. Unfortunately, the southern founded Democratic Ku Klux Klan was opposed and prohibited blacks from attending schools to attain intellect which would enable blacks to think for themselves. Instead the Democrats indoctrinated most African Americans, especially in the southern states, it was not necessary to apply self-esteem; regards to intellectual moral values because the U. S. Government will subsidize for the inability to comprehend the unique formidable principles America was established on. Most blacks have been complaining for three hundred and ninety three years about racism. The white man won't let me do this because I am black. Their philosophical demeanor; related to skills are inadequate; based on bias, distorted, philosophical, assuming agendas somebody is going to do suptin for us. Because the white folks is keeping us down; because us is black; because mama and papa told us when us was kids; they voted for Democrats and us should to because Democrats have always given us relief checks so us can have babies and us check git bigger, so us can take care of us babies daddies. Us folks told us never to vote for Republicans because day aint nuttin but racist. Day hate black folks and day aint never did nuttin to help blacks. Day want all da money for dem selves and don't giv us nuttin for ourselves.

Unfortunately, this is a common denominator utilized by most blacks for over seventy five years dictated to them by the Democrat President Franklin Delano Roosevelt's political regime. He sat and allowed approximately eighteen blacks to be lynched each year of his first eight years in office as president. It is terribly sad and extremely politically incompetent for the vast majority of ethnic people who were brought to America approximately four hundred years ago. Not being capable of analytically deciphering the differences between the two major political parties existing in America; regard to which party has assisted in their causes for moral liberty. Today their political intellect is parallel to the first twenty Africans brought to America during sixteen nineteen. Many publically demoralized and humiliated themselves with political and bias distortion based on philosophical incompetent lying agendas. On MSNBC the last word with Lawrence O'Donnell and Melissa Harris Perry appeared on March 28, 2011: supposedly a historian from some university, grinning like a jackass eating thorny briars; related to Dred Scott of eighteen fifty seven and his Supreme Court case to attain liberty from his owner, Sanford. This little, dysfunctional brain, jackass, grinning black woman, Melissa Harris Perry, equated the occurrence to racism, related to President Barack Hussein Obama. I would like to know when Obama was denied his civil liberties. It was the southern Democrats who imposed these barbaric sanctions on southern African Americans; not Republicans. Fortunately it was the Republican congress who quelled these incendiary violent barbaric acts of Democratic cynicism by implement of the thirteenth, fourteenth and fifteenth amendments to the U. S. Constitution ratification firmly establish this fact.

There was an established law in most southern states controlled by Democrats and their Ku Klux Klan where owning blacks was a legality of law; pertaining to all blacks who resided within those states. Dred Scott filed his law suit in a state where this guideline did not exist because he was opposed to being taken back to a state where this law existed; enforced by staunch Ku Klux Klan Democratic regime which bought and sold blacks for profit: a global African nation prodigy commodity; which the southern Democrats utilized for their capitalistic wealth. Dred Scott sued to get away from this Democratic Ku Klux Klan barbaric ordeal doctrine which is extremely unfortunate and terribly politically bias; also ignorant and philosophical incompetent. Exalted, educated and illiterate African Americans over seventy five years have not deciphered the techniques and scrutinized Democratic political bias distorted, symbolist, philosophical traditional traits based on an agenda of destructive, ambiguous and demoralizing trite which has indoctrinated most African Americans; to be their political alimentary canal slurps; regards to their voting capacity. They are on every available airway possible; mimicking, Democratic strategy of racism, directed at the Tea Party and Republicans. Apparently the upper, elite of Democrats are totally frustrated because they assumed after the election of Barack Hussein Obama all ethic people in America are as politically inept and incompetent as blacks; not being capable of differentiating between Republican and Democrats. Trust me. It has been determined without reasonable doubt they, the Democrats, have an elected official who is their leader and president, Barack Hussein Obama. Who is nothing more than a narcissistic, demagogic, political, bias, distorting, philosophical, deranged flippant who has disdain for the Constitution and American whites. Most Democrats are aware of this incompetent charade. Realistically the November election caused a Democrat political hemorrhage from their alimentary canal. It is still gushing, caused by a heavy dose of tea served by honorable American citizens who love our country, America, who have the will not to be intimidated because of racist, pathetic bias innuendos from black political incompetents and white sadists.

I am certain most have seen the Geico commercial with the fellow living under a rock. That is the strategy of Democrats; to utilize every black from under a rock, have them on every news outlet yelling and screaming racism pertaining to Republicans and authentic lovers of this nation; the citizens who honored themselves with the Tea Party which has been ridiculed. Trust me. President Barack Hussein Obama, ass is grass and they are the lawn mower; to include his radical regime; come two thousand and twelve. It is being assumed if radical whites herding with most blacks keep attention directed on racism; it will intimidate white voters from voting. Unfortunately for this void America nomad president, Barack Hussein Obama has politically self-destructed. Based on narcissistic bias, distorting incompetency, and the Democrats who are aware of this political tragedy are going to be affect immensely. The only recourse they have is an attempt to revive black power. Meaning: the airways are going to be inundated with blacks like horse shit around a cotton gin. During the early forties, utilizing propaganda, attempting to demoralize Republicans and all American citizens who disagree with their genetic heritage taught philosophical bias agendas. Fortunately, a majority of the loyal American citizens have discovered this president, Barack Hussein Obama, is a political child school yard and phony imposter fraud who has a vindictive, rebellious, philosophical agenda to sabotage the United States of America. He has run out of rhetorical and glamorous, deceptive speeches. As of April 3, 2011 his left wing vindictive, radical, alimentary, canal tongue lapping supporters are emulating Charlie Sheen appearing to be on crack cocaine because the Republican candidates for president are delaying their candidacy. The stupendous Democratic alimentary, canal slurps have excrement dripping from their mouths, anxiously waiting and wanting someone to sic the black and white heel hounds on with inspiring, bias, distorted accusations, impugning the integrity of Republican candidates based on their supposedly being racist against blacks and are responsible for blacks not having their equal rights today.

Most Democratic strategists never in the history of the Democrat Party have endured such a unique reforming philosophical challenge; to blame and outright lie on Republicans: they are racist and despise blacks. They have utilized this strategic doctrine to indoctrinate blacks against Republicans for over seventy eight years. Most Democrats are some of the strategic political diplomatic fast talking liars in unison on God's earth. The most politically violent, beginning with President Abraham Lincoln, the first president to be assassinated by a staunch Democrat, John Wilkes Booth. Initially, he formed a rebellious group of violent Democratic followers to kidnap President Lincoln, but this plot failed. He faithfully promised to eradicate the president for reasons he was a Republican and a nigger lover who intended for them to become citizens with voting rights, but not on his watch. He carried out this threat on April fourteenth at the Ford Theater.

This has been a tradition of Democrats for over one hundred and fifty years. If they can't convenience adherence to their philosophical ideology, they result to intimidation and violence. Fortunately there has always been the Republican Party to reach out to blacks with compassion and their cause in regards to moral diplomacy pertaining to liberties. Chronological records of significant events substantiate the validity; the Republican congress ratified the thirteenth, fourteenth and fifteenth amendments to the U. S. Constitution for African Americans. The Republican congress is responsible for the passage of the nineteen sixty four and five civil and voting rights for blacks. They are also responsible for affirmative action through Republican president, Richard Millhouse Nixon. Republican President George H. Bush selected the second black to serve on the U. S. Supreme Court against wishes of then senator, Joseph Biden, now Democrat vice president. Republican President George W. Bush chose the first two blacks ever to serve as Secretary of State: Colin Powell and Ms. Condoleezza Rice. Unfortunately there were two derogatory statements made about African Americans; one by the southern Democratic Ku Klux Klan during the year eighteen sixty eight. They accused blacks of being illiterate, stupid and incompetent who were trying to rise above their natural place of servitude and should never be nominated for any political position. This was during the time Republican blacks were being elected to the U. S. Senate and U. S. House of Representatives in the southern states; based on the Republicans ratifying the fourteenth amendment to the U. S. Constitution: giving all blacks their civil and voting rights. The Democratic Ku Klux Klan nulled this in eighteen ninety six based on trickery through the U. S. Supreme Court; endorsing the Jim Crow Rule; separate but equal.

The second implication was insinuated by FBI Director J. Edgar Hoover during nineteen fifty seven when he accused blacks of having brains twenty percent smaller than whites. There is always a reason for seemingly derogatory comments, especially pertaining to blacks. Immediately, most African Americans will assume it is because they are black. Unfortunately, most times it is because of their inability to decipher their philosophical intellectual genetic heritage traits. They constantly accuse others for their ignorant incompetency. The bona fide reason southern plantation slave owners accused blacks of being stupid, ignorant and incompetent was because they were. Southern white Democrat plantation owners taught blacks civilization and how to read and write. During the process, they utilized the opportunity to evaluate their intellectual skills; related to their philosophical, genetic traits from Africa. This is how they would determine plantation responsibilities. Their decisions were predicated on this premise; to label blacks stupid and ignorant: which is the definition of incompetency. During the time of eighteen sixty eight, blacks were elected to the U. S. Congress and would stroll into the congressional chambers with bare feet clutching to white women at their side. During nineteen fifty seven, the late FBI Director J. Edgar Hoover was given an assignment by Republican President Dwight David Eisenhower to infiltrate the Democrat Ku Klux Klan in an effort to quell the lynching of African Americans in the southern states; which he accomplished. While he was president, Eisenhower formulated the first civil rights bill for blacks in the south since the Republican congress ratified the fourteenth amendment to the U. S. Constitution for black's civil and equal rights approximately ninety years later. It was rejected by the Democratic controlled congress. However, he never gave up on liberties for blacks and utilized the nation guard to integrate southern schools. During this time blacks could vote in the northern states where they attended the Democratic convention in Philadelphia. They whooped it up and voted Democrats back in office who were lynching their ancestors in the south. This is when FBI Director J. Edgar Hoover made the statement he thought blacks brans were twenty percent smaller than whites; based on total frustration, in relation to black incompetency and ignorance pertaining to the political manifestations. There has been no change for over seventy five years. They are still the boot and alimentary canal licks for Democrats. The only thing the Democrats have reached out to blacks with is a rope with a noose on the end.

CHAPTER 11

During my life span as an adult, I have traveled over the United States of America and other countries. I have dialogued with most ethic people because tentatively it is a necessity to have some knowledge pertaining to the philosophical traits of others. There is not a single day when one is mobile they are not in contact with other people; regardless of the circumstances. If one should choose to enter the political arena and think he or she can continually avoid reality for the sake of a vindictive illusion, they will soon politically self-destruct based on their own philosophical ideology of incompetency. Our nation consists of approximately three hundred million diverse people. There have been numerous politically elected officials who were proven to be regrettable for a segment of citizens who reside in our nation. This is the unique established guidelines that are the prevailing continuity; based on our glorious constitution which offers citizens of our nation the necessary choice to make adjustments based on their philosophical ideologue. This is why the United States of America is the greatest nation on God's earth: individual choice, functional or dysfunctional. On April 5, 2011 I watched a segment of Morning Joe on MSNBC. There was a brief skit shown where a female news anchor person was convinced to lick her I-Pad hand set because she could and would smell and taste food. This was truly news worthy because it offered an explicit spectacle of what our nation consists of to date. There are millions who believe this philosophical myth who are sitting on their brains. These are the essential qualities of people who are responsible for the election of

Barack Hussein Obama to the presidency. At least she licked her I-Pad. For over seventy five years the Democrat Party has convinced most blacks to lick their alimentary canal.

President Barack Hussein Obama initiated his re-election campaign with a commercial photo'ing mostly young whites; appealing to those that lick their I-Pad screens for smell and of eatable food. He is aware most blacks and a segment of Hispanics are going to vote for him if he had a news conference smoking a crack pipe simply because he is black. Most haven't the slightest knowledge of political bias, distortion based on philosophical vindictive agendas.

I was born in the south and was subjected to the authority of Democratic guidelines; sitting in the rear of public transportation, drinking from colored only water fountains, sitting in the balcony of movie theaters. However these southern Democratic incendiary idiosyncrasy guidelines did not deter my love for the United States of America because I am of the opinion God created mankind in His own image; which means God had a brain which He passed on the humans with cells to control every phase of the body's motions. The most important cells are the ones which control intellectual moral values that dictate principles and communicated distinctions for thinking. If utilized appropriately, one can cast incompetent idiosyncrasies aside; minus rebellious vindictiveness, and utilize your God given intellectual talents. To research the validity of why certain occurrences occur if it is of concern to you not to assume, based on herding philosophical distorting bias agendas.

Most blacks never research anything. The get their information from black self-appointed leaders who dictate assumptions to them that the system is unjust and the white man is responsible for their failure in life; especially those racist Republicans. There has been a distinct inevitable disastrous and detrimental philosophical agenda for blacks in America that is eternal for most African Americans. Most haven't the ability to think in depth and decipher the validity of reality. They base their philosophical traits on herding assumptions. America is one of the most unique nations in the universe. Consisting of numerous logical elements to attain prosperity based on constitutional liberties. If understood and used appropriately with regards to adhering and conforming to moralistic traditions and pertaining to distinct dialogues of substance related to reality; which is the established standard of America. Unfortunately, there are those who utilize bias rebellious philosophical agendas to avert these traditional American standards, which in the next twenty months are going to be exploited at an alarming prevalent rate.

The re-election of Barack Hussein Obama, which Democrats are utilizing; this old Stone Age prehistoric strategy to seduce whites who lick their I-Pods for the smell and taste of food to unite with Democratic alimentary canal sucking blacks; in an effort to re-elect this political bias distorting philosophical incompetent narcissistic president who has intentions of sabotaging America. Based on erroneous assumptions related to African genetic heritage, controllability that has been responsible for most herding blacks in America for approximately four hundred years; which is a unique tradition stigmatically that only applies to most African Americans. This has been utilized by Democrats exclusively for demoralization and control of African Americans for centuries; beginning in eighteen ninety six after the Republican congress ratified the fourteenth amendment to the U. S. Constitution in eighteen sixty eight which gave all African Americans civil and voting rights. The out raged southern Democratic Ku Klux Klan strategically improvised a plan to rescind those rights. They knew most blacks were herders behind affluent other blacks; so they appealed to Booker T. Washington, the black president of Tuskegee Institute in Alabama. He appeased the southern Ku Klux Klan by giving speeches all over the highly populated black areas in the southern states such as Atlanta. He was encouraging southern blacks the Jim Crow Rule: separate, but equal, was inevitable and would be in their best interest. Most blacks began parading and yelling; he is the boss at a college; he know what is best for us. The southern Democrats and their Ku Klux Klan appealed to the U. S. Supreme Court; Plessey versus Ferguson; and convinced the justices; based on applauding blacks, this statutory should be ratified into law; which it was. Endorsing the separation of people by race was constitutional, as long as each race had appropriate subsidies. This was nothing more than initiating the reinstatement of servitude in a technical manner. Although the Democrats could not reinstate slavery, they could impose many of the slavery traits on blacks by rescinding their civil and voting rights. Public integration haunted southern blacks for approximately seventy years. Simply because of most black's stigmatic genetic traditional heritage of herding behind other affluent African Americans. However, most blacks have always wanted their own country within America. They were elated when the Supreme Court rules in the southern white Democrats favor during eighteen ninety six: the Constitution did not prohibit the segregation of race, as long as each race had compatible resources. This is why southern blacks had to sit in the back of the bus for sixty eight years; because all public bussing and the buses belonged to whites. After approximately one hundred fifteen years, most blacks still have a huge puzzling problem trying to figure out this resource thing: why most do not have resources comparable to whites. It is fairly simple. I think the lady who licked her I-Pod screen for smell and taste of food could figure this one out. Columbus discovered America during fourteen ninety two. Uncivilized Africans were brought here during sixteen nineteen; a hundred twenty seven years later. Oh, incidentally, civilization and resources were already profoundly established; which most blacks rebelled against for two hundred years; adhering to their genetic heritage traits from Africa.

During the year of seventeen fifty, there were approximately a half million Africans in America who came from different African ethnic tribal groups. Many spoke different tribal languages and performed numerous tribal rituals. They were extremely persistently violent. The significance of black rebellions became so intimidating for whites some southern states began consulting with the legislature in an effort to deport all Africans back to Africa. However it was quelled through debate. The existing circumstances to date are most African Americans are totally inept, or in dysfunctional denial. They do not realize America was established on the intellectual moral values of whites. The manual labor of most illiterate, incompetent blacks assisted in their efforts; regarding to accomplishments. They were rewarded according to their intellect. There were a large segment of whites incorporated within this same incompetent philosophical genetic chosen trait. Unfortunately for blacks, they were the only ethnic people who constantly try and convince others they are under rated because they are black. They have used this dysfunctional propaganda for approximately four hundred years; herding behind self-appointed black leaders who politically distort reality; based on philosophical inept incompetent agendas in an effort to deceive and camouflage for inadequacy. They gain this from understanding from Democratic incompetent whites and put into their own practical recourse of repertoire philosophical illusions; pertaining to deceit. This has been a genetic heritage tradition of most blacks for centuries.

Beginning in Africa and refined in the United States of America. Over a period of time, unfortunately it is a customary tradition of most blacks to emulate others because of the inability to concentrate comprehensibly pertaining to self-creative indulgence effectively on their individual merits. These expressed observations are not meant to demoralize; it is the authenticity of reality. I am a proud American with African heritage. I have carefully examined the philosophical genetic traits of others, black and white. The more we delve into our own individual philosophical genetic heritage and fully comprehend the objectives which will dictate our motives; evaluate the sensitivity based on intellectual moral values and reality; which will determine your anxieties and personal deliverance to attain desired objectives in life. There are only two choices in life: success or failure. Each of these representations of words begins at home while under the jurisdiction of parents. Parents are the bed-rock which establishes success or failure in children. These sentiments are embedded in genetic heritage controllability and careful denoted representation based on the standards of morality. These are principle standard guidelines established along with the enforcement of the law. Throughout the United States of America, if not understood based on adherence, your destination will be incarceration, Ghetto slums or both. Because the unique standards which formulate American diverse; society offers explicit opportunities to all those who qualify based on intellect not ethnics. Unfortunately, most blacks are of the assumed opinion they should have special privileges because of their ethnic of being black simply because of herding behind other affluent blacks and believe this philosophical fantasy.

To substantiate the validity of my accuracies, a facsimile was displayed on national television hosted by Ed Schultz on MSNBC April 10, 2011 along with Al Sharpton, which was a spectacle of the old Jim Crow Rule, initiated during eighteen ninety six: separate, but equal; established by the southern Democrats Ku Klux Klan when Booker T. Washington convinced blacks that separate but equal was in their best interest. They sat in the back of the bus for sixty eight years. This political philosophical episode was an identical replica of the Ed Schultz production; he being the southern Democratic Ku Klux Klan and Al Sharpton being the black traitor and Booker T. Washington. The only difference was the change in name. Instead of separate, but equal it is called Obama black America. With Al Sharpton leading the charge, insinuating day gwing to do suptin for us blacks because dare is disparity based on race and job cutting double for blacks.

Black people are being left behind. The need to galvanize this country so blacks can be equal: wit dem rich folks inside day ivory towers and dis is what dis black agender is all about. De congressional black caucus aint duing nuttin for us. Al Sharpton and Cornell West reminded me of a skit on Fox News, April 1, 2011. Tribes of New Guinea eating with cannibals;

where the magic man of the tribe, better known as the witch doctor, judge others who have committed some kind of offense. Their punishment would be cooked and eaten by other tribesmen. I was waiting for Ed Schultz to roll out the grill for Sharpton and West to experiment with this hostile, uncivilized endeavor. In essence, Democratic strategists have literally utilized ignorant, incompetent blacks, particularly in the southern states. Beginning with President Franklin Delano Roosevelt over seventy five years ago, a Democrat literally annexed blacks from the Republican Party which Republican President Abraham Lincoln had established for their best interest. By abolishing servitude he had introduced a legislative proclamation for congress to ratify; giving all black families forty acres of Democratic plantation owners land and a government mule.

Committable Republican President Abraham Lincoln truly was a person of outstanding, extraordinary character. He had a true compassion for blacks to become independent as U. S. citizens. His intent was to introduce them to a stage of American diverse civilization and the fundamentals which it was established on: the fortitude of having assets by giving them the land and a government mule for their independence to improve their living standards and educate their children. Unfortunately, blacks were deprived of this noble gift because a Democrat, John Wilkes Booth, assassinated President Lincoln prior to the ratification of his proclamation by congress. President Abraham Lincoln's vice president was a Democrat from Tennessee, Andrew Johnson. After he was sworn in as president, he rescinded the proclamation and gave the land back to the southern plantation owners. This was the beginning of a major destitution and compelled illiteracy for southern blacks. Because the Democratic Ku Klux Klan could not institute servitude again they utilized share cropping as a replica. Most blacks were illiterate and farming was all they knew. They had no other choice but to remain on the plantation and serve according to the guidelines of slavery. The plantation owners demanded their children not be educated because the premise of this theory was: if you cannot read, you have no other choice but to remain loyal to the plantation owners and serve according to authoritative regulations.

This was one of the most immoral tragedies to occur in the history of African Americans in America because it exploited illiteracy, ignorance and incompetency. In most ethnic blacks this is still prevalent today. The majority of blacks are totally inept or in denial to the fact it was the southern Democrat Ku Klux Klan who imposed this horrific, rebellious, destructive, preventative restriction on blacks in regards to attaining education. Another inequity occurred, imposed by Democrats in regards to slave trading and selling of blacks. Let's evaluate the validity of the circumstances. If a young African woman was brought in with three children and auctioned off; the mother was sold to someone from Tennessee, one of her children was sold to a buyer from Alabama, one to an Arkansas purchaser and one to a Mississippi buyer. Let's say this occurred during the eighteen forties. Republican President Abraham Lincoln abolished slavery during eighteen sixty five. Blacks were free to locate their relatives. Approximately twenty five years later the difficulty was created. Once sold and reaching their plantation of destination, their African names were changed based on the request of the plantation owners. Unfortunately, this caused utter chaos because through brain cell genetic controllability of close relatives such as mothers, fathers, sisters and brothers the genetic brain cells would dictate compassion and affection for each person. In essence, the fundamental reality of slave trading created a mass dilemma of incest internally with black ethnic people. This created the potential for dysfunctional children. Based on incestuous relations between relatives they were totally unaware of. Many miscellaneous health problems could have occurred related to same DNA genetic heritage.

CHAPTER 12

During the year seventeen eighty four, a white physician from Philadelphia, Benjamin Rush, quoted: slavery and the slave trade must be ended so Africans might become educated and useful citizens so America might become the beacon of freedom it professed to be. Republican President Abraham Lincoln dedicated his life to accomplish this sentiment. Unfortunately, the Democratic Ku Klux Klan was opposed to this moral civilized opinion. They eradicated the moral fabric of most blacks which is a fundamental stigmatization eternally. Most blacks do not have the political capacity to decipher alternatives. It was annexed by Democrats over one hundred forty years ago. During the plantation era, whites learned about the philosophical genetic heritage traits of blacks consisting of following leaders based on tribal instincts from Africa. Most plantations had thousands of cattle. Numerous times the cattle would break through the fence following a leader, mostly a female named a matriarch with a bell for the purpose of location. Once she was located, the balance of the cattle would herd behind her inside the broken fence. Southern plantation owners noticed this replica of a philosophical trait about blacks following behind black leaders so the plantation master literally named all blacks herders which is a genetic tradition in the philosophical heritage traits of most blacks today. This has demoralized their credibility almost to extinction, particularly in politics. Most blacks assume the Constitution is not in their best interest; it is only customized for the benefit of Caucasians. Their philosophical heritage traits dictate herding behind a self-appointed black assuming dictator which encourages rebellious asinine radical racist folklore. Most blacks have always had an infuriating complex in an effort to compensate for embedded personal convictions of incompetency. During the late eighteen sixties into the early seventies, southern Democrats and their Ku Klux Klan literally violently slaughtered black and white Republicans. They forced them from the southern states simply because they were trying to teach former slaves integrity and to read and write. They would literally lynch any black who supported Republicans. They intimidated and excoriated even to the extent of murdering whites. This was traditional until the election of Republican President Dwight David Eisenhower. He authorized FBI Director J. Edgar Hoover to infiltrate the Ku Klux Klan and quell this type of insane detrimental violence against people; especially blacks because they supported the Republican Party. This hostile environmental political bias distortion relegated to intimidation.

The Democratic Party controlled the U. S. Congress for forty years. Although President Dwight David Eisenhower succeeded in quelling the lynching of southern blacks, and integrated a segment of southern schools and legislated the first civil and voting rights bill for southern African Americans in eighty nine years, it was rejected by the Democratic controlled congress. During his administration, President Dwight David Eisenhower had sympathetic humanity for blacks equal to President Abraham Lincoln. He quelled the Democratic established Ku Klux Klan from lynching blacks and forcible use of federal military power over the Democratic governor of Arkansas, Orval Faubus' opposition by authorizing over a thousand one hundred First Airborne Paratroopers to protect nine black students to enter Central High in Little Rock, Arkansas. Most blacks and whites are generally incompetent to the fact that civil rights legend Dr. Martin Luther King and the legendary baseball star Jackie Robinson were staunch Republicans who supported President Eisenhower in his efforts to restore liberty for southern blacks. He initiated the premise during nineteen fifty seven for African Americans civil and voting rights to be restored in nineteen sixty four and five. Most blacks never understood the philosophical gratuitous accolades because most have always had an infuriating complex genetic heritage controllability which dictated comprehension. In an effort to compensate for embedded philosophical assuming and distorting reality based on incompetency which is responsible for high rise slum buildings all over the nation filled with rebellious illiterate blacks. There are approximately three hundred twenty five million people who reside in the United States of America where approximately thirty eight to forty million are African Americans.

The United States of America is the top incarcerating nation on the globe with approximately eight to nine million people incarcerated according to Wikipedia. African Americans are approximately three and one half to four million of all ethnic groups incarcerated. Blacks are the most single parents with children born out of wedlock along with most recipients infected with AIDS. It is quite obvious there is a genetic heritage dysfunction related to incompetency. They are the most school drop outs. Southern plantation masters discovered this hundreds of years ago. They utilized this deficiency to their advantage; especially when blacks became eligible to vote. The Democrats used strategic methods to politically indoctrinate most blacks with insinuations Republicans are rich, white, racists who despise blacks who are also responsible for their destitution because they have never reached out to blacks. Democrats utilized this sickening method of criteria to their advantage through victimization of Republicans for political control based on indoctrination comparable to an African Congo tribal chief with assistance from self-appointed black herding leaders. African Americans are the only ethnic people who reside in a justifiable society of liberty with a two major political party system. They choose to support he party which has only reached out to blacks with ropes having nooses on the end. Most African Americans have never chosen to closely study and systematically clarify or understand the credentials which our nation was established on with the accountability to decipher aspects in regards to the United States of America based on reality.

America is the greatest nation on God's earth simply because the founding fathers adhered to intellectual moral values which are embedded to support the structure of our diverse society based on philosophical agendas which should coincide with the established guidelines of our nation; especially if you are a politically elected official, either Democrat, Republican or independent, which is the essence of reality and the nature which guides the established system. If one of any ethnic group chooses to alter or eradicate this they obviously are philosophically embedded with rebellious, inept, dysfunctional illusions. It will never occur and there are dire consequences for those who attempt such radical philosophical ethnic agendas based on political gratification for dominating superiority over others. Chronological records of significant events dictates it has never appropriately succeeded because during the year of eighteen seventy four the southern Democratic arm force white league marched on the state house of New Orleans where black and white Republicans were located. In an effort to eradicate the Louisiana Republican state government; even to the extent of assassination and murder of Republicans for Democratic Ku Klux Klan white supremacy. The tragic violence escalated to eradicate the Republican Party in the southern states. In Vicksburg, Mississippi approximately three hundred black Republican supporters were literally slaughtered in an effort to dissuade support for Republicans and install Democratic Ku Klux Klan political control. In South Carolina, there were white supremacies calling themselves red shirts and rifle clubs tormenting and terrorizing black citizens in an effort to restore white Democratic political control from Republicans. Prior to these homicidal attacks to sabotage the Republican Party in the southern states, within the Republican system African Americans had made numerous political advantages. Hiram Rhodes Revels became the first black U. S. Senator from Mississippi; Blanche K. Bruce—the first black Republican to serve a full term in the U. S. Senate elected in Louisiana. There were many other black Republicans to succeed in politics. Over six hundred black Republicans served in state legislatures. Twenty were elected to the U. S. House of Representatives. They were working together with white Republicans for some Democrats to rebuild the south.

The southern Democratic Ku Klux Klan regime was intent on reinstating Democratic white supremacy of servitude which the Republican congress had abolished by ratifying the fourteenth amendment to the U. S. Constitution in eighteen sixty eight which gave all southern blacks their civil and voting rights. The southern Democratic Ku Klux Klan became rebelliously enraged because blacks had been given their liberties. This resulted in belligerent slaughtering of black and white Republicans which drove them from the southern states. Most blacks who could not afford to leave were forced to become Democrats if they were not lynched which a form of servitude was reinstated for southern blacks. This debacle persisted for approximately thirty years. During eighteen ninety six, the southern Democratic Ku Klux Klan, through the U. S. Supreme Court implemented the Jim Crow Rule: separate but equal guideline where southern blacks civil rights were revoked for sixty eight years; until nineteen sixty four and five when the Republican congress rose to the occasion and over-rode Democratic Senator Robert Byrd; a former Ku Klux Klan filibuster, against southern black's civil rights being restored. This is the year of two thousand eleven, forty seven years later after the restitution of civil and voting rights for southern blacks. Politically inept African Americans;

illiterate educated and supposedly highly educated are constantly sucking the alimentary canal of Democrats and rewarding them with approximately ninety five percent of their votes. As a gratuity for depriving their ancestors of liberties and intellectual moral values they were slaughtered because of their philosophical traits of being affiliated with the graciousness of the Republican Party. Why African Americans were loyal to the Republican Party is simply because Republican President Abraham Lincoln, through the brilliancy of his integrity, engaged troops into battle. Most of all he sacrificed his life in order that blacks could have liberty to choose their own destiny in life. In an effort that future generations could explore and determine their philosophical traits in a free society which is the embedded factor in the U. S. Constitution pertaining to all people.

If it were not for the Republicans none of the Democratic politically inept incompetent black idiots would be on national news networks on all phases supporting Democrats. There are numerous people globally who have ethnic idiosyncrasy deficiencies. Most African Americans deserve the Medal of Honor for being the most philosophical eccentric dysfunctional incompetent ethnic in the universe. These statements are not meant to demoralize or criticize based on derogatory remarks and has absolutely nothing to do with bias philosophical racism. It is to stipulate the validity of facts related to philosophical political ineptness of most blacks and a large segment of whites pertaining to the inhumane occurrences which transpired in our nation over hundreds of years ago. They are affirmed by the validity of factual reality related to chronological events. Unfortunately this has been politically distorted based on bias philosophical agendas in an effort to deceive and deter reality for political control over others. You can watch southern incidents portrayed twenty four hours daily pertaining to African Americans during the past years being assaulted in the southern states in an effort to redeem their civil liberties from southern Democrats not the Republicans.

There are two major political parties in America with Democrats being affiliated with liberalism and Republicans with conservatism. I have listened to radio and watched television for over sixty years. Never once have I heard or seen the news media distinguish or establish the truth accuracy related to the reality of the southern Democrats being the culprits who were torturing and eradicating African Americans simply because they were Republicans who wanted their liberties according to the Constitution. To substantiate the validity of my acclaim; during eighteen sixty eight, under Republican President Ulysses S. Grant's administration the Republican controlled congress reacted to southern Democratic Ku Klux Klan violence and slaughter of black and white Republicans. The Ku Klux Klan used murder as an intimidation to discourage black and white Republicans from voting. During the spring of eighteen sixty six, the violence became atrocious through the south; slaughtering black and white Republicans to prohibit their voting structure. The southern Democratic Knights of the White Camilla, the Pale Face Brotherhood and the Ku Klux Klan all vicious white terrorists determined to sabotage the Republican Party. Any white southerners who allied with blacks became Republicans were called scalawags and carpet baggers and were targets for assassination. They invaded Republican delegate halls in places such as New Orleans and Memphis. Unfortunately it was open season on southern Republicans. Under the regime of then Democratic President Andrew Johnson; until he was succeeded by a Republican president: Ulysses S. Grant. During the early eighteen seventies he consulted with the Republican controlled congress and they established numerous anti-Klan violated laws which President Grant signed into law in an effort to quell the murdering violence of Republicans.

During eighteen seventy one President Grant suspended the writ of habeas corpus in nine South Carolina counties where the Ku Klux Klan was most active. This initiated the efforts of arresting white Democratic Ku Klux Klan terrorists. The Republican controlled congress launched an intensive encroached investigation. Federal officials arrested and indicated hundreds of Democratic Ku Klux Klan and their terrorist supporters who were poor illiterate whites, educated whites, doctors, lawyers, ministers and college professors. This included Democrat Wade Hampton who served as governor and U. S. Senator from South Carolina who explicitly stated and urged his Democratic colleagues in the name of white supremacy: we must control Negro Republican voters; even assassinate to deter. The authenticity of our nation, Sweet Home America, consists of contrasting political party philosophical bias agendas. This book is not written to judge as a critic, but to offer an explicit psychoanalysis of chronological events based on reality. It has absolutely nothing to do with fiction or racism. I leave the conclusions entirely up to the readers.

There have been numerous episodes of violent events encroached in America related to political aspirations for dominate supremacy over others. Our forefathers were quite familiar with these philosophical agenda of traits because they ratified a deterrent on July 4, 1776: the Declaration of Independence; the action of the second continental congress; the unanimous declaration of the thirteen United States of America. When in the course of human events it became necessary for one people to dissolve the political bands which had connected them with another and to assume among the powers of the earth the separate and equal station to which the laws of nature and of nature God entitle them. A decent respect to the opinions of mankind requires they should declare the causes which impel them to the separation.

We hold these truths to be self-evident; that all men are created equal. They are endowed by their creator with certain unalienable rights. Among them are: life, liberty and the pursuit of happiness to secure these rights. Governments are instituted among men; deriving their just powers from consent of the governed. Whenever any form of government becomes destructive of these ends it is the right of the people to alter or to abolish it and institute new government. Laying its foundation on such principles and organizing its powers in such form as to them shall seem most likely to affect their safety and happiness. Prudence, indeed, will dictate governments long established should not be changed for light and transient causes. Accordingly all experience hath shown mankind are more disposed to suffer while evils are sufferable than to right themselves by abolishing the forms to which they are accustomed. When a long train of abuse and usurpation, pursuing invariably the same objects, evinces a design to reduce them under absolute despotism it is their right. It is their duty to throw off such government and to provide new guards for their future security. Such has been the patient sufferance of these colonies; and such is now the necessity which constrains them to alter their former systems of government. The history of the present king of Great Britain is a history of repeated inquiries and usurpations; all having in direct object the establishment of an absolute tyranny over these states. To prove this; let facts be submitted to a candid world. He has refused his assent to laws, the most wholesome and necessary for the public good. He has forbidden his governors to pass laws of immediate and pressing importance; unless suspended in their operations till his assent should be obtained; and when so suspended he has utterly neglected to attend to them. He has refused to pass other laws for the accommodation of large districts of people unless those people would relinquish the right of representation in the legislature; a right inestimable to them and formidable to tyrants only. He has called together legislative bodies at places unusual, uncomfortable, and distant from the depository of their public records for the sole purpose of fatiguing them into compliance with his measures. He has dissolved representative's houses repeatedly for opposing with any firmness his invasions on the rights of the people. He has refused for a long time, after such dissolutions, to cause others to be elected; whereby the legislative powers, incapable of annihilation, have returned to the people at large for their exercise; the state remaining in the meantime exposed to all the dangers of invasion from without and convulsions within. He has endeavored to prevent the population of these states; for that purpose obstructing the laws for naturalization of foreigners; refusing to pass others to encourage their migrations hither and raising the conditions of new appropriations of lands. He has obstructed the administration of justice, by refusing his assent to laws for establishing judiciary powers. He has made judges dependent on his will alone, for the tenure of their offices, and the amount and payment of their salaries. He has erected a multitude of new offices, and sent hither swarms of officers to harass our people, and eat out their substance. He has kept among us, in times of peace, standing armies, without the consent of our legislature. He has affected to render the military independent of and superior to the civil power. He has combined with others to subject us to a jurisdiction foreign to our Constitution and unacknowledged by our laws; giving his assent to their acts of pretended legislation: for quartering large bodies of armed troops among us; for protecting them, by a mock trial, from punishment for any murders which they should commit on the inhabitants of these states: for cutting off our trade with all parts of the world: for imposing taxes on us without our consent: for depriving us, in many cases, of the benefits of trial by jury for transporting us beyond seas to be tried for pretended offences: for abolishing the free system of English laws in a neighboring province, establishing therein an arbitrary government, and enlarging its boundaries, so as to render it at once an example and fit instrument for introducing the same absolute rule into these colonies: for taking away our charters, abolishing our most valuable laws, and altering fundamentally the forms of our governments: for suspending our own legislatures, and declaring themselves invested with power to legislate for us in all cases whatsoever.

He has addicted government here, by declaring us out of his protection and waging war against us. He has plundered our seas, ravaged our coast, burnt our towns, and destroyed the lives of our people. He is, at this time, transporting large armies of foreign mercenaries to complete the works of death, desolation, and tyranny, already begun with circumstances of cruelty and perfidy, scarcely paralleled in the most barbarous ages, and totally unworthy the head of a civilized nation. He has constrained our fellow citizens taken captive on the high seas to bear arms against their country, to become the executioners of their friends and brethren, or to fall themselves by their hands. He has excited domestic insurrections amongst us, and has endeavored to bring on the inhabitants of our frontiers, the merciless Indian savages, whose known rule of warfare is undistinguished destruction, of all ages, sexes and conditions. In every stage of these oppressions we have petitioned for redress in the most humble terms: our repeated petitions have been answered only by repeated injury. A prince, whose character is thus marked by every act which may define a tyrant, is unfit to be the ruler of a free people. Nor have we been wanting in attentions to our British brethren. We have warned them from time to time of attempts by their legislature to extend an unwarrantable jurisdiction over us. We have reminded them of the circumstances of our emigration and settlement here. We have applied to their native justice and magnanimity, and we have conjured them by the ties of our common kindred to disavow these usurpations, which would inevitably interrupt our connections and correspondence. They too have been deaf to the voice of justice and of consanguinity. We must, therefore, acquiesce in the necessity, which denounces our separation, and hold them, as we hold the rest of mankind, enemies in war, in peace, friends. We, therefore, the representatives of the United States of America, in general congress, assembled, appealing to the supreme judge of the world for the rectitude of our intentions, do, in the name. and by authority of the good people of these colonies, solemnly publish and declare, that these united colonies are and of right ought to be, free and independent states; that they are absolved from all allegiance to the British crown, and that all political connection between them and the state of Great Britain, is and ought to be totally dissolved; and that as free and independent states, they have full power to levy war, conclude peace, contract alliances, establish commerce, and do all other acts and things which independent states may of right do, and for the support of this declaration, with a firm reliance on the protection of divine providence, we mutually pledge to each other our lives, our fortunes, and our sacred honor. The fifty six signatures on the declaration appear in the position indicated.

I referred to our Declaration of Independence because those fifty six unique ingenious men, over two hundred and thirty five years ago, prescribed antidotes transpiring in our nation today. Their objectives were related to the philosophical traits of agendas of political objectives that are inevitable and it transcends into the Constitution of WE THE PEOPLE to determine our own political fate. We as a nation have the greatest combined principles on God's earth embedded within the Declaration of Independence and the Constitution. The Declaration of Independence dictates principles and guidelines based on morality pertaining to all people. The Constitution demands adherence to morality; which includes political parties that are entrusted to the dignity of the citizens who reside in the United States of America. One may philosophically distort reality for bias agendas and mislead some of the people, some of the time; but, not all the people all the time. This consists of two major political parties: Democrat and Republican. Each party supported by dedicated constituencies and independents who determine the outcome of elections based on their chosen candidate; initiated with a primary election to determine a representative from each party which either one can be either elected to the presidency of the United States of America.

I have monitored and observed this American tradition for over sixty five years. But never anything like two thousand eight; when a political distorting bias philosophical socialistic imposter, American sabotaging black man was elected president of the greatest nation on God's earth. Simply because he is black and has a self-taught distinct deceptive vocabulary. He superbly utilized this to politically distort; based on bias philosophical innuendoes to accomplish his rebellious agenda. An agenda to demoralize and sabotage the United States of America based on political inept incompetency by not being capable of deciphering the alternative between Democrat and Republican in regards to sympathy for African Americans during their traumatic Democratic southern Ku Klux Klan adventures. During the eighteen sixties they were literally lynched and slaughtered simply because they were Republicans attempting to utilize their civil rights in accordance with the Declaration of Independence and the Constitution which the Republican congress ratified by the fourteenth amendment of the Constitution on July 9, 1868: for all citizens of the United States of America inclusively for African Americans; which specifically stipulated: all persons born or naturalized in the United States and subject to the jurisdiction thereof are citizens of the United States and the state wherein they reside. No state shall make or enforce any law which shall abridge the privileges or immunities of citizens of the United States; nor shall any state deprive any person of life, liberty, or property without due process of law; nor deny to any person within its jurisdiction the equal protection of the laws.

The United States of America has some of the greatest intellectual moral valued opinioned thinkers on God's earth with extraordinary concepts embedded and ratified in our Declaration of Independence and the Constitution. Unfortunately, there are political opposing perceptions related to the general population, and the necessity for opinion clarification is established into the interior of a two party system; Democrat and Republican. The consistency is inevitable in an effort to eliminate a monarch or socialism in the United States of America.

For years I have researched to substantiate the philosophical political ideological motivated agenda of the Democratic and Republican parties in an effort to determine which party was duly in compliance with the Declaration of Independence bas on established American formality; and has used the Constitution to ratify for justice pertaining to the validity of the United States of America citizens because God, principles, values and morality was an adherence to our forefathers. According to chronological records of significant events, the Republican Party denotes these ethics. Ladies and gentlemen of America, I solemnly inject we are allowing our home sweet home (America) to be demoralized and principles are being abandoned for savagery and Congo philosophical distorted bias agendas. WE THE PEOPLE are still in control of our own destiny. The election of two thousand twelve is the most important in American history. We as a people have only two choices while it still exists: to think positive in regards to utilizing common knowledge based on facts of events; to evaluate the fundamentals of the current Democratic administration led by President Barack Hussein Obama. This administration has only one philosophical bias retaliated agenda which is to sabotage the United States to the brink of disaster so he can gloat over how he, being a single black man, persuaded and out-smarted all those stupid ass whites; especially the wealthy who brought their chickens home to roost. He sat with his church pastor for twenty years. His pastor emphatically and publically implied God damn America; the controlling rich white man's chickens are coming home to roost. He considered nine eleven to be a prototype as to what America should be plagued with. Prior to him being elected president, Barack Hussein Obama was affiliated with a home grown terrorist who actually carried out acts of bomb attacks in America. They claim it would have been more devastating and refuse to apologize. In essence, pragmatic voting constituency in America, WE THE PEOPLE discretion is being challenged to determine our future: continue supporting a philosophical bias distorting rebellious agenda with intentions of eradicating the Declaration of Independence and our Constitution.

Ladies and gentlemen, citizens of the United States of America, politically we are at a dead end crossroad: either turn right or left. Turn left and maintain the status quo of sabotaging America and establish a Congo chief monarch, also negated liberty. Turn right and maintain the Declaration of Independence and our sustaining constitutional ability to liberty. The thinking capacity of most Democratic whites are equivalent to most black's. The embedded teachings of the southern Democratic plantation masters and their intellectual teachings were based on ethnic traditional heritage of herding, meaning this is what I heard so pass it on. The United States of America is the most unique controversial nation on God's earth simply because of its ethnic diversity. Inherently within each ethnic internally derive an individual or individuals that excel with specific, explicit, terminology which appeals to other ethnics. Through inventing, manufacturing or politics and politicians are the solidification of all endeavors pertaining to people in general. Theoretically you are engaging in a philosophical agenda of you ideology to solicit with the intent for others to either purchase of support.

Politics is quite unique. You are soliciting support from all ethnics. There are numerous categories which require elections for state and federal administrations. Our forefathers established the credible guidelines for America on the basis of majority rules. The procedures are characterized within our Constitution which addresses many miscellaneous guidelines: beginning with *WE THE PEOPLE*. The highest political office to attain is the presidency of the United States of America. Most candidates will utilize any method possible to attain this office to the extent of outright lying to the American people in an effort to convince them of his or her qualifications. There have been numerous candidates, over hundreds of years, to attain the presidency, beginning with the first president, George Washington in seventeen eighty nine. Since then there have been multitudes of political bias, distorting, philosophical strategies formatted to confuse constituencies in an effort to attain their confidence in regards to their voting support. The political candidate will utilize any method of extremism to delegitimize their opponents.

During the eighteen hundreds, the Democrats utilized murder and assassination to prevent black and white Republicans from being participants in the voting process. The sentiments of the process have changed based on time, modern technology and adherence to the Constitution, enforced by demand from authoritative personnel. Unfortunately the system is not perfect. Idealistically this is all we have to sustain humanity. There are those candidates who will utilize political bias distortion based on philosophical agendas of enormous deceit. Who will numerous of times galvanize and motivate segments of ethnic people to support their agenda of covert delusions: they are going to change the philosophical versions of America to their best interest. Most are inept to the distinguishing fundamental established peculiarity of the United States of America. How is it possible to change the philosophical embedded overall traditions of America when they are philosophical distorting bias dictating deficient individuals who know absolutely nothing about the chronological established events of ethnical fortitude which has existed for hundreds of years? Most are estranged to and have alienated themselves based on political bias distortion which is based on philosophical agendas of change; and is inept to the fact the standards of America are inevitable, eternal and a gift from God.

CHAPTER 13

I begin this chapter with an explicit explanation in regards to the Democratic Party and African blacks; beginning with a statement from the prominent, former Democratic governor of Pennsylvania, Ed Rendell on MSNBC on April 9, 2011. He gave a trustworthy opinion free from deception when he emphatically stated: We Democrats hardly have thrifty philosophical traits on anything. In a winning fashion, we have to wait until the Republicans generate ideas and we seek to distort and delegitimize their efforts. In an effort to stabilize our credibility which he was ambitiously wanting the government to shut down so he could blame, bash and ridicule Republicans, simply for Democratic bliss. This is the cornerstone of Democratic legacy. They never have any relevant resolutions to adequately resolve anything politically. However, once the Republicans render a solution, the Democrats are dissecting and attempting to delegitimize their efforts as they have a better plan. The strategy is only to politically distort with bias philosophical radical agendas in an effort to confuse and frustrate the American people under pretenses they are elites over the Republicans. This is only demagoguery to impress because chronological records of significant events dictate the Democrats have never had plans of appropriate essential justification related to the American people. The never consider what is in the best interest for the people who elected them. Their strategy is to confuse the American people into thinking it is the Republicans who are the culprits. They have utilized this covert strategy tactics on most African Americans for over one hundred and forty years.

The substantiating evidence is available for the entire world to witness. In a society of liberty with a major two party system consisting of Democrat and Republican, one ethnic people, who are black, vote ninety five percent for Democrats. Obviously, this is unprecedented in a liberated ethnic civil society. It is based on dysfunctional genetic heritage due to herding. Democrats utilize herding to their advantage to maintain superiority over political inept blacks who enhance their philosophical bias agenda to scathingly censure Republicans in regards to racism against African Americans. Along with white radical monolithic surrogates who are exiting racism in an effort to appeal to whites based on solidifying votes related to compassion for stupid ass blacks. I mean this literally because the research written in this book substantiates the validity of my claim.

There are those who are going to assume their opinions such as: he ain't nuttin but a white man nigger; he is against us and by God the Republicans really brainwashed that nigger to lie about his own folks, especially Barack Obama. Unfortunately, they are the small dysfunctional brain, philosophical aloof Democratic alimentary canal sucks; totally inept to the intricacy of our Declaration of Independence and Constitution. They are also lost in humanity based on political bias distortion relative to philosophical agendas, categorical on assumption, dispelling reality. These are ethic people black and white who only vision remedies in life from their exclusive generalities based on arrogant, argumentative premeditations and evading morality, distorting reality, theoretically based on assumptions, minas research.

There are certain ethnic people who utilize the scenario of assumptions in an effort for others to think they are marked with wit and ingenuity. They are dysfunctional and incompetent to the magnitude they will attempt to convince others George Washington was not the first president and Abraham Lincoln was a racist Republican president who despised blacks and persecuted them until the Democrats forced him to abolish slavery. Thomas Jefferson had nothing to do with the Declaration of Independence. Dr. Martin Luther King was a white man Negro and a turncoat and is why civil rights was so long coming. This is the greatness of America. These people are embedded in a civil society. Some are illiterate or highly educated, black and white; also financially stable; yet they are out of touch with reality: misinformed, rebellious and inept to the fact if it wasn't for the Declaration of Independence and the Constitution of this great nation, the United States of America along with the Republican Party their chances of where they are would have been next none. This is why the

United States of America is heaven on earth. One can be a dysfunctional, small brain, rebellious, incompetent idiot and still obtain success related to all merited intervals in America.

Although there are numerous times qualifications are not determined until after the fact, the evaluation for selections or elections could emulate dire consequences. The validity of this analysis is sitting in the White House as president of the United States of America, Barack Hussein Obama. Selections, failures or successes are determined by an individual or individuals elected. Success or failure are determined by the people who elected one to office primarily based on promise and expectancy of intellectual, moral and loyal values. The American standard tradition is your voting constituency determines success or failure based on your accomplishments only. Unfortunately black and white Congo hyenas are slobbering at the mouth with President Barack Hussein Obama; alimentary canal excrement, screaming racism. This is nothing more than political bias distortion based on philosophical agenda of strategic illusions illustrated by ambiguous extremist Democrats in an effort to compensate for President Obama's incompetency and narcissistic, rebellious, demanding arrogance. It was politically inept, stupid ass I-Pod lickers for food, taste and smell whites who elected him to the presidency. The American people are some of the most collective, comprehensive, compassionate, intellectual American citizens globally. Many politicians take this for granted; goodwill and assume their supportive voting intentions based on political bias distortion estimated on philosophical agendas of duplicity.

The current administration led by President Barack Hussein Obama is slowly eradicating based on self-destruction from political power. Their philosophical agenda is for some amicable Republican to legitimately enter the two thousand twelve race. If he or she wears black shoes the porch monkey Democratic alimentary canal sucking blacks and whites are going to inundate the airways with philosophical agendas of distorting radical lies of contempt accusing Republicans of being racist against blacks. For hundreds of years, the Democrats have never had a strategic format for the best interest of our nation. Their general consensus is to wait until the Republicans institute amicable legislation which has merit pertaining to the security and stability of our nation.

The Democrat methodology behavioral agenda is inscribed in chronological records of significant events. When they literally terrorized, murdered and slaughtered black and white Republicans during the early eighteen seventies; simply because they wanted to exercise their civil and voting rights in regards to their liberty in the southern states. That had been ratified to the Constitution by the Republican congress. The fourteenth amendment was ratified July 9, 1868. The Republican Party was literally violently driven from the southern states. This was over a hundred and forty years ago. Since then, southern blacks demonstrated in an effort to have their civil and voting rights (which the Democrats voided in eighteen ninety six with the Jim Crow Rule; separate but equal through the Supreme Court). Then along came Democratic President Franklin Delano Roosevelt during the early thirties and solidified black voters into the Democrat Party eternally with a philosophical agenda of social programs providing relief checks along with social security monitoring the philosophical traits of how blacks uniquely vote in a bloc in the northern states. President Roosevelt utilized the monolithic heritage of herding philosophy of blacks to compliment for the advancement of other blacks. He utilized this dysfunctional black trait to his advantage. He promoted two military blacks: Benjamin C. Davis from colonel to general and William Hastie to staff or war secretary Stimson.

Most northern blacks who had supported Republicans switched to supporting Democrats assuming that he was for blacks. Over seventy five years later, most are still slobbering the alimentary canal of Democrats with their constituency support. In essence, not being ware, the first seven years of the Roosevelt presidency approximately eighteen blacks were lynched annually. In Duck Hill, Mississippi two blacks were blow torched to death while a crowd of whites applauded. Democratic President Franklin Delano Roosevelt was a unique politician. There will never be another to duplicate his philosophical agenda. He was quite familiar with the basis of the system and how it was formulated and utilized it to his advantage. He was a president who was committed to his philosophical agendas and manipulated other politicians, of authority, to attain goals. He was liked for his enduring stamina to succeed. He was an individual who was committed to judging ethnic traits which determine the distinguishing quality of people in general. He evaluated people based on their merits not what institution they graduated from; simply because he chose a vice president to serve along with him; Harry S. Truman; who had no formal education. He characterized the ethnic heritage traits of blacks: who voted in a bloc; and was gratified when other blacks were appreciated with promotions. This was his clue, to eliminate the black Republican Party which President Abraham Lincoln established by promoting two military blacks: Benjamin C. Davis and William Hastie.

To really seal the deal of sabotaging African Americans from the Republican Party, he chose a black congressman from Illinois, Arthur Mitchell, for the first time ever to address the Democratic convention. He praised President Roosevelt for his relief benefit programs for African Americans. President Roosevelt was an individual who premeditated the philosophical ethnic traits of people in general. He coordinated his efforts accordingly with the spheres of the established government. He virtually controlled the U. S. Supreme Court. The major news networks applauded him. He solicited Republicans into turncoats. However, he never abused the Constitution or attempted to eradicate. He was the longest sitting president ever. He accomplished his philosophical political agendas by manipulating people who were elected officials; such as the U. S. Senate, congress and U. S. Supreme Court. Most foreign leaders admired and applauded him. There was one exception: Adolf Hitler.

During the cold war of the forties to the present, numerous of former presidents of the United States of America were protégés and emulators of President Franklin Delano Roosevelt with philosophical traits of ideology pertaining to astuteness. Among them was Harry S. Truman who became his vice president and later, after his demise, succeeded him as president. Others include John F. Kennedy, Lyndon Baines Johnson, Dwight David Eisenhower, Jimmy Carter, Richard Millhouse Nixon, George H. Bush, Gerald R. Ford, Ronald Reagan, William Jefferson Clinton, George W. Bush and current president Barack Hussein Obama who is the first African American president of the United States of America.

CHAPTER 14

Presidents of the United States of America should be the epitomizing optimist for the people of our nation because the philosophical, traditional guidelines were established July 4, 1776 with the Declaration of Independence and the Constitution September 17, 1787. These two inspiring ratifying methods are the stability which unites the United States of America which is the greatest nation on God's earth. America has intricacies of two major political parties: Democrat and Republican which fortify democracy in the United Sates consisting of five hundred and thirty five elected congress personnel. One hundred senators are elected to serve six years. Four hundred and thirty five congressional representatives are elected to serve two years. Each political body is independent of the other. Most consolidate by certain margins to approve or disapprove ratification of laws for the best interest, improvement and security of our nation. If an occurrence arises to be debatable there is the independent branch of our government, the Supreme Court. The Supreme Court consists of nine justices with life tenure who are appointed by the sitting president of the United States and confirmed by the member of the senate based on majority consent. The responsibility of those nine justices, led by a Chief Justice, is to appropriately resolve disputes based on their discretion. Their resolve is for the entire fifty states in the United States; only if judges and lower courts have not reached a conclusion. If they should choose to accept cases for ruling it is based on majority of the nine justices; nine because it eliminates the possibility of a deadlock.

The executive power shall be vested in a president of the United States of America. He shall hold his office for a term of four years together with the vice president chosen for the same term. Their authoritative philosophical, political agendas are related to the carrying out of decisions, plans or laws; not ratifying to become law. Since the first president George Washington, there have been numerous candidates challenging to become president of the United States of America: Democrats, Republicans and others. Most will rely on the utilization of political bias, distortion based on philosophical agendas of lies and deceit to get elected. Once they are elected, they suddenly realize the complexity and how difficult it is to fulfill political bias, distorted philosophical agendas of deception. His political, bias accomplishers (mostly within his political party) in an attempt to legitimize his erroneous, political bias distortions based on philosophical agendas of deceiving the American people into thinking it is they who should accept his incompetent ideology because he is president and their commander and chief who knows what is best for their future. He is a graduate of Harvard, Yale or another major university and he has the solution for all American people's problems and will resolve them and determine their future with change.

There have been forty four U. S. Presidents to include; George Washington the first in essence every creature on God's earth derived from genetic heritage; including mankind, God created with a brain especially for thinking so to communicate verbally. Based on taught moral intellect these distinctions are derivative from all ethnic people. These philosophical characteristics are embedded in each genetic ethic heritage eternally. Inevitably each individual illustrates and demonstrates their philosophical genetic heritage traits passed on from line of descent and the acquaintance with heritage. It is a guide line which will determine one's philosophical traits. Beginning with biological parents, there are ethic people universally who have numerous illnesses and behavioral distinguishing qualities which is dictated through genetic heritage controllability. This is a unique paradoxes, but inevitable. This also applies to animals. In essence, when a woman has three to five children fathered by different men each child has a contrasting genetic heritage because when a child is initially conceived the first body structure to develop (with special functions) is the heart. Later the brain uniquely takes control of the unborn child's body and determines the abilities by characterizing genetic heritage from each parent throughout the child's body. Neither of the four or five children (fathered by different men) is genetically ideologically identical. This creates philosophical contrary mannerisms and dispositions of individuals by not having the same father and is a phenomenon which is eternal. This determines genetically, functional competency or dysfunctional incompetency pertains to all people and animals.

Most African Americans are a unique ethnic people who have philosophical genetic heritage traits which are estrange dictated through genetic heritage over a thousand years from Africa based on herding around tribal chiefs. This distinguished quality still exists today with most blacks. I am of the opinion they are totally unaware of these embedded philosophical genetic traits. In essence most ethic whites in America have never evaluated the philosophical emotions of blacks based on their perceptions related to the ethnic of whites. It has not changed for most in approximately four hundred years. This is simply because of their traditional genetic heritage embedded from Africa, herding behind tribal chiefs for guidance. This is not a racist or derogatory remark. It is the chronological events of reality which is substantiated based on history related to genetic controllability pertaining to most blacks. Realistically, it is a chosen tradition for most blacks to congregate with sympathetic conjecture in support of self-appointed black leaders. I will clarify legitimacy in regards to demonstrating and pertaining to African Americans: Dr. Martin Luther King. His cause was to rectify and restore civil and voting rights for southern African Americans who southern Democrats had murdered, sabotaged and rescinded during eighteen ninety six with the approval of the Supreme Court on the Jim Crow Rule: separate but equal for African Americans only. Dr. King philosophical motive was to restore those rights which every other ethnic people in America was privileged to. Once those rights were restored, during nineteen sixty four and five, the case should have been closed period! Unfortunately, along came the cynics, self-appointed black replicas of a Congo tribal chief claiming injustice and to damn stupid and incompetent to realize the Democratic Party (which they support; approximately ninety five percent) were and are the perpetrators of all atrocities which occurred to southern African Americans. The inherent philosophy is terribly flawed with inept, dysfunctional, incompetency pertaining to most blacks who reside in America. A large segment have progressed immensely in regards to success; graduating from every major university in America. Many have law degrees and/or are law professors who have numerous other degrees. This is prevalent on every air network available like horse shit around a cotton gin during the early forties. Most are utilizing their African Congo heritage of tribal philosophical traits of being controlled by a chief. Most have chosen the Democrat Party as their adviser, replica to a Congo chief, led by black self-appointed, Congo plantation slave drivers.

CHAPTER 15

In an effort to clarify my accuracies, I am going to revert to sixteen nineteen; the first introduction of Africans to the colonies of America. In Virginia, twenty aboard a Dutch ship docked. The captain was out of supplies and funds. He appealed to the colony people for supplies. Their answer was: no funds, no supplies. The ship captain suggested he had twenty Africans on board. The colony people accepted the twenty Africans for supplies. After the ship departed, the colony people suddenly realized these people were uncivilized, illiterate and could not speak a word of English. What do we do with them? They can't survive being uncivilized. The colony people chose to place them on a tobacco farm, feed, house and clothe them for their labor tilling the tobacco farm. This was the initial introduction of Africans to the British Colony in North America. This process was deemed to be very lucrative because tobacco was the stability of the colony. Additional Africans were brought into Virginia to work the tobacco farms for food, clothing and housing. There were also whites in the same category; indentured servants. There were no regulations for African labor in the British American Colonies during the early part of the seventeenth century; whites and Africans served accordingly while race relations were in the process of being injected for formulation. Unfortunately, Africans had a unique perception about race relations. They refused to conform to the adherence of American culture. Instead they practiced their African heritage genetic traits for over two hundred years. This estranged their relations with whites which brought integration to a screeching halt. Whites began to segregate from Africans. As the African population grew there were African Congo Congolese warriors brought to America. They began to instigate rebellious tactics with some of the local Africans. The Africans who refused to rebel, supported the efforts covertly. Most Africans began to organize behind self-appointed African leaders. They began to covertly instigate a takeover of America from whites. Whites became leery of an African revolution.

During the sixteen sixties, the Chesapeake Colonies of Virginia established distinct racial formulated regulations by banning interracial marriages. Northern states began to ban interracial marriages also: namely Massachusetts and Pennsylvania. During sixteen ninety one, South Carolina initiated British North America with a code; which was the first to introduce slavery and owning and selling Africans as property. It was submitted to the British Island Colony of Barbados by South Carolina. After seventeen hundred, other British North American Colonies ratified the same law. Strict guidelines were initiated for African plantation workers because of their philosophical Congo agenda to practice African traditions of rebellious, violence and ignore American civilized traditions. Their own herding, choosing to remain loyal to an African Congo genetic heritage herding philosophy. After approximately four hundred years, these philosophical African traits still exist relating to most African Americans in the current society. Current philosophical heritage traits are displayed by most blacks who reside in the United States of America. This dictates a radical bias agenda and is more prevalent than ever before. The American people were duped by a slick talking black man into electing him president of the United States of America: Barack Hussein Obama. They have identical perceptive bias, philosophical dysfunctional Congo ideological traits to change the traditional fundamentals America was founded on to a replica of African Congo ideology; where tribal chiefs are in control of whites. Most older whites; particularly Democrats, are aware of this black idiosyncrasy ideologue; especially southern senior whites because this is where this debacle began hundreds of years ago. They are also totally aware of the fact it will never occur. Democrats have always understood the incompetent ignorance of most blacks in general. They have utilized their dysfunctional stupidity to their political advantage for hundreds of years literally. The southern Democrats blow torched blacks to death and murdered them for petty insinuations, denied them civil rights, sold blacks into slavery like cattle and molested black women in the presence of their families.

The southern Democrats founded the Ku Klux Klan in Pulaski, Tennessee during eighteen sixty six. Lynching blacks was a hobby; literally forcing blacks into share cropping with the ruling of the Supreme Court ratifying the Jim Crow Rule: separate but equal; denied black children the right to be educated during the thirties and forties. In essence, the Jim Crow Rule (separate but equal) revoked the civil rights of all southern blacks. This meant they had to sit in the back of the public transportation and were totally segregated from all white facilities in the south. During the fifties and sixties era the southern Democrats and their Ku Klux Klan would sic dogs on blacks. They also blasted them with water hoses; bombed a church in Birmingham, Alabama (which gruesomely blew three little black girls to bits). During nineteen sixty four, Senator Robert Byrd (a Democrat and former Ku Klux Klansman) and some other Democrats assembled the longest filibuster in senate history (against southern African Americans' civil rights being restored).

Let's revert back in history. During September 9, 1857, U. S. Supreme Court Justice (a Democrat and slave owner) read the opinion concluding the Dred Scott case; a black man sued for his liberties from his slave owner. He lost his bid for freedom by a 7-2 vote. Chief Justice Roger B. Taney added in his opinion reading: African Americans had never been and never could be American citizens. During the senate debate for election during eighteen fifty eight between Republican Abraham Lincoln and Democrat Stephen A. Douglas, Lincoln stated: African Americans were included in the Declaration of Independence because it stated: all men are created equal. Democrat Stephen A. Douglas' reply was: American was made by white men for the benefit of white men and their posterity forever.

During eighteen seventy six, there was a U. S. Presidential election between Democrat Samuel J. Tilden and Republican Rutherford B. Hayes. Republican Hayes won the election and the Democratic controlled congress literally refused to certify his election unless he agreed to remove U. S. federal troops from the south that were protecting blacks so they could be in control of deciding stability and litigation civility for blacks. The U. S. Supreme Court removed federal protection for blacks in the southern states and the Democratic establish Ku Klux Klan began lynching blacks at their discretion without consequences. In previous years the Republican controlled congress ratified the thirteenth amendment to the constitution by a vote of one hundred twenty one to twenty four. This stipulated: neither slavery nor involuntary servitude, except as a punishment for crime whereof the party shall have been duly convicted, shall exist within the

United States or any place subject to its jurisdiction. The most devastating economical atrocity occurred in African American history and the dysfunctional traits are more prevalent today than ever before.

When John Wilkes Booth (a staunch Democrat) assassinated President Abraham Lincoln at the Ford Theater on April fourteenth, he was filled with rage because of the confederacy defeat. He leaped from the balcony on to the stage and commented: now the Democratic south is avenged. Be it so to all tyrants no niggers will become citizens in the southern states. Why this was so devastating to African Americans was because he was truly a sincere advocate for their causes. Not only did Republican President Abraham Lincoln abolish servitude, he also initiated lucrative incentive plans for the future of all African Americans based on true convictions from his heart and his trust in God. At age nineteen he was on a trip to New Orleans. While there he happened to observe a mulatto woman being auctioned at a public auction. He suggested to his cousin Dennis Hanks; by God if I ever get a chance to hit slavery, I am going to hit it hard enough until it is revoked. Which, in later years he did accomplish. During the year of eighteen sixty five, he philosophically understood the traditional illiteracy embedded in black ethnics. His intent was to give them an opportunity to improve, based on their having civil liberty incentive. He was aware the only custom blacks were accustomed to was farming. President Lincoln, on September 22, 1862, issued the Emancipation Proclamation declaring freedom for all blacks enslaved in areas still rebellious against the United States as of January 1, 1863. The emancipation also granted each African American family forty acres of confiscated confederate land and a government mule. This was in the process of being confirmed by the government placement responsibility act of refugees when President Lincoln was assassinated.

During the spring of eighteen sixty five, Lincoln's vice president Andrew Johnson (a staunch Democrat) was sworn in as his replacement. Immediately Johnson began granting amnesty to former confederate military personnel and wholesale pardon to white Democratic racist confederate southerners. The only requirement was to state they would support the thirteenth amendment of the constitution and all their land was returned. In essence President Johnson rescinded President Lincoln's Emancipation Proclamation and returned the promised land for blacks to the southern plantation owners. This was one of the most egregious, devastating acts of atrocity to ever occur to African Americans; pertaining to their incentive. However, as God created mankind in His own image;

the philosophical characteristics of people are inevitable to repeat; personal or politically, based on God created mankind in His image and the philosophical characteristics of all people are inevitable to repeat; based on ethnic genetic heritage. Chronological records of significant events support those initial occurrences.

During eighteen sixty six, the Republican controlled congress moved vigorously to accommodate the liberty for southern African citizens. They formulated guidance to this initiative. They began with the thirteenth amendment; ratified to the constitution on December 6, 1865. Democratic President Andrew Johnson was extremely dissatisfied with the Republican congress because they chose not to admit confederate former military patriots to serve in the senate or a congressional representative. In the interim, the Republicans were consecrating on how to improve on the Emancipation Proclamation that President Lincoln issued and became effective on January 1, 1863 freeing slaves in all territory that was still at war with the union. During this time, President Johnson vetoed the legislation for the first time. The grand old party rose to the occasion and assembled enough votes to over-ride his veto and passed the civil rights act of eighteen sixty six which established southern blacks as American citizens and prohibited discrimination against them. Later the Republican congress ratified the fourteenth amendment to the constitution on July 9, 1868. All persons born or naturalized in the United States and subject to jurisdiction thereof are citizens of the United States and of the state wherein they reside. No state shall make or enforce any law which shall abridge the privileges or immunities of citizens of the United Sates; nor shall any state deprive any person of life, liberty or property without due process of law; nor deny to any person within its jurisdiction the equal protection of laws. The Republican congress also ratified the fifteenth amendment to the Constitution on February 3, 1870; which stipulates the right of citizens of the United States to vote shall not be denied or abridged by the United States or by any state on account of race, color or previous conditions of servitude.

CHAPTER 16

It is so terribly incredible and ironic the Republican Party (during their existence) is for all American citizens not just a segment. Chronological records substantiate the validity of their remarkable traits; specifically for all political bias, stupid ass distorting, dysfunctional, small brain, philosophical Congo ideological blacks. If it wasn't for the Republican Party the blacks would not be crawling from under the rocks all over the airways that exist insinuating Republicans are radical and racist against blacks. It is as simple as this: if not for the Republican Party the cotton picking machine would not have been invented because the black asses sitting around on all airways bashing Republicans in their little tight suits and dresses would still be dragging cotton sacks in the southern states. Why the derogatory remarks? I suspect when God created ethnic people He experimented with blacks because there is something missing in most of their brains. There are numerous blacks who have graduated from a conglomerate of colleges all over this nation. They still cannot determine and distinguish the difference between Democrat and Republican. In regards to which is responsible for their liberties to attain success in the United States of America through attending colleges which include common sense illiterates with no formal education.

The Republican Party is creative. They have engineered solutions pertaining to the stability of our nation since inception. Their unique ability to endure political bias distortion based on an agenda of philosophical, horrendous, and hypercritical lies is creative. Their stamina is due to intellectual sequences passed on through genetic heritage to excel over opposition to continue attaining stability of the United States of America against all arduous philosophical, cynical demagoguery is truly a remarkable feat generated by President Lincoln. He was inaugurated as the sixteenth president of the United States of America on March 4, 1861. He began his crusade of justice and liberty for all Americans to determine their individual destiny in life by choice, not guidance from Democratic southern plantation owners or slave drivers.

In an effort to deter this kind of malicious behavior he issued the first Emancipation Proclamation on January 1, 1863 with the intent to quell servitude of blacks. The confederate southern Democrats labeled President Lincoln: a black Republican, nigger lover; simply because he was anti-slavery and wanted liberty for blacks. Jefferson Davis was president of the Democratic southern confederate states and supported and demanded slavery of blacks be continued in the south. In an effort to defend their philosophical ideology, on April 12, 1861 the southern Democratic confederacy in Charleston Harbor literally shelled federal Fort Sumter with artillery. The war began. Due to the courage of President Lincoln, the United Union States defeated the confederate states and slavery was abolished in the south for blacks. Fortunately the Republican controlled congress adhered to President Lincoln's philosophical ideology: that all mankind are created equal and reserve the right to establish their individual traits during their life and not be controlled by dictators. To prevent this from occurring, the brilliant Republican controlled congress ratified the fourteenth and fifteenth amendment to the Constitution: for all people who reside in the United States of America especially African Americans.

Unfortunately there were some Republican renegade rhinos. During nineteen fifty seven Republican President Dwight David Eisenhower formulated the first civil rights bill for blacks in eighty five years. It was rescinded by the Democrat congress. But they did not have the necessary votes in their party structure to repeal. Twelve Republicans crossed over and annulled the civil and voting rights bill for southern blacks. Most Republicans are consistent with the philosophical traits of President Lincoln: that all people should be free to make decisions based on their individual philosophical agendas.

Chronologically, history has determined by ratified events to verify which is constantly repetitious based on replica scenarios; but obviously transparent enough to determine the intent. For instance, approximately one hundred fifty years ago, the Republican Party utilized their distinguishing qualities to rectify an in-justice perpetrated against blacks by the southern Democratic founded Ku Klux Klan that maimed, lynched, and blow torched blacks and also confined them to slavery. Chronological records establish the truth. It was Republican presidents and Republican controlled congresses who quelled these atrocious acts committed against southern blacks by Democratic Ku Klux Klansmen. There is a phrase most commonly used by a former NBA player who currently analyzes NBA games. Numerous times he will comment after an outstanding play: mama there goes that man again. This statement is derived from African American community living based on a married couple with a cheating wife. While the husband went off to work the lover would sneak by. The nosey neighboring kids would run to their mothers and state: mama there goes that man again.

I am going to rephrase and utilize that statement in a more political challenging manner. In essence, President Barack Hussein Obama; here comes that grand old Republican Party again. Why Obama? Because, he is the president of this great nation. Time consists of transitions. That is inevitable and the criteria of revolutions are persistent based on self-confidence. Political leaders, if determined not to be appropriately manifested is reason for concern based on political philosophical guidance of our nation pertaining to adhering to the legitimacy of our Declaration of Independence and Constitution. The southern Democrats and their established Ku Klux Klan violated these principles pertaining to southern African Americans. He is now president of the Democrat Party which committed all of those violet atrocities against innocent African Americans.

George C. Wallace was the Democrat governor of Alabama who stood in the doorway at the University of Alabama and stated segregation now and segregation forever. The Democratic Ku Klux Klan blew three innocent little black girls to bits inside their church in the city of Birmingham, Alabama. During Republican President Dwight David Eisenhower's administrative reign during nineteen fifty seven, Democrat Governor Orval Faubus of Arkansas initiated one of the most racist and furious provocations of President Eisenhower's term in office. He ordered the assembly of the National Guard around Central High School in Little Rock, Arkansas to prevent twelve African Americans from entering. President Eisenhower was persistent and arranged for federal troops on October twenty third to allow twenty three blacks to enter Central High.

After the school year's end, Governor Faubus closed the school entirely to eliminate blacks from attending. However it did open again in nineteen fifty nine and was integrated.

It is essential ethnic people who reside in the United States of America as citizens understand the basic philosophical traditions of chronological events. There are ethnics who are not disciplined to the cultural trends. They rely on speculations which characterize them as being dysfunctional and incompetent and other ethnic people utilize bias distortion to capitalize on their ignorant misguidedness. Most immigrants who migrated to America were civilized and eager to conform to the philosophical guidelines that are evident traits established in the United States of America hundreds of years ago. Unfortunately it is incomprehensible Africans were brought to American British northern colonies approximately four hundred years ago and most have never made the indispensable resolution to adhere with dignity and support he fundamentals America was founded on. If any ethnic people choose not to conform to the traditions established by the founding fathers to justify credence in the United States of America there is a bias rebellious, ignorant discord claiming the system is against blacks; which creates political bias, distorting, philosophical, inept, dysfunctional, incompetent, egotistical behavioral summations such as most African Americans have. These comments are not based on racism or color. It is the reality of genetic heritage, generated from Africa and embedded within all African Americans. The awareness of this unique validity escapes most all ethnic people. Genetic heritage is inevitable and eternal; created from God and related to all mankind and animals. The initial inventive nation of heritage is eternal pertaining to ethnic formality.

If a Chinese baby is brought to America and grew up adhering to American customs and not aware of his Chinese line of decent his motivations are controlled by his genetic heritage from China which dictate philosophical traits in regards to characteristic demeanor; to evaluate the genetic heritage custom similarity of Africans brought to the British colonies of North America during sixteen nineteen in Virginia and equate African Americans philosophical traits compatible to date.

Beginning in Africa, over a thousand years ago, they were savagely uncivilized, illiterate, extremely persistent and loyal to their tribal customs controlled by a tribal chief. Along with numerous other tribes, many practiced different customs such as cannibalism (braided hair is an established custom of Africa); some tribes matted their braids with human dung to maintain stiffness. There were constant tribal war fares to exterminate other tribes. There were no faculties (personal or monetary) in tribal areas. Their recourses for survival was maintained by free living off the land; such as hunting animals, fruits and vegetables from jungles, sharing within the tribe. Their tribal instincts consisted of herding around their tribal chief for instructions, advice and guidance. Their loyalty was monolith. The tribesmen utilized several women as wives and had children immensely. Their wearing apparel consisted of sloppy, loosely affixed with body and clothing adornments. Most tribal chiefs were rude and narcissistic. Numerous of ethnics pertaining to integrated society in a nation are an asset. That is what made the United States of America so great a nation; this lucrative, pragmatic endeavor has never existed in tribal Africa and never will. Unfortunately the philosophical, genetic heritage traits from Africa are embedded in most African Americans.

In an effort to verify these characteristics commonness, I begin during the sixteen nineteen's era with the initial beginning; when the first twenty Africans were brought to British North America colonies in Virginia (over time others were brought). They literally refused to integrate with other ethnics and formed their own entitle facsimile of tribes from Africa, advised by a self-appointed leader. The formatted this process for over two hundred years. In the interim, as population grew from other Africans being brought to Virginia, their philosophical agenda was to replicate their African heritage in America. As their population increased, they began to formulate African tribal like groups, following leaders who were hostile and rebellious along with some Indians who were joining their Congo tribal activities. During sixteen ninety one, South Carolina chose to eradicate civil liberties for Africans and Indians through a legislative process which ratified all Africans and Indians to be sold into bondage. Other British North American colonies agreed and joined their ratified legislation. This process eliminated trouble makers because if he or they behaved rebelliously, they were traded or sold until the U. S. Congress ended the African slave trade in eighteen hundred and eight. After this congress repeal, blacks began to organize rebellious groups of African tribesmen. One such group was led by a leader named Jemmy. With trained Congolese African former soldiers they staged an act of murdering whites during seventeen thirty four along the Stone River in South Carolina. The South Carolina militia was called out and they were killed. During eighteen eleven, a tribal leader of blacks named Charles Deslondes led a military rebellion through New Orleans. Marching in cadence they slaughtered whites. The state and local militia killed them off, severed their heads and placed them on poles along the Mississippi River. During eighteen twenty nine, rebellious anti-white radicals David Walker and Henry Highland (self-appointed black leaders) incited violence against whites by stipulating: we hate whites, this is more our country than theirs. This inspired Nat Turner in eighteen thirty one to stage a rebellious revolt around Virginia. The governor had to call on the state infantry and the U. S. Navy to quell his revolt by killing his followers. However, there was a somberness ending; whites retaliated and killed hundreds of innocent blacks in one day. Laws were ratified in the southern states; it was a misdemeanor for a white to kill a black.

Let's revert back to Africa and relate to those philosophical, chronological events in an effort to substantiate African genetic heritage traits which are embedded in most African American society today, pertaining to compatibleness.

(1) Beginning with constant ethnic conflict: exterminating each other for control of miscellaneous philosophical, genetic assumptions. These sequences of monolith, irresistible impulses are an instinctive genetic replica of heritage passed on from Africa over a thousand years ago. They are in unison with most blacks today who reside in the United States of America.

(2) The authentic reversions which exist in Africans are prevalent genetically in African Americas: inevitably and eternally. In essence, for a child to perceive intellectual, moral values he or she has to begin schooling at ages of approximately four to six years old and continue through numerous of years; based on their philosophical traits of endurance. Africans were brought to British North America in Virginia during sixteen nineteen with none of these values being adults. After their arrival, the southern Democrats restricted their learning for approximately another two hundred and fifty years. This is the logical reason for the density of most African Americans today. Obviously, President Barack Hussein Obama and Attorney General Eric Holder firmly agree with this precise validity. Recently they authoritatively demanded test scores be lowered at Dayton, Ohio police department (for blacks only) to secure their opportunity for passage to become police law officers for the city of Dayton.

(3) After approximately four hundred years (during sixteen nineteen) the initial introduction of Africans to British North

America, just listen to the dialect of appropriate English verbiage of most African Americans nationwide who graduate from high school and college. It is a distinctive combination of African and American mixed traits which Africans formulated in the southern states hundreds of years ago. Informal, nonstandard vocabulary of dis, dat, aint and dem. I could go on and on, but this is a philosophical heritage trait (origin from Africa) which is inevitable and eternal; having absolutely nothing to do with race or derogatory remarks; but the facts of reality. The United States of America is a nation of philosophical standards which requires appropriate attire based on moral community life and the ability to communicate with respectful dignity. These are the inevitable, required attributes sustaining philosophy based on humanity and principle which is the stability of the United States of America pertaining to all ethic citizens who reside in America. There are approximately three hundred twenty five million ethics citizens who reside in the United States. Black ethnics number approximately thirty eight to forty million. Unfortunately, of this forty million, most have chosen to allow a monolith, replica of a Congo tribal African tradition to determine their philosophical, bias, distorted political destination by uniting and adhering to affluent leaders. Some are self-appointed who dictate their assumed policy and procedures as an African tribal Congo chief would.

(4) There are numerous sets of moral principles embedded in American history. The Declaration of Independence and the Constitution are the philosophical principle guidance of stability which makes America the greatest nation on God's earth. Unfortunately, there are numerous individuals within ethnics who are opposed to the existing philosophical standards. America consists of many ethnic nationalities who determine the distinguishing quality of America through their voting capacity (related to a two party system, Democrat and Republican). Each ethnic denomination determines a winning political candidate through a process of voting percentages of deviating; based on party affiliate candidate of their choice. This is the traditional guideline which is entrusted to the citizens of the United States of America granted by

the Constitution. Every ethnic race of immigrants who have migrated to America for hundreds of years has conformed and made the necessary adjustments, and have invested their talents in regards to intellect in an effort to attain lucrativeness based on proud to be an American citizen.

Chapter 17

The uniqueness of Africans brought to British colonies of northern Virginia during sixteen nineteen is an exception because over three hundred and ninety years most blacks have never (then or now) conformed to the general principles established by our forefathers: the Declaration of Independence and the Constitution. Deriving from Africa their traditional customs are estranged based on distinguished quality they are an ethnic people who consist of tribes that are obligatory to a tribal chief for guidance. This distinctive, philosophical trait is embedded in most African Americans from genetic heritage.

African Americans are an ethnic people with overbearing density. They rely on guidance from self-appointed dictators for advice. The dictators in America are utilizing prehistoric diction in an effort to indoctrinate the general public; blacks are underprivileged and white superiority is responsible for their living in destitution and change is the only solution. Most blacks are sophisticated, distorting liars who rely on their ability of deception for personal gain. It is a monolithic, philosophical bias trait in regards to herding together, endorsing miscellaneous occurrences pertaining to their scope of ideology which is politically motivated based on bias distorted agendas of radical racism to justify overbearing density of African genetic heritage.

The unique tradition of most blacks congregating to support self-appointed black leaders (for hundreds of years) has created a human debacle for most blacks because those political, inept black leaders are dictating dysfunctional myths who are out of touch with reality simply because their narrative is distorted with how whites are denying blacks equal rights based on discrimination. In essence, this is nothing more than a political ploy which is a philosophical trend utilized by most blacks to attain attention in an effort to convenience people they are resourceful with ingenuities; when their philosophical traits are marred in overwhelming, dysfunctional, overbearing density. There are approximately three hundred twenty five million ethnic people who reside in America. The ethnic African Americans are approximately thirty six to forty million total. There are philosophical established identifying records accredited to blacks only (the most ethnic incarcerated for committing miscellaneous crime; the most ethnic with babies born out of wedlock; the most school dropouts; the most ethnic who have contracted AIDS; the only ethnic people who reside in the United States of America who voted ninety five percent for one political party—Democrat (who have lynched, slaughtered, blow torched, seriously wounded and disfigured African Americans for hundreds of years). Blacks have allowed white philosophical, distorting Democrats to utilize deceitful strategies to manipulate self-appointed black replicas of African Congo tribal leaders to convenience their monolithic black followers they (the Democrats) are completely innocent; it was the Republicans who committed all these violent atrocities. Records of significant events empathically hold to determine it was the southern Democrat Party who persecuted blacks and disallowed their development, mentally and morally; which is responsible for most black's overbearing density today.

Most whites in America are totally inept to the distinct inner emotionalism most African Americans are driven by. It is a genetic replica derived from African traditions over a thousand years ago; herding behind a tribal chief for his guidance of dictating cynicism. Most are totally politically monolithic adhering to self-appointed black leaders who offer advice of vindictive, rebellious, racist, overbearing density which they learned from the white southern Democrats: if you do not have an answer to problems just wait until someone else has a solution to the problem. Then philosophically utilize bias, distorted, radical, overbearing, dense demagoguery in an effort to deceive for attainability. This is and has always been Democratic strategy. Most African Americans are overbearing with density to literally decipher the difference between Democrat and Republican; simply because they characterize all whites as being monolith as they are, and are so damn stupid, incompetent, and dysfunctional to realize if it wasn't for the Republican presidents and Republican controlled congress, as of to date, they would still be dragging a cotton sack and slopping hogs on master's southern Democrat plantations. Yet they blame all Republicans for their dense, incompetent, dysfunctional, philosophical African heritage traits with stigmatic verbiage such as: dem dare white foks aint fur us black foks, day helt us back, whence us kno moe bout runnin dis contry dan day do. Blacks are irresponsible and are inept in regards to reasoning and personal responsibility.

Let's equate the solidarity between the Democrat Party and African Americans. The Democrat Party is equivalent to African Congo kings who founded slavery (owning and selling people as a commodity globally for trinkets and blankets). They utilized Congolese soldiers to raid jungle tribes and bring to the Gold Coast for sale over the globe. As of to date, there are black emulators of these African Congolese soldiers embedded and controlled within the Democrat Party who has united with the worse political, bias, distorting, white trash to slide out of a uterus with a philosophical agenda to re-elect a narcissistic, overbearing, dense, dysfunctional, incompetent president, Barack Hussein Obama. He has typical distinguishing qualities of an African Congo tribal chief. Through direct genetic heritage President Obama was in Ireland exploiting his Irish genetic heritage from his white mother (why not do the same about his African heritage from his father?). This was nothing more than political bias distortion based on a philosophical agenda in an effort to establish credibility based on heritage (one side of his genetic ethnic). It would not surprise me if he put to the test of the American people his parents are a replica of Mary and Joseph and he was created without a father. This certifies his intentions of seducing the American people, once again, into accepting his philosophical African traits of Congo tribal chief agenda; of opposing the Declaration of Independence and the Constitution. Ninety five percent of African Americans are estranged to both the Declaration of Independence and the Constitution. They have denounced each authoritative controlling sentiment for America. They have more loyalty to a Congo tribal chief's ideology from Africa. This continuing circumstance has been in existence for approximately four hundred years, with guidance from inherent, self-appointed black dictators, constantly politically distorting with bias philosophical agendas of deceitful, radical racism. It is astoundingly mythical, and quite mysterious, that a black ethnic people brought to British North American colonies three hundred ninety two years ago. Most have never formally conformed to the established general principles according to the United States of America; the greatest nation on God's earth.

There is an explicit explanation for this embedded overbearing density. It began in Africa over a thousand years ago. African tribal traditions are monolithic to their custom; under the guidance of a tribal chief with him being the only dictator of tribal customs, based on prehistoric, savage, uncivilized, philosophical, illiteracy. This is the genetic heritage introduced to the northern British colonies of America during sixteen nineteen with rebellious, hostile, violent temperaments. As the population increased, they secluded on southern plantations and practiced African cultural heritage traits for over two hundred years. This ethic genetic heritage portrayal is still in existence currently, and more prevalent than ever. Most African Americans are totally unaware of their African, genetic heritage of overbearing density. The sequences are identifiable in most philosophical mannerisms. African Americans congregate monolithic, adhering to self-appointed black, dictating leaders such as Jessie Jackson, Al Sharpton and others; especially black men claiming the transcend from supremacy relating from the bible. Most dictate philosophical traits; in general consensus on how the established procedures in America should be. Based on assumptions, which is totally contrary and divisional pertaining to the incorporated ratified standards of the United States of America.

The United States of America is a nation consisting of diverse immigrants who migrated to America to freely utilize their special talents in accordance with the established guidelines; to resourcefully succeed, or fail, based on their individual meritorious agenda; not adhering to a dictating replica of a Congo tribal chief who is distorting reality pertaining to the Declaration of Independence and the Constitution (which does not discriminate; there are no special privileges for any ethnic people). Unfortunately, most African Americans are adversely contrary to the founding father's evidence of qualifying authority. For approximately four hundred years, most have been trying to invent and establish a black America, instead of blacks residing in America. According to chronological records of significance, Columbus discovered America during fourteen ninety two; Africans were brought here during sixteen nineteen. According to any mathematical methods utilized, this is a hundred twenty seven years later. Yet, the philosophical, ideological traits of most African Americans have chosen America as a definitive black America by stipulating: dis is us country and us aint got us equal right us need de play feld levred so us is equal to white folks. This is prehistoric, monolithic, over-rated, dense incompetency. In an effort to malign other ethnics with political, bias, distortion based on philosophical agendas of sentimentality, by constantly referring to slavery and blacks being victimized; yes; there were barbaric acts of atrocious violence against southern blacks. Unfortunately, the philosophical specifics have never been explored and revealed to the general public and characterized based on the validity of essentiality there had to be a specific notably particularly reason for the Democrat established Ku Klux Klan; lynching, maiming and eradicating blacks in the southern states.

I grew up in the south, so I am quite familiar with southern traditions. The southern Democratic Ku Klux Klan set guidelines for blacks; such as yes mam and yes sir to all whites; absolutely no pestering white women; all public places (such as eateries, hotels and public buses) were segregated, including drinking fountains. Most blacks who resided in the south tolerated these standards. Numerous times they had relatives visit from northern states; they would insist they behave accordingly. Unfortunately there were some who chose not to; there were consequences, sometimes severe; perpetrated by the Democratic Ku Klux Klan. The most significant reason for blacks being lynched was when it was exposed they supported the Republican Party; and other occurrences were due to rudeness, rebellious implications and lying thievery. Blacks were not eradicated for being black; they were involved in numerous activities which the Democratic Ku Klux Klan disapproved of; and not for trivia incidents.

From eighteen sixty six (when the southern Democrats brought the initial Ku Klux Klan into existence) their philosophical established laws controlled the southern states with an extension to the state of Indiana. Their tactical procedures were to infiltrate police law stations because a segment of those police officers were Ku Klux Klansmen which was the most politically influential powerful organizations in America at the time. Until nineteen fifty seven, when Republican President Dwight David Eisenhower wrote the first emancipation for southern blacks in eighty nine years, the Democratic senate controlled their leader, Lyndon Baines Johnson, and rejected the civil and voting rights for southern blacks. President Eisenhower was persistent. He authorized FBI Director J. Edgar Hoover to infiltrate the Democratic Ku Klux Klan and quell the lynching of southern blacks. He accomplished this mission. Over the protest of Arkansas Governor Orval Faubas, President Eisenhower's military forced school integration took place in Little Rock, Arkansas. During the time, FBI Director J. Edgar Hoover evaluated African Americans brains as being twenty percent smaller than whites. This is not a racist hatred, derogatory remark for blacks. FBI Director Hoover was disappointed, frustrated and totally confused because of all the hell they endured while attempting to restore civil rights for southern blacks, quelling the Democratic Ku Klux Klan, the lynching of blacks, and integrating southern schools for blacks.

Northern African Americans who were privileged to civil and voting rights were herding around Democrats at their convention in Pennsylvania; voting for Democrats who established the Ku Klux Klan in the southern states which was mutilating, lynching and destroying their southern ancestors. This ethnic, genetic heritage portrayal is currently in existence and has been for approximately eighty years; and as of to date more prevalent than ever. Most African Americans are totally unaware of their African genetic heritage of overbearing density because theoretically the Congo tribal traits are technically being utilized philosophically in a monolithic congregating tribal manner, adhering to self-appointed black leaders, miscellaneous church ministers, and many institutions of learning who dictate disparaging philosophical monolithic monologue, advocating blacks are underprivileged solely because of the white man's injustice. This consists of nothing more than a black uniformity routine tradition for attentive notoriety in an effort to compensate for overbearing density. There is a cohesive, rebellious, philosophical trait embedded in most ethnic African Americans to the generalization of fundamental principles American was established on. The former assassinated President John F. Kennedy analyzed our nation in a formal attribute. He stated: ask not what your country can do for you, but what you can do for your country. This statement was most gratifying because it offered an explicit explanation which profiles the United States of America. The stability of America greets any ethnic people with a dignified philosophical ideology of individual participation in any adventure of your choice. However, the first choice should be to become familiar with overall unique established principles granted through the Declaration of Independence and the Constitution because they are the controlling factors in all citizen lives who reside in the United States of America. With non-coercing, America is a nation of liberty to choose destiny. These two emancipations offer the security to all ethnic the utilization of their God given talents to execute in accordance with their philosophical traits if utilized appropriately, adhering to our Constitution, along with intellectual and moral values. By being a moderate citizen, gainfully employed; then as an ethnic you are rewarding your country for the granted liberty privileges to succeed based on your individual perception pertaining to your philosophical agenda of merit. If you are a success in America, you are doing it for your country because you adhered to the prevailing established standards to include military service. In essence, it was so eloquently phrased by former President John F. Kennedy: ask not what your country can do for you, but what you can do for your country.

Unfortunately and sadly appalling, are the miscellaneous ethnic U. S. citizens who repudiate and rebel against the established standards of the United States of America. Particularly and notably most African Americans who monolithic congregate along with their self-appointed black leaders who are dictating slave drivers for the Democrat Party. However, it is their philosophical agenda to serve their plantation, political dictating, and distorting black masters. Unfortunately this kind of behavioral conjuncture is an indication of overbearing density because it reverts back to genetic heritage which is an equivalent to the Congo tribes of Africa; herding around a tribal chief who dictates an authoritative outline of policy conduct.

African Americans are the only ethnic who reside in the United States of America, and globally, who support one political party as a voting constituency bloc; over ninety five percent who live in a liberated society continuously for approximately eighty years. This is an illustration of a philosophical dysfunctional, overbearing density beyond reproach. It is extremely crucial to offer an explanation to the philosophical traits of Africans and African Americans which is replica through genetic heritage which have never been exposed to scrutiny with regards to whom they are and their philosophical distinguishing quality. Blacks have been under the radar sense being brought to America during sixteen nineteen. All you ever hear about is what whites did to them because they are black; which is the biggest damn lie that has ever been fabricated in the United States of America. Being black is one thing; having philosophical traits of denial, dysfunctional incompetency and being black is another; which is applicable to all ethnic people. Most blacks deserve the Medal of Honor because most African Americans have never inclined favorably and disposed in their mind there are numerous ethnic people who reside in America and our Declaration of Independence and Constitution prohibit partiality for either ethnic national character of people. Most African Americans have a vindictive philosophy pertaining to the intricacy of the Constitution. Their perception is: it should be altered to accommodate their philosophical agenda based on their being black and was abused during servitude.

CHAPTER 18

It is an established fact most Africans/African Americans have never philosophically adhered to the established ratified lawful guidelines of America. Their political philosophy has and still is: they should attain a separate principle, more to their acceptance, varying from the Constitution because they are black and different from whites in regards to philosophical traits. Their entire ideological agenda, for approximately four hundred years, has been to take control of America in an effort so they can have their laws compatible to a Congo tribal chief dictator who can advise them of their standard conduct instead of the Constitution based on state and federal laws. This is an embedded philosophical, African, genetic heritage and is inevitably eternal. Most blacks are totally unaware of this traditional ideological, African genetic trait.

I am going to describe these African philosophical traits embedded in African Americans based on chronological events, past and current rebellious attempted agendas. The definitive philosophical distinguished quality of all African Americans is a replica of African genetic heritage occurring over thousands of years ago; uncivilized, lawfulness, hostile, brutal, illiterate and constant tribal warfare, killing each other and other tribesmen. These were our ancestors brought to America during sixteen nineteen who were embedded with these eternal philosophical genetic heritage qualities. I will make an analysis of these genetic traits embedded in most African Americans beginning with herding; a name given to Africans by plantation masters, describing their philosophical traits related to cattle. Cattle herd behind a matriarch. If she is driven over a cliff, they all will follow. Most African Americans are of this identical human mentality; following self-appointed black leaders; and a segment of whites who politically utilize this herding process of most blacks to their advantage; such as Democrats.

There are approximately forty million blacks in American to date; for over eighty years, over ninety percent have been a voting constituency for Democrats only. This is for certain an overbearing density politically with the inability to decipher on an individual basis intellectually. This reverts back to Africa based on genetic heritage controllability; where the Congo tribal chief made decisions for all his tribe to follow.

Most African Americans, and a segment of whites, for hundreds of years, are in denial to the philosophical ratified authoritative guidelines of state and federal laws which exist in America.

For instance:

During the year of sixteen seventy six, a white Virginian named Nathaniel Bacon organized a rebellious revolution of black and white anarchist. Bacon's army of crusaders burned the colonial capital and drove the governor from his dwelling in an attempt to take possession of American lands in Western Virginia. The Virginia Militia eradicated Bacon's rebellion with mostly blacks being killed who were herding behind their radical leader.

During seventeen thirty nine, Congolese Africans brought to America contrived a rebellious revolution at the Stone River in South Carolina. Their leader was an African named Jemmy. The governor alerted the militia and they were defeated. The colonies of British South Carolina implemented laws against blacks such as: if a white murdered a black it was a misdemeanor and blacks were not allowed to testify under oath.

During the year eighteen eleven, an African named Charles Deslondes organized a brigade of rebellious African followers in an attempted revolution of New Orleans. The local militia won victory over them and severed many of their heads and staked them along the Mississippi River as a warning to other militants.

During the eighteen twenties, an African named Denmark Vesey plotted a rebellious revolution near Charleston, South Carolina with hundreds of black followers claiming blacks were God's chosen people. Vesey and his herding followers had planned to burn the city of Charleston. Before his plot could exist, a military force discovered his intentions of revolution and foiled their plot. Vesey and approximately thirty to forty blacks were convicted for plotting treason and lynched.

During eighteen twenty six, a northern black from Boston, Massachusetts named David Walker and his tribal followers established the Massachusetts General Colored Association. They incited militant violence against whites (especially southern whites) because initially Walker was from North Carolina. He instigated militant statements against whites such as: you whites, we hate you; America is more our country than you whites, we blacks are going to stand firm against you. This caused southern whites to become intense because Walker condemned America and insisted on a black rebellious revolution. In essence, David Walker's bias, radical, demagoguery caused the southern whites fears to come true.

During eighteen thirty one, a black named Nat Turner plotted and carried out one of the most devastating insurrections against southern whites around Southampton County, Virginia. Turner was supposedly a religious person who saw black and white blood on corn stalks. He saw spirits of blacks and whites in battle and streams flowing with blood. He believed God had chosen him to eradicate whites. Turner began his incredible rebellious revolution with blacks herding behind him from numerous plantations. Many whites were of the opinion this was the rebellious revolution David Walker instigated from Boston. The Virginia governor called out the U. S. Navy and state infantry. The state militia had to be reinforced to defeat Turner's attack. After it was over, he escaped to the swamps. He was located, tried and lynched. A team of surgeons removed his skin and manufactured shoes and purses from it. Unfortunately, there was another horrible tragedy to occur when white retaliated; they killed every black they came in contact with from Richmond through Southampton County. They killed approximately one hundred and fifty blacks in one day (many were innocent) because whites assumed this was the all black rebellious revolt David Walker had predicted.

During seventeen seventy five, a young black known as Colonel Titus from New Jersey organized a band over eight hundred black rebellious guerrillas who called themselves the King of England soldiers. They terrorized, burned and raided plantations for over fifty years.

The stability of mental capabilities is the most philosophical attributes God inherently created in mankind. If not understood and used appropriately, it can create human disaster which is inevitable in numerous capacities based on American exceptionalism. It is a vile handicap to not have the intellectual ability to decipher the required perseveration to determine; philosophical agendas which hinder based on distorted bias hypothetical demagoguery.

For over one hundred forty years, the ethnic African/African Americans have created their internal herding density dilemma by not being adaptable to the general exceptionalism of America. (American exceptionalism refers to the theory that the United States is qualitatively different from other countries.) Their distinguishing qualities have been grossly overrated based on intellectual moral values; because for approximately three hundred and fifty years most blacks have engaged in an attempt to modify America to their satisfaction. Meaning: a black America, established within America, under their jurisdiction. Most are insidious narcissistic because they are taught nationally, at a very early age from their families and churches they are God's chosen ethnic people and will control the universe one day. Most African Americans who reside in America are illiterate or semi-illiterate and are hindered by these philosophical, overbearing densities which create the inability to grasp or decipher. Most who attend institutions of higher learning either drop out or are given a pass because they are black, philosophically aloof and utilize racism as a camouflage for overbearing density. Most have always lived in combative seclusion and never acclimated into the fundamental traditions America was founded on. They never research anything for the actual validity; it is always what they are advised by someone else. They constantly utilize racism in an effort to convince others their philosophical ideology is compatible to the general consensus of American traditions. Unfortunately, their genetic traits are to the contrary with overbearing density which is never exposed until they are hired into private industry or politically elected by a constituency. Most then begin to embellish in their accomplishments with narcissistic tendencies of self-control related to authoritative Congo tribal chief indication doctrines pertaining to herding: that blacks are superior over other ethnics. This is an inevitable psychological problem of overbearing density which has dominated most African/African Americans for centuries. This began in Africa with black king rulers and tribal chiefs capturing other tribes for sale between Europe and Africa during the fourteenth century; trading Africans for beads and miscellaneous textiles. There were slave castles along the coast of West Africa where African kings utilized them for

European nations to transport Africans globally. African kings were applauded as lucrative because before the fifth century the Romans paid astronomical prices for North African slaves. The name slave and owning people was founded and originated in Africa. In essence, there is a vast philosophical difference between other ethnic people and Africans. Other ethnics choose to migrate to America because they were civilized and seeking liberties in an effort to attain capitalistic prosperity based on their individual intellect and were eager to attain comprehension of America's unique viable standards for a better life America had offered for hundreds of years.

Chapter 19

The ethnic of Africans were brought to America against their will while African slaves were being ship transported to miscellaneous segments of the glove. If allowed on ship deck, many would commit suicide by jumping overboard. The first African slaves were brought to British Colonial North America during the year sixteen nineteen with twenty aboard a military Dutch war ship which docked in Jamestown, Virginia in desperate need of food supplies. The ship's captain negotiated with the colonial people to trade the African slaves for food supplies.

African slave was initially labeled to all Africans by African ruling kings. This was transcribed to America during later years which the plantation masters were identified with. The initial twenty Africans brought to Jamestown were not referred to as slaves. They were characterized as indentured servants; same as poor whites. Unfortunately for Africans, they could not adjust to existing Virginia colony laws over a period of seventy two years which had consisted of an African population explosion. South Carolina was equivalent to a West African tribal ethnic which they never sort to veer from their philosophical African genetic heritage to attain American exceptionalism. Their alternative was to engage in a rebellious revolution, herding behind Nathaniel Bacon, during sixteen seventy six when many Africans lost their lives in defeat.

The rebellious revolutionary revolt was one of the most devastating tragedies in the history of America for Africans/African Americans. The consequences were during sixteen ninety one. The South Carolina

Colonial British North America legislative assembly negotiated in understandable system of laws and guidelines the ethnic Africans could be sold and traded into bondage; the same as animals. This became a vast sensational commodity throughout America, mostly in the southern states that remained in existence until eighteen hundred eight when congress abolished selling and trading of Africans. This southern atrocity legacy altered the entire lives of most Africans/African Americans inevitably and eternally. Most African Americans to date haven't the slightest idea of who they are, where they came from, or what transpired based on their philosophical ideological genetic heritage traits. This instigated determining decisiveness based on over-rated density is constantly prevalent in most African American ideological agenda today: pursuing non-existing assumptions based on herding behind self-appointed extremists. Most African American's ambitions have always been related to a Congo ideology of sharing; like food from the jungles with other tribesmen. Their philosophical genetic heritage traits from Africa has always dictated: America should be shared, pertaining to their profiled identity as black America which most blacks commonly utilize the verbiage: white man's America; which is nonsensical and over-rated density because America is a unique nation and stands alone with numerous of ethnics residing here and are constantly migrating.

Illiteracy is one of the most devastating phenomena in human life. Inevitably you are obligated to others for guidance and having not gone to institutions for learning you are dense to their motivations which can lead to misguided destruction. To be educated and incompetent is equivalent to illiteracy. These philosophical traits demand manual serving or accusing others for your over-rated density to intellectually excel which is a replica of verbal indentured deficiency. American English is one of the most unique languages on God's earth because of the variables to equate same scenarios. Most African Americans never acquired the intellect to speak appropriate English. If you can't speak it, you sure as hell can't understand the correlated verbiage. Illiteracy and the inability to conform to ratified, established laws and constantly adhering to African traditions and attempting to establish an African monarch in America created slavery because Africans were brought to America during sixteen nineteen. Their philosophical African genetic heritage dictated adverse to change; instead of conforming to established American guidelines which they rebelled against.

Most Africans consistently practice Congo ideology for approximately two hundred years because initially there was no slavery for seventy two years in the south. After seventy two years, the African population had grown tremendously and they choose to segregate and organize a replica of Africa in Jamestown. On the North American mainland where slavery had never existed, or been considered, because there were inter-racial marriages whites and Africans were treated equal as illiterates while performing their chores. However, Africans were adhering to their sensuality rebellious witchcraft Congo traits. It was of extreme concern to the Virginia colonial authorities. During sixteen seventy six their worst fears occurred. A radical Caucasian named Nathaniel Bacon organized an illiterate troop of rebellious Africans. They pursued a revolution to appropriate native lands in Western Virginia. They were eradicated by the Virginia Militia after the brigade of African revolt. The Virginian colonial authority became immensely alarmed in regards to other covert planned attacks by Africans. They began planning strategies to prevent Africans radical revolts because over a period of seventy two years they had never attempted conformity to British colonial ratified established laws. During sixteen ninety one, the South Carolina British North America legislature ratified codes to sell and trade Africans. Other British North American colonies accepted and implemented the identical procedures. Not because they were black African slaves unfortunately, but because they refused to accept the fact that America is controlled by numerous ethnic people eternally and they rejected philosophical traits of Congo herding ideology. Africans were held accountable for their atrocious altercation actions which created an African disaster because they were sold and traded into bondage throughout America. This became a lucrative commodity that made many southern whites very wealthy. Nathan Bedford Forrest, a Mississippi horse trader who moved to Memphis, Tennessee, was one and began trading Africans. He became one of the wealthiest men in the south. Africans were transported all over the south to plantations which were controlled by plantation masters who appointed black slave drivers.

Then, along came the political organization during eighteen twenty eight known as the Democrat Party. They formulated southern traditions pertaining to African slaves that still philosophically adhered to and prevalent with most African Americans today. During the eighteen thirties, African slave population had increased immensely, particularly in the southern states. The state of Tennessee had a population of over one hundred fifty thousand; Mississippi over seventy thousand. The southern plantation masters were cohesive with the newly formed Democratic Party. They utilized the illiteracy and incompetency of African slaves to their utmost advantage through whatever method they deemed authoritative; such as lynching and miscellaneous slaughtering. Though these violent doctrines of infiltrated philosophical indoctrinations created a genetic heritage throughout most ethnic African Americans; an irrational microcosm of folklore has been devastative for most African Americans for hundreds of years and are more prevalent today than ever.

For every philosophical occurrence in life pertaining to people, there is a reason for every philosophical occurrence in life pertaining to people. To assume without certainty, demonstrate dysfunctional incompetency or illiteracy which is a potential philosophical trait embedded in every ethnic people who reside in the United State of America. Unfortunately, most Africans, African Americans, and blacks have lived in an over-rated density, fantasy illusion in America with an imaginary vision which was mostly denoted during eighteen ninety six when most southern blacks herded behind Booker T. Washington, the president and founder of Tuskegee Institute in Alabama. He literally traveled to African American populated areas over the southern states, coaxed and encouraged blacks to accept the Democratic Ku Klux Klan Jim Crow Rule: separate but equal and insisted it was inevitable. During eighteen ninety six, he was the most choice elite black in America. Many black families were naming their children after him. He was lacking sufficient knowledge and skill to decipher and determine the philosophical agenda of separate but equal imposed by the southern Democratic ku Klux Klan.

The southern Democrats had analyzed the philosophical ideology of blacks as if they were domesticated animals kept for pets. They knew blacks had never wanted to socialize with whites unless it was an affair for gratuity. During eighteen ninety six, most southern blacks were illiterate and incompetent so they assumed separate but equal was a compromise to equate their status compatible to whites with no resources other than a cotton sack. Blacks backed themselves into a corner by herding behind Booker T. Washington claiming he was educated and he knew what was best for them. This is why the fourteenth amendment to the Constitution on July ninth, eighteen sixty eight (giving all southern blacks their civil rights) and ratified by the Republican congress was revoked by the Democratic Ku Klux Klan through the Supreme Court jurisdiction that ruled separate but equal was constitutional based on compatible quantities pertaining to equal assets. This ruling compelled all southern African Americans to be separate from whites in all public facilities and to sit in the rear of all public transportation for sixty eight years. Being equal did not prohibit African

Americans from manufacturing their own public facilities and busses. The ruling from the Supreme Court separate but equal approximately one hundred fifteen years ago was an emphatic ruling to inform all ethnics: this is the United States of America not black or white America. Unfortunately, most African Americans have never come to this conclusive perception due to a philosophical innate over-rated density and dysfunctional traits of genetic heritage related to illiteracy and incompetency which is a genetic controllability that is eternal.

Illiterate indicates you are not capable to read and write. Incompetent indicates you can read and write but lack sufficient knowledge to determine the validity of what you read. This has been a tradition of most African Americans for hundreds of years. They assume and distort based on their philosophical bias agenda and constantly accuse others for their over-rated density.

CHAPTER 20

The Declaration of Independence and our Constitution of America are two of the most intellectual documents known to mankind on God's earth because they represent liberty; the philosophical established intellectual guidance to the greatest nation on the globe; the United States of America. One of the most terribly saddest, repulsive dysfunctional ideological behavioral ethnics in America is most Africans Americans; illiteracy has handicapped blacks for hundreds of years. Of those who can read and write (supposedly educated) most are incompetent because they can read but cannot decipher the validity in order to establish guidance which is equated to over-rated density. Most African Americans have disdain for the established guidance of the Constitution.

Today is Saturday, July 2, 2011. Monday is July 4th and I am reminded of the Declaration of Independence of July 4, 1776;

> *We hold these truths to be self-evident, that all men are created equal, that they are endowed by their Creator with certain unalienable Rights, that among these are Life, Liberty and the pursuit of Happiness.—That to secure these rights, Governments are instituted among Men, deriving their just powers from the consent of the governed, —That whenever any Form of Government becomes destructive of these ends, it is the Right of the People to alter or to abolish it.*

This theory was emphatically endorsed by the Constitution on September 17, 1787 when stipulated:

WE THE PEOPLE *of the United States, in Order to form a more perfect Union, establish Justice, insure domestic Tranquility, provide for the common defence, promote the general Welfare, and secure the Blessings of Liberty to ourselves and our Posterity, do ordain and establish this Constitution for the United States of America.*

Article I

Section1. *All legislative Powers herein granted shall be vested in a Congress of the United States, which shall consist of a Senate and House of Representatives.*

As I write these segments of the Declaration of Independence and the Constitution, I became emotional; because if you can read and decipher the meaning and are not reverence by these declarations then you or they are a threat to our nation in regard to our liberty.

Fortunately, America is balanced with a political power structure written within the Declaration of Independence which stipulates that governments are instituted among men. Whenever any form of government becomes destructive of these ends it is the right of the people to alter or abolish. These philosophical ideologues are committed with confidence to a major two party system; Democrat and Republican, under the jurisdiction of the people pertaining to city, state and federal governments in an effort to determine destiny.

The ethnic of most African Americans for hundreds of years have chosen their own destiny because of illiteracy and political bias distortion based on philosophical agendas of motivated incompetency; herding behind self-appointed leaders. The vast majority of Africans/African Americans/Blacks adhered to their traditional Congo tribal African beliefs for approximately two hundred years in America. Most blacks have literally refused to conform or consider incorporating into American established traditions, guaranteed according to the Declaration of Independence and the Constitution. These declarations offer tremendous liberties and advantages no other nation can compete with. Other ethnics, migrating immigrants, illiterate and educated has conformed and utilized the advantages the United States of America has to offer to their advantage; while ethic African Americans who reside in America are constantly trying to literally establish a black America for hundreds of years to no avail. This tribal Congo ideology, based on he is one of us and us got to stick together, is an illiterate, incompetent, genetic delusion heritage from the tribes of Africa. It is inevitable, also eternal, with most blacks who have devastated and will continue to destroy the enthusiasm of most African Americans to understand and participate in the fundamentals of what the United States of America has to offer based on individual merit.

This book is not written to demonize or demoralize the integrity of all blacks; but to offer an explicit explanation to their philosophical, genetic heritage traits which is unique to all other ethnics who reside in the United States of America pertaining to conforming to traditions. However, it is without question there are millions of African Americans who have given the ultimate sacrifice in honor of America. There are those who have chosen to enter into the philosophical traditions of American and have performed spectacularly in various professional endeavors throughout America, for hundreds of years, related to practically every employment classification in the United States of America to include private owned businesses, corporate industries and politics. Unfortunately, politics have always been an Achilles heel for most African Americans; simply because of their inability to decipher the contrasting complexity written in the Constitution due to illiteracy and incompetency. Unfortunately, due to southern Democratic Ku Klux Klan compulsory was utilized for control of blacks based on their illiteracy and incompetency during servitude, the Democratic Klan used violent, brute force to control African Americans related to their superiority and dominance.

The plantation master chose two other hierarchy; a white workman in charge of the plantation and a black slave driver in charge of other salves. They supplied him with high boots and a whip to maintain superiority dominance over other slaves which on numerous occasions could be brutal; even death. The brutality, at times, could become so severe the plantation master would have to chastise the slave driver. In essence, based on philosophical traits of southern Democratic Ku Klux Klan indoctrinating over hundreds of years, this genetic heritage is embedded in the philosophical traits of most blacks today. Let's just illustrate the philosophical agenda of Democrats in general. Realistically, during eighteen sixty six, they founded the Ku Klux Klan. They were committed to white supremacy and determined to eradicate the Republican Party. During this era, practically all African Americans were Republicans and worked harmoniously along with white Republicans nationwide. In an effort to deter this Republican relationship, the Democratic terrorist Ku Klux Klan during eighteen seventy four in Vicksburg, Mississippi slaughtered over three hundred African Americans to discourage their affiliation with the Republican Party. They literally murdered and drove white Republicans from the southern states. The remaining southern African Americans were literally violently forced to become Democrats or be lynched.

One hundred thirty seven years later, based on illiteracy and incompetency, they are still supportive of Democrats. The Republican congress ratified the thirteenth, fourteenth and fifteenth amendments to the Constitution for their liberties, civil and voting rights during the eighteen sixties and seventies. The southern Democratic Ku Klux Klan rescinded all civil and voting rights for southern blacks during eighteen ninety six through the U. S. Supreme Court, which ruled in their favor, that separate but equal, the Jim Crow Rule was constitutional: all southern blacks had to sit in back of bus transportation for sixty eight years.

Dr. Martin Luther King lost his life to have civil rights for southern blacks restored. When it occurred, during nineteen sixty four and five, former Democratic Ku Klux Klansman Senator Robert Byrd filibustered for over seventeen hours against southern blacks civil rights being restored. Once again the grand old party, Republican congress, rose to the occasion and over-rode Senator Robert Byrd's filibuster to restore southern African Americans civil and voting rights. After this restorative episode of nineteen sixty four, the Democrats devised a new strategy of political control over illiterate and incompetent, dysfunctional African Americans which was equivalent to servitude; minas the physical labor with the cotton sack. Unfortunately, it is political bias distortion based on philosophical agendas to maintain their traditional herding of voting capacity which in essence the Democrat Party is equivalent to the southern plantation slave owners. They physically manipulate illiterate and incompetent African Americans through the liberal bias media by constantly utilizing those incompetent black slave drivers of modern times to convenience other African Americans it was those racist Republicans who was, and is, responsible for all their questions to be resolved.

Let's delve into two of the validity resolving accolades in the history of African Americans. During eighteen sixty five, Republican President Abraham Lincoln abolished slavery. Unfortunately he was assassinated and replaced by his Vice President Andrew Johnson (a Democrat from the south) who rescinded legislation President Lincoln had proposed; to give each southern black family forty acres of southern plantation master's land and a government mule. Andrew Johnson gave the land back to the plantation masters. Most African Americans are totally inept to the analogy between Democrat and Republican parties (particularly Republicans). Republican Ulysses S. Grant replaced Democratic President Andrew Johnson during eighteen sixty eight. President Grant suspended the Writ of Habeas Corpus in nine South Carolina counties where largely Ku Klux Klansmen concentrated. He installed federal troops to quell the lynching of blacks by the Democratic Ku Klux Klan. The Republican congress launched an all-out investigation of the Ku Klux Klan in the southern states. They arrested and indicted approximately several hundred white Ku Klux Klansmen in Mississippi, South Carolina and North Carolina. The Democratic Ku Klux Klan was highly distraught and retaliated with verbiage: all blacks were ignorant, illiterate, incompetent and trying to rise above their philosophical traits and should remain loyal to servitude because they will never advance in the political arena.

The fourteenth amendment of the Constitution was ratified on July 9, 1868 by the Republican congress authorizing civil rights for all people (particularly African Americans who were citizens of the United States of America). Unfortunately, most African Americans were illiterate and incompetent (I used the terms loosely) because the initial Africans were transported to America were hostile, uncivilized and illiterate. During slavery this was compounded because the slave masters taught Africans school wasn't for their benefit because they would be taken care of for life. This genetic heritage is prevalent in African American community life today. Of all ethnics residing in America, African Americans have the highest rate of school drop outs.

During eighteen sixty eight, after the Republican congress ratified the fourteenth amendment to the Constitution, white and black Republicans (even some Democrats) worked tirelessly to rebuild the southern states during the end of the Civil War. Approximately six to eight hundred African Americans served in the state legislature. Twenty to thirty were elected to the U. S. House of Representatives; two to the U. S. Senate. There were over five thousand schools open in the south for black and white students. During eighteen seventy seven there were more than seven hundred thousand African American children in elementary schools. Black judges and sheriffs were appointed. Unfortunately, the southern Democrats and their Ku Klux Klan were determined to eradicate all Republicans and replace them with white supremacy Democratic Ku Klux Klan political power. They did accomplish this mission by slaughtering approximately three to five hundred Republican African Americans in Vicksburg, Mississippi and finally expelled all black and white Republicans from the southern states during the early eighteen seventies.

For over ninety years any black suspected of being a Republican was lynched by the controlling southern Democratic Ku Klux Klan. The remaining southern blacks were forced to become Democratic supporters. As of the year two thousand eleven, approximately one hundred forty years later, most blacks were still slobbering over the alimentary canal of Democrats. Most haven't the slightest idea why. I have asked blacks all over America as to why they support Democrats. All I get is: My granddaddy was a Democrat, my daddy was a Democrat, my mama was a Democrat and I am going to be a Democrat until I die. This is the genetic heritage; forced indoctrination passed on through genetic controllability southern Democrats intimidated African Americans into adhering to. It is inevitable also eternal with most. Unfortunately, most African Americans, being illiterate and incompetent, have been gullible and allowed Democrats to politically utilize bias distortion, based on philosophical agendas of contrive rebellious demagogic lies to malign Republican as civilians who have contempt for all African Americans. In essence, if it were not for Republican presidents and Republican controlled congresses, the ethnic of African/African American/Blacks would have been literally eradicated, or still enslaved by the southern Democratic established Ku Klux Klan. It would not have been necessary to create the cotton picking machine because the Democratic Ku Klux Klan Party in the south had ambitions to continue slavery and have blacks pick the cotton.

There has been numerous speculations as to why the southern Democrats founded the Ku Klux Klan during eighteen sixty six in Pulaski, Tennessee. Prior to eighteen sixty six, there were the white terrorist called the Knights of the White Camilla and the Pale Face Brotherhood. Their resolution was to eradicate the stability of the Republican Party in the southern states because the Republican congress ratified the fourteenth amendment to the Constitution where southern slaves had their civil and equal rights. This caused hysteria from the Democratic Ku Klux Klan because blacks had become united in alliance with northern Republicans who came to the southern states to teach former slaves to read and write which had never existed prior to the Civil War. The Democratic Ku Klux

Klan was established for two systematic reasons: to eradicate Republicans from the south and reinstate slavery. They utilized every brutal method possible. There was a terrorist armed forced named the White Man League during eighteen seventy four. They marched on the New Orleans state house where black and white Republicans were in session. They intimidated and demanded they were going to overthrow the Louisiana state government and install Democratic Ku Klux Klan white supremacy. Wade Hampton served as South Carolina's governor and U. S. Senator demanded everything possible should be executed to prevent Republicans from voting, especially blacks, including murdering them; unfortunately the lynching of blacks continued by the Democratic Ku Klux Klan through the seventeenth century to the mid nineteenth century.

During Democratic President Franklin Delano Roosevelt's first eight years in office, seventeen to eighteen blacks were lynched each year. One of the most tragic, disastrous, manipulating, misfortunates occurred to southern blacks during the eighteen seventy six presidential elections between Democrat Samuel J. Tilden and Republican Rutherford B. Hayes. Republican Hayes won the election and the Democratic controlled congress refused to certify his election unless he removed federal troops from the southern states who were protecting the blacks from being lynched by the Democratic Ku Klux Klan. Once the troops were removed, the southern Democrats persuaded the U. S. Supreme Court to annex the protection for southern African Americans to include their civil and voting rights. The Democratic Ku Klux Klan resumed their terrorist acts of violence on African Americans. The torturer doctrine, under the superiority of the Democratic Ku Klux Klan continued in existence for seventy seven years until Republican President Dwight David Eisenhower was elected on October 22, 1953. He presented the first civil rights bill legislated for southern blacks in eighty nine years. It passed the House of Representatives, but was rejected by the senate where Lyndon Baines Johnson was the leader of the senate. President Eisenhower was truly a remarkable, indulgence for African Americans. He instructed FBI Director J. Edgar Hoover to infiltrate the Ku Klux Klan and quell the violent lynching of African Americans.

During his presidency he chose one of the most precarious endeavors ever introduced in the south by any president since the Civil War. He was determined to integrate southern schools for blacks. One of his greatest challenges was Democratic governor of Arkansas: Orval Faubus, who literally refused to cooperate. Also, Democratic U. S. Senators Lyndon

Baines Johnson, who implied there should be no troops brought in and Senator Olin Johnson suggested if he was governor of Arkansas he would fight to the bitter end. While there were uncontrolled white racist mobs, over several thousands, yelling lynch the niggers; claiming President Eisenhower was trying to destroy the social order of the south. Governor Orval Faubus denounced the decision of the U. S. Federal courts to integrate central high. Republican President Dwight David Eisenhower was persistent and determined. He ordered federal troops to escort black students into Central High in Little Rock, Arkansas on October 23rd. In the school year of nineteen fifty nine they were admitted without incident. In essence, Republican President Eisenhower established the fundamentals for the nineteen sixty four and five restoration of civil and voting rights for southern African Americans which eradicated the Democratic Ku Klux Klan's violent maiming attacks against southern black and white Republicans.

There is a replica of philosophical bias distorting cynicism portrayed verbally by numerous Democratic liberals today. It is equivalent to the philosophical traits of the Democratic plantation masters and their white plantation overseer along with the black slave driver dressed in high boots and black jacket with a whip. These conjunctions are prevalently equated as a scenario over the United States of America pertaining to political bias distortion based on philosophical agendas of verbal abuse for Republicans not violent eradication which was executed during the eighteen hundreds and mid nineteen hundreds. The verbal implications duplicate the philosophical intentions to demoralize the repulse Republicans for political gain which is redundant over most news outlets. Utilizing fallacious demagoguery to impugn the integrity of others is equivalent to the southern Democratic Ku Klux Klan during the eighteen sixties. During that era, most who indulged in those barbaric atrocities simply for political superiority were illiterate and densely incompetent.

There is a definitive difference between illiterate and incompetent. Illiterate is defined: unable to read and write. Incompetent is defined: without adequate ability, knowledge, fitness, etc.; failing to meet requirements; incapable; unskillful; not legally qualified; lacking strength and sufficient flexibility to transmit pressure, thus breaking or flowing under stress: said of rock structures—an incompetent person; esp., one who is mentally deficient.

One can be a Harvard or Yale graduate and be incompetent because one can read the Declaration of Independence or the Constitution, but is incapable of deciphering the structure and interpret based on their philosophical agenda of bias distortion, is an incompetent idiot; and because of the variables gaining wealth is not deterred.

This is why America is so unique; regards to complexity, because the founding fathers chose the people to make a judgment choice and bring to a conclusion of our destiny, which consists of numerous ethnics based on individual choice, not a monarch ruler, or one political party doctrine. The Democratic Party of America has constantly utilized every tactic accessible; including slaughtering people of the opposing Republican Party. Beginning over one hundred eighty years ago, their philosophical ideology was to abort free speech and capitalism in an effort to implement a form of government control of production and distribution of goods for the people. The criteria which motivated the philosophical ideology of Republican agendas are to allow people to think for themselves and determine their own destiny in accordance with the specification of the Declaration of Independence and Constitution of the United States of America.

Abraham Lincoln was inducted to be president of American March 4, 1861. He was scandalized as being a Republican president and nigger lover by southern Democratic confederacy. President Lincoln stated: the states where slavery existed he had no philosophical agenda to interfere. Unfortunately, until the confederate military attacked federal Fort Sumter on April 12, 1861, President Lincoln retaliated with a barrage of military force to quell the rebellion in South Carolina. This was the beginning of the Civil War. There were a number of slave states such as Virginia, Arkansas, Tennessee and North Carolina who withdrew their status from the United States and joined the southern confederacy. The war ended within approximately four years with the union being the victors with Confederate Commander Robert E. Lee's surrender to U. S. General Ulysses S. Grant at Appomattox Court House in Virginia.

Republican President Abraham Lincoln issued an Emancipation Proclamation for all enslaved blacks to have their liberties from slavery on January 1, 1863. Most blacks had to be advised what it was because of wholesale illiteracy due to southern Democratic prevention of blacks being schooled. During eighteen sixty five the Republican controlled congress ratified the thirteenth amendment to the Constitution on December 6, 1865 by a vote of one hundred twenty four to twenty four. This initiated the total abolishment of servitude for blacks in accordance with the Declaration of Independence on July 9, 1868. They also ratified the fourteenth and fifteenth amendments on February 3, 1870. President

Lincoln was a true American patriot who set the ameliorate standards for liberty. His philosophical ideology was equality for all mankind pertaining to liberty for all ethnics who were Americans, particularly blacks because of their overwhelmingly illiteracy and incompetency; based on dysfunctional overrated density.

President Lincoln was quite aware of these philosophical traits of blacks instituted by Democratic southern plantation owners. Their resolution; if you can't read and write, you can't leave the plantation. However, President Lincoln had devised an appropriate resolution to the criteria. His philosophical objective was schooling and self-sufficiency in an effort to they could determine their individual destiny pertaining to human quality and adhere to the central importance and the necessity American was founded on. President Lincoln knew not being capable of reading and writing or incompetent was one of the worst tragedies known to mankind if you are inept to the validity of effects. Unfortunately, President Lincoln's life was snuffed out by a murderer; especially for political reasons by John Wilkes Booth (a staunch rebellious southern confederate Democrat) at Ford Theater on April 14, 1865 in Washington, D. C. with a bullet to his head. Once Booth committed this hideous crime, he jumped over the balcony and yelled hale to the Democratic confederacy. This is vengeance for losing the war and no nigger will ever become a citizen or vote in this country.

President Johnson gave pardons to all the Democratic confederate plantation slave owners and returned their plantation. Although blacks were no longer slaves, due to the thirteenth amendment to the Constitution ratifying the Republican congress, blacks were illiterate or incompetent and had no place to go but back to their plantation owner for assistance. Blacks not being a plantation slave any longer were subjected to inordinate consequences. The plantation owners passed new regulations which consisted of prohibiting blacks from attending school. Also, if any black displayed intellect or dressed well, addressed any white with yes or no, responded negatively to being called boy or girl, being a senior citizen, most commonly used was nigger or darkie, old Uncle Tom, blacks were to address whites at any age, yes sir and yes mam. Many Democratic southern states enacted black codes; limiting freedom for blacks, imposing fines for jail time for unemployment; in essence subject to be lynched for any of these offenses which was a replica of servitude and worse.

The Republican congress attempted to protect African Americans from these atrocities, but Democratic President Andrew Johnson quelled their efforts. The Republican congress was extremely persistent in their opposition against President Johnson previous dictating for Democratic southern supremacy over southern African Americans. The Republican congress passed the fourteenth amendment to the Constitution giving all African Americans their civil rights; ratified July 9, 1968 and the fifteenth amendment giving blacks their voting rights; ratified February 3, 1870.

CHAPTER 21

During the eighteen sixties, after the Republican congress ratified the fourteenth amendment to the Constitution to give blacks their equal and civil rights as American citizens, they began to enter politics in the southern states after Republican President Ulysses S. Grant replaced Democratic President Andrew Johnson. Republican African Americans made political progress in the south. Oscar J. Dunn became Lieutenant Governor of Louisiana. Hirman Rhodes Revels became the first American Black U. S. Senator in Mississippi. Blanche K. Bruce served as U. S. Senator during eighteen seventy four. Jonathan Gibbs served as Florida's Secretary of State. Egbert Sammis was elected to Florida's state senate. Francis Louis Cardoza served as South Carolina's Secretary of State. Pickney Benton Stewart Pinchback became America's first African American Governor of Louisiana. There were over twenty blacks elected to the U. S. Congress. They united with white Republicans in hopes of rebuilding the south. They built schools in an effort to enroll black and white illiterates. Unfortunately, these dreams and hopes were shattered by the Democratic founded Ku Klux Klan. They literally slaughtered black and white Republicans driving them from the southern states and specifically stated African Americans were stupid illiterate and incompetent by trying to rise above their natural place of servitude.

The Democratic Ku Klux Klan revoked civil and voting rights for southern blacks by initiating the Jim Crow Rule separate but equal; primarily based on their illiteracy and incompetency curing eighteen ninety six by their not being capable of deciphering the verbiage separate but equal: which means if you applaud separatism you are still equal to others, according to the Constitution. However, it is the resources that separate one or miscellaneous groups from others.

There are numerous ethnics residing in America who are plagued with illiteracy and incompetency. However, it is African Americans who have suffered the consequences drastically opposed to other ethnics. For over three hundred and ninety years southern Democrats have formulated strategies; including wholesale slaughter to take advantage of illiteracy and incompetency of blacks; these philosophical genetic heritage traits are embedded in the distinguishing quality of most African Americans and is more prevalent today than ever.

Slaves from Africa were brought to the British Colonies in Virginia, North America during sixteen nineteen. They were illiterate and uncivilized. There was no slavery. They were introduced to the tobacco farms along with mostly illiterate whites. Their responsible servings were equal; they worked the fields and homes of the farm owners. This was a tradition for fifty seven years. Until sixteen seventy six, when a band of interracial illiterates chose to organize a rebellious revolution led by a white, Nathaniel Bacon. They burned the colonial capital, desecrated the governor and drove him form the capital. However, they were defeated. The elite whites of Virginia colonial authority were deeply raged because over fifty seven years the British Colonies of Virginia had grown tremendously with Africans being brought from western and central Africa and also natural born in America. They never conformed to British North American traditions. They constantly adhered to and practiced their African heritage and were opposed to conforming American methodology which became very disturbing to the British North American Colonies.

Fifteen years after the revolution of sixteen seventy six staged by revolutionist Nathaniel Bacon and his followers, during sixteen ninety one South Carolina provided British North America with an initial slave code. The code stipulated: all negroes mulattoes, etc., were to be sold into bondage. Over eighteen hundred other British North American Colonies engaged in the same philosophical agenda. It was seventy two years before Africans were introduced to slavery in America simply because of illiteracy and incompetency not because they were black.

Due to illiteracy and incompetency, along with unsettling temperaments of violence, during eighteen sixty six, the southern Democratic Ku Klux Klan announced blacks were politically inept, illiterate and incompetent and should refrain from engaging in the political sphere of activity. During nineteen fifty seven, FBI Director J. Edgar Hoover assumed blacks brains were smaller than whites by twenty percent. These philosophical accusations were based on traits of dysfunctional illiteracy and incompetency which is an embedded genetic heritage from Africa which most African Americans are characterized with to date.

Most people residing in the United States of America are totally unaware of this distinguishing quality of most African Americans because it is consistently disguised by false pretenses of day to dis to us because us is black. Most African Americans have never, and never will, decipher the importance of the Declaration of Independence and Constitution because most are still busy trying to write their own black legislation as they began over three hundred and thirty years ago following Nathaniel Bacon. Based on illiteracy and incompetency this same scenario of a covert replica exists today; minas violence. Most African Americans haven't the slightest comprehension of who they are, pertaining to the sum of personal convictions of their nation of origin; based on genetic heritage and how most are affected by these philosophical traits.

These writings are offering an explicit introduction to past and current African/African American/Black identity and philosophical body of beliefs that was caused by illiteracy and incompetency. The southern Democratic Ku Klux Klan doctrine of violent intimidation of blacks in an effort to indoctrinate over hundreds of years was a political bias distorting success; based on a philosophical agenda of mind control due to illiteracy and dysfunctional incompetency which dictates the philosophical traits of most African Americans in current society today. Because blacks are the only ethnic who reside in a liberated society in the United States of America who supports the Democratic Party approximately ninety five percent as a voting constituency. This exemplifies illiterate incompetency as the southern Democrats predicted during eighteen sixty eight. FBI Director J. Edgar Hoover was so frustrated during nineteen fifty seven he was quoted as suggesting the brains of blacks were twenty percent smaller than whites. During Republican President Dwight David Eisenhower's administration, he formulated the first civil rights bill for southern blacks in approximately ninety years. Unfortunately the congress was controlled by Democrats and it was rejected. President Eisenhower quelled the lynching of southern blacks by Democratic Ku Klux Klan and the exploding of churches with little black girls inside. He initiated southern integrated schools for blacks. During the interim northern

African Americans who could vote were supporting Democrat candidates to be elected while their southern ancestors were being lynched and being blown to bits in churches by the southern Democratic founded Ku Klux Klan.

The southern Democrats knew of this dysfunctional illiterate incompetency of most blacks because they specifically acknowledged it during the early eighteen seventies. It has been proven they were absolutely correct because there was no schooling for southern blacks on plantations. Blacks were not allowed to attend any place in the southern states. There were more illiterate, incompetent whites over the southern states than blacks that were instructing blacks. Blacks thought they were educated because they were white. The only difference was illiterate, incompetent whites were free to travel the states and become engaged in political bias distortion based on their philosophical agenda. This is why America is the greatest nation on God's earth because of exceptionalism.

Illiteracy and incompetency is an infinite duration in society for all ethics past and current. Changing times and modern technology have eradicated illiteracy pertaining to expedient success. However, incompetency has escalated in our society to the extent of dire concern for the moral fabric and dignity of our great nation based on political bias distortion and sphere of philosophical agendas.

The United States of America consists of numerous ethnics who are characterized as the most intellectual, moral valued people on God's globe. I suspect we have been politically lulled based on distorted philosophical agendas into dozing at the wheel. I am a proud American with African heritage that is a heart conscious patriot of the United States of America which is embedded in my genetic controllability; beginning with my great grandfather, Mr. Dowen Jones. Born in eighteen forty seven, he utilized his God given manual talents. He trained himself to be a carpenter and built one of the first cotton gins in Marengo County, Alabama. He purchased land in eighteen eighty three which I inherited and is still there in Demopolis, Alabama. I dedicated my first book in his honor *"Political Self Destruction of Most African Americans"*; which is available at Trafford Publishing and other book sellers along with a photo of my great grandfather and his land deed. He, in my opinion, is an inspiration of what exceptionalism in the United States consists of; providing you are capable of deciphering the founding fundamentals and conform to the adherence of capitalistic endeavors as he accomplished one hundred and sixty four years ago.

There is a code of ethics standardized as a tradition in the United States of America; reading, writing, arithmetic, competent intellect and moral values. Initially these philosophical fundaments skills are taught in the home of a child and expanded on within the school system. These are the philosophical characteristic standards which are inevitable in an effort to determine progress in America. If you choose not to adhere to and avoid these philosophical American traditions, it is quite obvious your destination probably will be decided by a judge and jury to determine how much time you get or stacked in high rise slum dwellings like sardines screaming and herding behind self-appointed black leaders who tell you it is the racist white man who has caused your failure in life. In essence it is illiteracy and incompetency which has and can cause destitution. Being illiterate it is difficult go get employment. Being incompetent means there is a very distinct possibility you will lose employment based on deficiency. Unfortunately, illiteracy and incompetency has caused destitution in all ethnics and a major incarceration.

The southern Democratic Ku Klux Klan and plantation owners prohibited most southern blacks for approximately three hundred and forty five years from largely attending schooling centers to obtain an education. This was a philosophical trend which is largely due to most African Americans illiteracy and incompetency today. The southern Democratic plantation owners held blacks hostage. There were an extraordinary amount of illiterate whites who were preoccupied with rebellious intentions after the Civil War. There were two southern elites in this category: Nathan Bedford Forrest and President Andrew Johnson. Nathan Bedford Forrest, through his ability to sell slaves became lucrative for him and President Johnson rescinded the order President Abraham Lincoln had proposed to give African American families forty acres of plantation owner's land and a government mule. This revoking coded African Americans into plantation servants for ninety six years.

There were illiterate and incompetency combined between black and whites, sharing a goal of dysfunctional illiteracy. Most whites egressed. Unfortunately, most blacks are still stigmatized with illiterate, dysfunctional, incompetency prevalent in current society and with most it is eternally. Most blacks have always been followers; herding behind a tribal Congo chief in Africa thousands of years ago. This is a genetic heritage embedded in most African Americans today that they are totally unaware of.

In an effort to clarify my summation: there were numerous illiterate and incompetent whites throughout the southern states who were proud of the eleven confederate states which seceded from the U. S. during eighteen sixty and sixty one. After they lost the Civil War, they became enraged and rebelled against everything the U. S. instituted, including the Declaration of Independence and the Constitution. Once Democratic President Andrew Johnson returned the forty acres of land Republican President Abraham Lincoln had chosen to give blacks along with a government mule illiterate whites became belligerent against blacks; molesting their wives and family members in their homes. Illiterate and incompetent whites taught illiterate blacks philosophical rebellious traits against the Constitution and it was those Republicans who started the war and caused their problems. Southern blacks being illiterate and afraid were indoctrinated based on political bias distortion in an effort to accomplish philosophical agendas.

Over a period of one hundred forty six years they cloned blacks to their ideology: there is only one political party in the United States of America which is Democrats. In essence mission accomplished: through illiteracy and incompetency. Most African Americans support and vote approximately ninety five percent Democratic constantly nationwide. This illustrates gross dysfunctional, incompetent insanity because most haven't the slightest idea of why, other than my granddaddy was a Democrat, my daddy was a Democrat and I will be a Democrat all my life and teach my children to be Democrat. This stigmatic revelation is equivalent to an African Congo tribal controlling chief over his tribe. He is their guiding spokesman who determines their philosophical destiny. A philosophical replica of standard has been adopted by most African Americans in regard to the Democrat Party; as their plantation masters along with self-appointed black slave drivers.

Let's revert back to the eighteen hundreds and equate African Americans of today. Pertaining to the southern Democratic Ku Klux Klan during the eighteen hundreds they utilized brute human slaughtering tactics in an effort to force blacks to conform to their philosophical agendas of illiterate incompetency related to bias political propaganda to eradicate Republicans. Today's modern strategic methods are to utilize the airways minas violence in an effort to verbally sabotage the integrity of Republicans. This kind of character assassination is equivalent to southern Democratic Ku Klux Klan and a facsimile of the white plantation bosses who supervised the black slave drivers. Most African Americans who were lynched by the Democratic Ku Klux Klan in the southern states were not lynched because they were black. Their problems occurred because of being affiliated with the Republican Party.

Let's evaluate the existing circumstances of today. Beginning with a few elite facsimile white Democratic Ku Klux Klansmen, utilizing the airways to malicious demagogue and impugn the integrity of Republicans. Beginning with a few: Chris Matthews, Ed Schultz, Rachel Maddow, Keith Olbermann, Wolf Blitzer, Lawrence Odonnell, Ed Schultz, Bill Maher, Dylan Ratigan, John Stewart, Martin Bashir, Alan Colmes. These are just an elite limited few of facsimile plantation bosses of the eighteen hundreds who reported to the plantation owner masters. The black plantation slave drivers reported to him with all pertinent information concerning plantation slaves. He advised which slaves were to be sold or lynched.

The listing below is some of the facsimile replicating blacks of today; equating black plantation slave drivers of the eighteen hundreds, licking the alimentary canal of the white plantation supervisors and were responsible for the sale of thousands and lynching of slaves by the southern Democratic Ku Klux Klan. In essence dysfunctional, inept, illiteracy and incompetency is a patent trade mark of most African Americans because slave drivers were utilized by the plantation owners and white supervisors to betray other slaves during the eighteen hundreds to be lynched by the Democratic Ku Klux Klan.

Today is August 4, 2011, one hundred thirty nine years later. The Democrat Party is still utilizing the betrayal of African Americans. Unfortunately, today it is the Republican Party they are constantly demoralizing and rebelling against instead of lynching blacks. Let's explicitly define what each political party contributed to the security and liberty of African Americans. The two political parties came into existence during the mid-eighteen twenties: Democrat and Republican.

Let's begin with the Republican Party.

Republican President Abraham Lincoln abolished servitude for southern blacks in eighteen sixty five.

Republican President Ulysses S. Grant ordered military troops into southern states. They arrested, indicted and prosecuted Democratic Ku Klux Klansmen in an effort to quell the lynching of blacks in eighteen sixty eight.

The Republican controlled congress ratified the thirteenth, fourteenth and fifteenth amendments to the Constitution to give all southern African Americans their civil, equal and voting rights on December 6, 1865, July 9, 1868 and February 3, 1870.

Republican President Dwight David Eisenhower, during nineteen fifty seven, established the first civil rights bill for southern blacks in eighty nine years. He quelled the Democratic Ku Klux Klan from lynching southern blacks and integrated southern schools during the fifties.

Republican President Richard Millhouse Nixon established affirmative action for blacks during the sixties.

Republican President George H. Bush chose the second black to serve on the U. S. Supreme Court.

Republican President George W. Bush chose the first two blacks, male and female, ever to serve in his cabinet as security advisor and secretary of state.

Now let's evaluate the Democrat Party's contributions for security and liberty for African Americans.

Beginning with a rebellious Democrat, John Wilkes Booth who assassinated Republican President Abraham Lincoln for abolishing slavery for southern blacks in eighteen sixty five.

The southern Democrats founded the Ku Klux Klan in Pulaski, Tennessee during eighteen sixty six and began whole sale lynching of southern blacks simply because they were affiliated with the Republican Party.

Democrat President Andrew Johnson succeeded President Lincoln after the Booth assassination and rescinded the legislation President Lincoln had chosen to give each black family forty acres of southern plantation owner's land and a government mule during eighteen sixty five.

During eighteen ninety six, the southern Democrats, through the U. S. Supreme Court implemented the Jim Crow Rule: separate but equal which eradicated southern blacks civil and voting rights. They were forced to sit in the back of public transportation, enter rear doors, drink from separate colored water fountains, sit in balconies of movie theaters, and older blacks had to address young whites yes sir and mam. These codes were enforced for approximately sixty eight years in the southern states. The codes ended during nineteen sixty four and five. When forwarded to congress for ratification, a former Ku Klux Klansman (U. S. Senator Robert Byrd, racist Democrat) filibustered for over seventeen hours against southern blacks having their civil and voting rights restored. Fortunately, the Republican congress joined forces and rose to the occasion and nullified the filibuster.

CHAPTER 22

I am going to delve into the responsibility of the black slave driver during slavery and equate current day black Democratic Party political slave drivers.

The slave driver during servitude was the most important slave on the plantation. He was the eyes and ears of the plantation master and the white over-seer. All plantation over-seers were white. The black plantation slave driver reported to him as a Congo tribal southern plantation leader over other slaves. Most were dysfunctional and illiterate. These philosophical, repetitious genetic traits are still equated by black political Democratic Party slave drivers in current society. Their responsibility is to politically bias distort, based on philosophical agendas of herding most blacks into the Democrat Party and most are supposedly educated blacks; attorneys, law professors, doctors, news Pulitzer Prize winners, congress people and college professors. Unfortunately, this dysfunctional, incompetent, black alimentary canal slobbering for the Democratic Party is an incompetent replica of the white Democratic Ku Klux Klan lynching blacks in the southern states during eighteen sixty eight.

When Republican President Ulysses S. Grant utilized the military to arrest them, many were doctors, school teachers, lawyers, store owners and college professors tutoring illiterate whites on what blacks to lynch. These historic equated verbal scenarios are prevalent today in regards to black's affiliation with the Democrat Party. They are scattered all over the broadcast news networks like horse shit around a cotton gin during the forties, slobbering the alimentary canal of their white plantation news facsimile Democratic Ku Klux Klan anchors as they did white plantation supervisors during slavery; tattling on which black to lynch.

As of to date, Democrats have assigned them a new tattling assignment. It is to sabotage and degrade Republicans. Unfortunately, this has stabilized incompetency equated to the illiterate black slave driver of the eighteen hundreds because it is a ratified established code: that Republican presidents and controlling Republican congresses liberated southern African Americans from southern Democratic Ku Klux Klan extinction or eternally on a southern plantation illiterate slopping hogs and dragging a cotton sack.

Illiteracy, dysfunctional incompetency is the worst disastrous fate known to the human race because you are living in a fantasy world of hope, dreams and blame, because of not being capable of deciphering the codes of reality. This has been the destination of most African Americans for approximately three hundred ninety two years. This stigmatic philosophical genetic trait was caused by the southern Democratic Ku Klux Klan regime. It is inevitable also eternal because if you are in denial or haven't the slightest idea of what caused a problem, you sure as hell do not have the skillful ability to resolve occurrences.

I am going to list a political elite herd of African Americans who have answers to all black destitutions, incarcerations, school dropouts, babies born out of wedlock and the highest rate of unemployment. In essence, most blacks assume to resolve these black ethnic problems embedded through genetic heritage is to adhere to the doctrines from the Democratic Party which is to sabotage and eradicate those old, rich white racists against blacks (Republicans). While blacks are railing against Republicans they will never offer an explanation to their success.

Elite, successful African Americans include: Jessie Jackson, Al Sharpton, Tavis Smiley, Juan Williams (MSNBC), Eugene Robinson, Marc Lemont Hill, Carl Jeffers, Michael Eric Dyson, Van Jones, James Clyburn, Charles Rangel, Shelia Jackson Lee, Cornel West, Elijah Cummings, Charles Blow, Russell Simmons, Maxine Waters, Eric Holder, Ben Jealous, Whoppie Goldberg, Tamron Hall, Tom Joyner, Joe Madison, Roland Martin, and Cynthia McKinney. These are just a few current day facsimile. Eighteen hundred Democratic Ku Klux Klan black plantation slave drivers that politically bias distort reality; based on a philosophical agenda of political inept dysfunctional incompetency in an effort to seduce African Americans to remain loyal to the Democrat Party. The discernible ratio between the two major Democrat and Republican Parties is their philosophical ideological traits are negative to most African Americans.

Initially, during eighteen sixteen, there was the Federalist Party (which was a combination of Democrat and Republican). There was a split during the mid-eighteen twenties which gave severance to the national Republican and Democratic Parties. The Democratic Party endorsed and enforced slavery of Africans. The Republican Party was intensely opposed to slavery. Slavery began during sixteen ninety one when South Carolina established the code: all Negroes would be sold into bondage. Seventeen hundred British North America colonies joined this code. Unfortunately, these atrocities occurred due to African illiteracy and violent characteristic frame of mind due to their traditional African tribal chief genetic heritage beliefs. They completely ignored American conformance simply because of their inability to read and write. The southern Democrats utilized this dysfunctional stigmatic trait to their advantage.

Three hundred years later it is currently prevalent based on political dysfunctional incompetency of most African Americans. Realistically, most blacks are totally inept to the philosophical arranging characteristics America was founded on; deriving from the Declaration of Independence and the Constitution ailing with intellectual moral values and capitalistic resources. If you are in denial, illiterate or incompetent obviously you are incapable of deciphering the intricacy of these historical conglomerations pertaining to all ethnics who reside in the United States of America which is the controlling factor in an individual's life.

To continually scream and advocate racism is no solution. However, it does imply artfully inept, dysfunctional incompetency of not understanding the unique methodology of our great nation, the United States of America. We, as a proud affluent capitalistic nation, are at the crossroad of a disastrous destiny. The first three words of the Constitution are: *WE THE PEOPLE.* The Declaration of Independence emphatically stipulates: *governments are instituted among men, deriving their just powers from the consent of the governed, that whenever any form of government becomes destructive of these ends, it is the right of the people to alter or to abolish it, and to institute new government.*

I reference the crossroad. We are there as a nation with three choices: either turn left, straight ahead, or turn right. Left turn is a dead end. Straight ahead is endorsing the current administration determined to replicate the famine in Somalia Africa where President Barack Hussein Obama's ancestors might be living. Turn right and you are in compliance with the Declaration of Independence and the Constitution which emphatically stipulates: *WE THE PEOPLE*. It is the right of the people to alter or abolish destructive governments.

I am of the opinion there is going to be an attempted effort to desecrate and demoralize the integrity of America along with the Republican Party. As I have predicted, inept ignorance, dysfunctional illiteracy and incompetency are the worst mankind disasters. Our nation is beginning to get top heavy with these kind of people produced over the last hundred years from all ethnic who reside in the United States of America. Accountability is slowly dissipating, along with the comprehension of intellectual moral values to determine hypocrisy and philosophical demagoguery through political speeches of bias distortion based on agendas to manipulate in regards to their philosophical ideology to eradicate the Constitution and replace it with a Congo emperor instead of a president.

There are numerous news media anchors and commentators, liberal and conservative, inquiring about the demeanor of President Obama and the confronting problems our nation is experiencing. It appears they are becoming frustrated in regards to his inability to resolve. The fundamental nature of quality; if you are incompetent to the philosophical identity of problems it is quite obvious you are inept to a solution. President Obama is a direct line descendant from Africa who has genetic traits which dictates his philosophical ideology of tribal heritage which is opposed to American traditions for hundreds of years. Although he is a graduate of Harvard, genetic traits tend to override numerous of teachings and revert back to cultural line of descent body of beliefs.

Chronological records of significant events do not lie. All other ethnic people chose to migrate to America were civilized and conformed to the philosophical traits of America. During sixteen nineteen, Africans were brought to America against their will. During sixteen seventy six they rebelled; herding behind the revolution of Nathaniel Bacon, a white Virginian. They were illiterate, white and black servants rebelling to take possession of native lands in western Virginia. Fifteen years later, during sixteen ninety one, Africans were still practicing their African heritage traits and refused to conform to American formability. Being illiterate, they had no other choice but remain in the initial area of Virginia. The Virginia colony authorities were fearful of another revolution. The authorities of the colonies had utilized every method possible in an effort to conform Africans in regards to American traditions to no avail.

Unfortunately, after seventy two years, they chose to remain loyal to their African traits of animalistic sensuality. In an effort to reduce the population of illiterate, rebellious violence, during sixteen ninety one, South Carolina chose to legislate and provide British North America with an initial slave code. All Africans would be sold and traded into slavery. They were dispersed primarily over the southern states as plantation slaves. For approximately one hundred and seventy four years, until Republican President Abraham Lincoln issued his Emancipation Proclamation (abolishing servitude) most southern blacks had no idea what it was because of illiteracy. If you have no idea of where you came from, the idea of where you are going is extremely remote. The southern Democratic terrorist organizations such as the Knights of the White Camilla and the Pale Face Brotherhood united into the Ku Klux Klan during eighteen sixty six; supposedly led by Nathan Bedford Forrest. Southern plantation Democratic confederate owners held blacks into slavery for one hundred and seventy four years. They prohibited education and freedom of speech like it or not, those were our past ancestors of illiterates and incompetents. These philosophical genetic traits were passed on to every African American born in the United States of America. Most current day African Americans are totally inept to the causes of slavery and what transpired and the length of time from beginning to end.

Slavery was enforced by the southern Democratic Party and assisted by a brute force of their established Ku Klux Klan. Southern blacks were lynched on numerous occasions for a verbal dispute in a dialogue with whites. Because of this exploitation, most African Americans have and always will experience complex difficulty of the unique appropriate American exceptionalism because of the African genetic line of descent were illiterate or incompetent and literally rejected our Declaration of Independence and the Constitution based on complacency.

Blacks were largely responsible for many vindictive atrocities by creating disparity based on a mentality of Congo hostile ideology. Africans chose to rebel against learning civilization and to become acclimated in an effort to speak appropriate English. This has been a stigmatization which still exists for most blacks that is inevitable and eternal.

Read and come to your own conclusion. Jessie Jackson and Al Sharpton ran for the presidency and never were successful. Jessie Jackson wanted to sever Barack Hussein Obama's balls off. The United States of America is a unique elite and most remarkable nation on God's earth simply because of its ethnic diversity and the extraordinary philosophical distinguishing quality of people; particularly senior citizens. Many were frustrated during the election of two thousand and eight, especially with John McCain and Hillary Clinton, because each had over-stayed their welcome in Washington. He being a rhino Republican and she married to a political pimp. There was Barack Hussein Obama, a trained professional actor with political bias distortion based on his philosophical agenda to sabotage America. While older whites sat on their couches and allowed ninety five percent of African Americans and eighty five percent of Hispanics and a segment of small dysfunctional brain whites elect him president. This was one of the most over-rated density occurrences in the history of America.

People are motivated by numerous philosophical traits dictated through genetic heritage which is inevitable and is consistent over generations. To know something about their line of descent (especially political individual's line of descent) usually determines their characteristic qualities. There is no way to determine their purpose pertaining to political aspirations. However, *WE THE PEOPLE*, as a free independent society must delve into politician's genetic heritage. Their mothers, fathers, grandfathers, and grandmothers and their responsibilities are legally obligated persons. A combination of heritage dictates the potential of mankind and animals.

We, as a people of America, have the constitutional responsibility of controlling our own destiny in an effort to maintain stability of the United States of America through our voting process. Unfortunately, we, as a nation, have allowed our common sense to be influenced through modern technology is an obsession; radical distorted aggression for entitlements based on bias demagoguery. Unless we revert to the fundamentals of faithful portrayal of circumstantial reality, our nation is in peril of credible dysfunctional incompetency globally.

There have been political skirmishes before. Parallel to current circumstances, during eighteen sixty five, Andrew Johnson became president after President Abraham Lincoln was assassinated. Democratic President Andrew Johnson's philosophical ambitions were to reconstruct the confederate southern states while congress was not in session. He pardoned all confederate personnel under his supervision. After congress reconvened in December of eighteen sixty, the southern states had reconstructed. Although slavery had been abolished, black codes were being regulated to prohibit blacks their liberty. The Republican congress was belligerent and moved vigorously to impede and change Democratic President Johnson's programs. The Republican congress fought vigorously to gain the support of northerners who were discouraged because southern states were improvising plans to maintain slavery. The Republican congress refused to seat any senator or representative from the confederacy. They also passed codes dealing with former slaves. President Johnson vetoed the legislation. The Republican congress struggled like hell to establish enough votes to override his veto. This was the first time in history the congress had overridden a president's important legislative bill. This was the passage of the civil rights act of eighteen sixty six which was the fourteenth amendment ratified to the Constitution on July 9, 1868 establishing blacks as American citizens and prohibiting discrimination against them.

During March of eighteen sixty seven, the Republican congress strategically planned their own reconstruction, placing southern states under military rule. They passed codes placing restrictions on President Johnson; the military rule was to prevent the Democratic Ku Klux Klan from lynching blacks. President Johnson violated one of these codes; which was the tenure of office act. He dismissed Secretary of War Edwin M. Stanton. The house voted eleven articles of impeachment against him. He was tried by the senate during the spring of eighteen sixty eight and was acquitted by one single vote.

Incidentally, during the time the Republican congress was fighting like hell to give blacks their civil rights and prevent Democratic Ku Klux Klan's lynching, they were labeled as radicals.

CHAPTER 23

One can politically distort, based on philosophical bias agendas, be in denial, demagogue with radical slander, but chronological records of significant events are inevitable and repetitious.

One hundred forty three years later a replica of the President Andrew Johnson debacle is developing in Washington with President Barack Hussein Obama. The only difference is President Johnson was white and chose to disregard congress during their recess and reconstruct the southern states in an effort to continue slavery controlled by the Democratic Ku Klux Klan lynching and murdering blacks at their discretion. President Obama is black and is attempting to disregard congress and socialize America to a Congo tribal chief's formality. Andrew Johnson was virtually illiterate; Barack Hussein Obama is a Harvard University graduate. In essence their philosophical characteristic traits are identical; attempting to disregard congress (particularly Republicans). Most Republicans are intellectual, moral, shrewd people. Most Democrats are like schools of catfish (all mouth and no brains). Because of the persistent factor, our nation is in deep, deep turmoil. Trust me, when the Republican congress overrode and vetoed Democratic President Andrew Johnson's legislation one hundred forty three years ago to give African Americans their civil and voting liberties.

Article one, section one of the Constitution, specifically stipulates: *All legislative powers herein granted shall be vested in a congress of the United States, which shall consist of a senate and house of representatives.* The

Republican congress, along with the support of the people, will die and go to hell before they allow this incompetent black president Obama to sabotage our nation into socialism. We have allowed our nation to become an antiquated appeaser held hostage by black power, guilt generated by those facsimile Democratic Ku Klux Klan anchor newscasters and their herding black slave drivers.

During nineteen fifty seven, FBI Director J. Edgar Hoover accused blacks of having brains twenty percent smaller than whites. Due to over-rated density of blacks, Republican President Eisenhower assigned Hoover to quell the Democratic Ku Klux Klan from lynching southern blacks which he succeeded. President Eisenhower coded the first civil rights bill for southern African Americans in eighty nine years. The Democratic controlled congress rejected it. Eisenhower utilized military force to integrate southern schools for blacks. During the interim, northern blacks who could vote, were at the Democratic convention in Pennsylvania whooping it up voting Democrats into office who refused to certify the civil rights bill. Their ancestors were constantly lynching blacks prior to the FBI Director's quelling. Fifty four years later, these are the small dysfunctional brain people who are being coaxed by their white news media facsimile Democratic Ku Klux Klan plantation bosses; it is those old white racist Republican Tea Party folks who are causing problems.

All African Americans born in America are initially from the south in regard to speculative ancestry. Unfortunately illiteracy and incompetency has immensely destroyed their practicality through genetic heritage. Our ancestors were programmed by mostly southern illiterate and incompetent southern Democratic racist confederate whites. For approximately two hundred eighty eight years, beginning with a white Virginian named Nathaniel Bacon. He convinced illiterate Africans during sixteen seventy six to wage a rebellious revolution war against the Native American lands of western Virginia. They were slaughtered like chickens. The population of Africans had increased beyond control and they could not relocate because of illiteracy. Fifteen years later, during sixteen ninety one, South Carolina established a legislative slave code for British North America. This definitive stated: all Negroes will be sold into slavery. This was in existence for one hundred seventy four years under southern Democratic Ku Klux Klan confederate control until Republican President Abraham Lincoln abolished slavery during eighteen sixty five for all southern blacks.

During this time the abolishment of slavery was only a symbolic abstract code because southern plantation slaves were shut off from the civilized world. Many rebelled against educating their children when it became available because plantation slaves were taught by plantation white bosses and black slave drivers education, reading and writing was for white folks only. If they would continue to inquire they were given a whipping by the black slave driver, or lynched by the southern Democratic Ku Klux Klan who controlled the southern states.

The majority of plantation slaves were determined to suffer the consequences of slavery. Unfortunately, many committed suicide; especially the young who were traded. Many escaped from the southern plantations and resided in the northern states; especially in Ohio. They began special trades and schooling. These are the pioneers who established the tradition of black education. There were thousands of blacks migrated to Canada during the eighteen fifties. There were some northern slave states, but none compatible to the brutality of the southern Democratic controlled Ku Klux Klan. Blacks who escaped to the northern states were illiterate. Later they began to enroll their children in schools. The children taught their parents to write their names. Over decades many blacks became educated.

During eighteen fifty nine in Oberlin, Ohio Abolitionist College was the first integrated college in the nation. During the eighteen thirties, the slave population in the state of Mississippi was approximately seventy thousand; state of Tennessee over one hundred fifty thousand. Unfortunately, during eighteen sixty three approximately ninety eight percent of southern black plantation laborers were illiterate; the same percentage of whites were either illiterate or incompetent to the fundamental principles our nation was founded on; such as the Declaration of Independence and the Constitution. Blacks could not read it and most whites could read it but ignored it. During eighteen sixty five the Civil War ended. Democratic Vice President Andrew Johnson succeeded the slain Republican President Abraham Lincoln. President Johnson granted amnesty to all former southern confederate military commanders and plantation owners. The only conciliate was to verbally agree loyalty to the United States and support the thirteenth amendment to the Constitution and their property and citizenry were restored.

Like it or not, or come to your own conclusion; but these accusations are based on chronological events related to our American history over one hundred and fifty six years ago. In essence these are the people who created the line of descent of millions Americans and abroad; black and white. Their great, great, great grandchildren are in numerous positions in American today: manual labor, business owners, private enterprises, doctors, lawyers, politicians, etc. However, genetic controllability is an inevitable eternal distinguishing quality for all mankind and animals. The heritage of most African Americans is illiteracy, over-rated density and incompetency because of their Democratic southern Ku Klux Klan bondage and deprived of education. There are segments of whites who have these identical characteristic traits. However, the philosophical extended general directions are capitalistic resources; whites are the establishers, blacks are the granted advantage users.

In essence, the ethnic of Caucasians supply the vast majority of employment in America. Based on necessity, they will hire the most qualified and loyal employees. Most small and large companies are staffed with majority whites. The loyal employees, black and white, always know someone illiterate or semi-illiterate. They are the representatives responsible for semi-illiterate employees for manual labor. Most are Caucasians and this is the absorbing factor of semi-illiterate whites throughout the United States of America. This is not a racist issue; it is a fact of reality. Most African Americans have a unique philosophical tenure: they are the world's greatest convincers based on cunning techniques of deception. This is embedded extended genetic heritage from Africa. African tribal groups continuously planned evasive techniques from the tribal chief because miscellaneous tribal chiefs had numerous punishments for not behaving to his guidance: tribal caning to death, and roasting for cannibalism. These were the mix tribal persons African kings captured and sold from deep in the jungles of Africa. Enslaving and owning people originated in Africa. Selling slaves was an institution; most Africans understood slavery.

During the fifth century, the Romans were purchasing slaves from North Africa. African slavery was hostile and brutal; particularly on slave ships where sixty or more slaves were attached together, locked in chains and irons. Transporting slaves was a dangerous business; Africans were wild and fought like animals. During sixteen nineteen, twenty were introduced to the British Colonial America in Virginia against their wishes, aboard a Dutch war ship. The captain was low on supplies and had no finances. The twenty Africans were traded for food supplies. This was the beginning of our ancestor's turbulent introduction to British North America; being hostile, illiterate and uncivilized, three hundred and ninety two years ago. The hostile, illiteracy and incompetent density still exists today for most African Americans. Africans never accepted American culture. Their ambitions were to formulate their Congo tribal chief advisory mentality along with American philosophical birthright.

I never make accusations unless there is sufficient evidence to vindicate them. There are numerous ethnics who migrated to America with the intent to conform to American philosophical traditional codes and gain by necessary efforts required to improve. Africans were brought here during sixteen nineteen; slavery did not exist until sixteen ninety one; seventy two years later. Unfortunately, Africans chose their African traditions over American distinguished quality by congregating in a monolith African Congo tribal content. During sixteen seventy six they chose to follow a white named Nathaniel Bacon in a rebellious attempt to take possession of American lands in western Virginia. They were butchered by the Virginia militia. Africans were given another fifteen years to reform from African traditional formalities which whites in Virginia regarded as intimidation for another rebellion.

To counteract another rebellion, during sixteen ninety one, South Carolina issued the first slave code: for all Negroes to be sold and traded into slavery. Unfortunately, this began their plantation scrutinizing trek to all southern states controlled by white plantation bosses and black slave drivers. This did not deter black rebellious revolutions. During seventeen thirty nine, hundreds (possibly more than a thousand) Africans led by an African named Jemmy to conquest South Carolina; beating military drums, flying African army flags. South Carolina called out the militia and they were eradicated. For two hundred years through the seventeenth and eighteenth centuries, most blacks in America remained loyal to their traditional African beliefs.

During eighteen hundred eight, congress abolished slave trading. During the late eighteen hundreds blacks attempted to establish themselves. They cherished and honored their African tribal Congo homeland and were opposed to our great nation: The United States of America, the greatest nation on God's earth.

These are some of the names they chose for their organizations and community.

During seventeen eighty in Newport, Rhode Island they established a mutual and society named The African Union Society.

During eighteen hundred in Philadelphia, Pennsylvania they established The Free African Society, The African Church of St. Thomas, Bethel African Methodist Episcopal Church, African Humane Society, African Masonic Lodge, African Free School.

During eighteen thirty one, black terrorist Nat Turner waged one of the most terrifying rebellious revolutions between black and white in the history of America. He was supposedly a religious person. He saw visions of blood on corn stalks. He had visions of black and white spirits engaged in war. He saw blood trickling down water steams. He also believed it was a sign of God to exterminate the white man. He began his insurrection. To accomplish his mission he routed the first militia reinforcements eradicated his forces. Unfortunately there was a heavy price to pay. When angry whites retaliated they slaughtered and tortured, shot and burned to death approximately one hundred and fifty blacks in one day. From Richmond to South Hampton County, Virginia Nat Turner was located weeks later. They tried and lynched him. Surgeons removed his skin and utilized it and his bones to make purses and trophies from his bones.

Based on illiteracy and incompetency, most blacks have never approved of the honorable, dignified, conglomerate legitimacy American was established on. If you are illiterate you can't read. If you are incompetent you tend to distort because you cannot decipher what you read. This has been the bona fide history of most African Americans who reside in our world's greatest nation: The United States of America, for approximately three hundred and ninety three years. As of to date, the black vindictive, alienating, misconceived, dysfunctional, illiterate, incompetency, ineptness still exists because of genetic heritage controllability. It is an established fact: if you do not understand the intricate meaning of our Declaration of Independence and the Constitution, or are not capable of differentiating the moral intellect established pertaining to our major two political parties system (Democrat and Republican) and the unique complexity they function on the diversity persists. Also capitalistic gratitude exists. In an effort to maintain progress based on God's will to preserve our great nation, The United States of American eternally.

The most idealistic phenomenon of reality known to mankind is the brain. Brain cells dictate sympathies which determine human reactions. Based on how it is utilized has affirmative or negative consequences. These are the dominating facts in human philosophical behavioral distinguishing quality. This is why it is so extremely important all individuals attend school beyond illiteracy in an effort to improve on their philosophical human qualities. Human life consists of deciding individual issues that are sufficiently appropriate to bring moral results. The most important intuition in human life is choosing. There are numerous times results can be disappointing. Unfortunately, it is inevitable. However one should evaluate the detriment of consequences to determine resolutions. For instance: I was at a produce market; they had watermelons on display; I chose to purchase one for six dollars. Once I arrived home, I cut the melon open. It was deteriorated, not good for eating; so I had to make a choice; either return the mushy melon or discard it. I chose to discard it because I would have used over six dollars in gasoline to return the melon and possibly this produce market was selling mushy watermelons. I chose another watermelon distributor and their melons were suitable for eating.

In essence, politicians are like melons. You do not know what is inside until you have bought it, so you have to make a choice. Discard, change to another, or remain with the status quo. Unfortunately, most African Americans residing in America live in a political mythical philosophical Democratic ideologue of dysfunctional demagoguery and illiterate incompetency which consists of Democratic party monolith herding; a replica of African Congo tribal chief codes, southern Democratic Ku Klux Klan, plantation white bosses and black slave drivers.

CHAPTER 24

Africans were brought to America during sixteen nineteen. They have had the greatest opportunity of any ethnic residing in America based on their choice to migrate. Illiteracy and incompetency ruined progress for most; also selfish, radical, racist, bigotry for whites and negativity pertaining to codes. Most blacks have never realized and acknowledged they are the minority ethnic in the United States of America based on population. There are approximately three hundred twenty five million people of numerous ethnics residing in America. African Americans are only thirty eight or forty million. Our nation is regulated in accordance to the Constitution; federal and state, under the jurisdiction of the congress consisting of a senate and congressional representatives which are elected by the general public through a process of choice based on majority rule.

The negligence and reluctance of most blacks to prepare and attain philosophical awareness of their constituent demagoguery is rotting away based on illiteracy and dysfunctional incompetency. Pertaining to the fundamentals America was established on; most have chosen not to gravitate to the idealistic formalities other ethnics have capitalized on with great success. America is a nation of intellectual challenges. Beginning at home with parents, their teachings should be marked with intellectual depth and insight. In order to succeed in America you must challenge the established requirements America exists on: intellectual moral values through communication with all ethnics. These are the following established customs of American compulsory implemented by the Declaration of

Independence and the Constitution. If you refrain from these American standards of true relationship of importance, the formalities of America will literally destroy you and your opposing intentions; which has occurred with most politically illiterate, inept, incompetent, dysfunctional African Americans for approximately one hundred forty three years. The African genetic heritage of Congo tribal chiefs controlling and dictating is prominent in most African Americans eternally. This influences their philosophical distinguishing quality. They are totally unaware of this unique genetic ancestor trait derived from Africa. These accusations are not racist distorted derogatory innuendo, but facts of reality that has stymied the progress of most blacks in America.

Illiteracy, density, gibberish, rebellious violence, gullibility, monolith endorsing, racist against other ethnics, ineptness in regards to the Constitution, bias distortion, undermining, thievery, narcissism, overly elaborate, underrated deciphering, braggadocious for attention, highly disagreeable, covert ferocious liars, intense emulators and extraordinary incompetency are the stigmatic philosophical genetic African traits of most African Americans that has impeded American progressive stability based on primitive initiatives and southern Democratic Ku Klux Klan intimidation. The temperament of whites has never coincided with blacks; particularly Democrats.

During eighteen fifty eight, prior to his presidency, Republican President Abraham Lincoln challenged incumbent Democrat Stephen A. Douglas for the Illinois Senate. During the debate Lincoln argued emphatically: all men are created equal and Negroes are equal within the Declaration of Independence. His Democrat opponent Stephen A. Douglas argued the Declaration of Independence made no mention of Negroes whatsoever and America was formulated by white men for the benefit of white men and their posterity eternally.

Chronological records reveal Republicans have always sympathized with illiteracy and incompetency of African Americans. President Abraham Lincoln stipulated, after the Civil War, ninety eight percent of southern blacks illiterate; all they knew was farming. He proposed legislation to give all black families forty acres of confederate plantation land and a government mule. The intent was for them to educate their children and obtain their own resources. Unfortunately, he did not survive to carry out his mission. He had chosen a southern Democrat for his vice president; Andrew Johnson from Tennessee. After he succeeded President Lincoln, he rescinded the Lincoln legislation and gave the land back to the southern plantation owners and blacks were returned back to a facsimile of servitude through share cropping.

The fundamentals of America were established on intellectual moral values and majority rule. For approximately two hundred seventy five years, southern Democratic terrorist groups such as: The White League, Rifle Club, Red Shirts, and the Ku Klux Kan deprived southern blacks of being included in the majority of American citizenry through violent tactics. After the Republican controlled congress ratified the fourteenth amendment to the Constitution during eighteen sixty eight, giving all southern blacks their civil and voting rights, the southern Democrat Ku Klux Klan became violently hostile.

During eighteen seventy four, The White League terrorist armed force marched on the New Orleans State House to eradicate the black and white Republicans. Louisiana state government, the southern Democrats were committed to: we the white people supremacy of Louisiana, will assassinate all Republicans to attain control of the southern states.

One of the most inhumane slaughters occurred in Vicksburg, Mississippi. Southern Democratic Ku Klux Klan murdered three or four hundred black Republicans to implement white supremacy.

Democratic Ku Klux Klan terrorists in South Carolina violently attacked black citizens and forced them to participate in Democratic voting process.

During eighteen seventy six, during South Carolina's governor election, blacks were literally forced to support Democratic candidate Wade Hampton, the Democratic Ku Klux Klan white supremacist prohibited voting by any white and black Republicans in the southern states.

During the eighteen seventy six presidential election, Republican candidate Rutherford B. Hayes won over Democrat Samuel J. Tilden. The U. S. Congress was controlled by the Democrats and they refused to certify his election until he authorized removal of troops from the states who were protecting blacks from being lynched and slaughtered by the Democratic Ku Klux Klan in the south.

Many dense and incompetent African Americans claim President Hayes abandoned blacks because he was a racist. Most blacks never research anything. It is constantly based on assumptions in regards to color. If President Elect Hayes had relinquished his title as President elect, it was a close race from the very beginning. A special committee had to determine the winner. So it is possible the runner up Democrat Samuel J. Tilden would have succeeded him and the troops would have been removed anyway. Unfortunately, our nation was in utter chaos waiting for the Democratic controlled congress to certify Rutherford B. Hayes as our nineteenth president.

However, after that debacle, the Democrats and their Ku Klux Klan possessed political power over the southern states. It has been reported the U. S. Supreme Court was partial in their favor because during eighteen ninety six the southern states implemented the Jim Crow Rule: separate but equal; endorsed by the U. S. Supreme Court in their favor; which deprived southern blacks of their civil and voting rights the Republican congress had awarded them during eighteen sixty eight.

The Democratic Ku Klux Klan awarded southern blacks the back of the bus; entering through back doors; yes mam and yes sir boss man; and nooses at the end of ropes for sixty eight years.

On C-SPAN-2 on September 4, 2011, I watched a segment of April Ryan's interview with Randall Kennedy, road scholar; Clerk for U. S. Supreme Justice Thurgood Marshall; Harvard law professor, initially from Colombia, South Carolina which he spoke of his father and equated him as being a characteristic replica to pastor Wright (Barack Hussein Obama's guidance for approximately twenty years) as a participant in church congregations. He quoted his father as having rebellious disdain for America with a negative philosophical agenda for military personnel defending America. He also gave a brief synopsis of he and his father returning to South Carolina and being stopped by a police officer for no reason other than his father was driving a new automobile and warned his father things are different down here and expected his father to answer yes sir.

Mr. Kennedy also revealed to Mrs. Ryan he did not share his father's ideologue pertaining to vilifying America. However, he did choose to relate to the Jim Crow Rule: separate but equal and delved into American history. The fact Herman Rhodes Revels was the first black to serve in the U. S. Senate that completed the term of Jefferson Davis who became president of the Confederacy in the southern states.

After the Republican controlled congress ratified the fourteenth amendment to the Constitution they began to venture into politics. The southern Democrats became incensed and accused blacks of being ignorant, incompetent people trying to rise above their natural place in society of being servants.

Most blacks who excelled in politics during the late eighteen sixties were schooled in the northern states. During this era, all blacks were

Republicans working cohesively with whites, even some white southern Democrats, in an effort to reconstruct the southern states after the Civil War. This segment will elaborate on some of the black Republican southern pioneers in American history during the eighteen seventies.

Blanche K. Bruce, the first African American to be elected to the U. S. Senate and served a full term.

Jonathan Gibbs served as Florida's Secretary of State and Superintendent of Education.

Egbert Sammis was elected to the Florida State Senate.

Francis Louis Cardozo served as South Carolina's Secretary of State. He also was State Treasurer and was appointed to the Treasury Department in Washington, D. C.

Pickney Benton Stewart Pinchback was the nation's first African American governor of Louisiana.

Approximately seven to eight hundred African Americans served as southern state legislatures; thirty to forty were elected to the U. S. House of Representatives.

Thousands of African Americans and white Republicans, businessmen, lawyers, teachers and doctors returned to the south from the northern states and Canada in an effort to assist in reconstruction of the southern states. There were thousands of schools open throughout the southern states for black and white students educating from kindergarten to college. Blacks and whites were attending these schools by the thousands. Unfortunately, this viable intention to educate black and white southerners was eradicated by the Democratic Ku Klux Klan. They literally murdered and slaughtered Republicans (mainly blacks) because the Democrats were determined to return their traditional white supremacy over African Americans. This was to the advantage of the plantation owners; for blacks to remain illiterate and loyal to farming.

Most blacks are just illiterate and incompetent as they were one hundred forty three years ago. They are politically entrenched constituents (slaves) for the Democratic Party; herding behind black self-appointed leaders such as Jessie Jackson and Al Sharpton who are largely responsible for the word incompetency being added to the dictionary. Most affluent blacks tend to adlib speculative issues; particularly slavery and the chronological events that occurred. This is an incompetent tactic agenda to influence others they are intellectually clever in an effort to maintain their Congo tribal chief status over other American blacks. There is a segment of whites, especially the young, who have fallen into the nonsensical, dense, deceitful, dysfunctional rhetorical gibberish about slavery and the Jim Crow Rule; which is nothing more than covert politics to influence based on assumptions to attain egotistical notoriety.

Most supposedly elite, sophisticated African Americans are so preoccupied being a plantation black slave driver for their white Democratic replica of the Ku Klux Klan, new anchors and slobbering over their alimentary canal, obsessed with their distorted demagoguery and lies about the Jim Crow Rule: separate but equal. This is an example: Jessie Jackson was at a gathering on national television execrating the Tea Party as being Republican; trying to rescind the thirteenth, fourteenth and fifteenth amendments to the Constitution in an effort to reinstate slavery. Obviously, he has eaten so much Democratic Ku Klux Klan alimentary canal dung over the years it has affected his brain not to know he would not be sitting there entertaining with Democratic demagogue lies. If it were not for the controlled Republican congress who ratified the thirteenth, fourteenth and fifteenth amendments to the Constitution during December 6, 1865, July 9, 1868 and February 3, 1870. These amendments pertain to all U. S. Citizens; but specifically for southern plantation African Americans; to give them their liberties from slavery and civil and voting rights within the southern states.

Al Sharpton was grandstanding on a podium some years ago and raised the issue: whatever happened to the forty acres of land and the government mule? It is astoundingly dysfunctional and incompetent for blacks to assemble and listen to distorted bias Democratic philosophical obsessed radical stupid innuendo. They know absolutely nothing about American history; particularly their beloved Democrats who lynched and murdered southern blacks for hundreds of years.

The fifteenth amendment to the Constitution to abolish southern Democratic slavery legislated by Republican President Abraham Lincoln. The confederate regime of white supremacy became so belligerent John Wilkes Booth assassinated President Lincoln. Prior to this assassination, President Lincoln coded legislation, and passed it on to congress, for their approval, giving black families forty acres of southern plantation owner's land and a government mule. Unfortunately, President Lincoln chose a southern Democrat to be his vice president; Andrew Johnson from Tennessee. Immediately after he was sworn in he began to pardon all the confederate officers and repealed the coded legislation. He gave the land back to the plantation owners. This was devastating for southern blacks because it reinstated plantation slavery through share cropping. Being illiterate, they had no other place to go but to remain on the southern Democratic plantation under the control of white supremacy plantation bosses and black slave drivers made a mockery of African Americans. Their children were not allowed to attend school. White Ku Klux Klan supremacies would enter black's homes and molest their family members. If blacks were caught trying to speak appropriate English or dress cleanly, they were whipped by the black slave driver.

CHAPTER 25

President Lincoln was truly one of the most remarkable projective presidents in American history. His life was taken because of his philosophical agenda for African Americans. He knew southern blacks were illiterate and uncivilized to American culture so his intentions were to give them the necessary valuables in farm land; based on they had worked those southern plantations for approximately one hundred seventy four years for clothing, shelter and food they grew themselves. His philosophical agenda was to allow them to slowly incorporate themselves into a civil society through schooling and individual merit, having their own assets in southern plantation lands.

President Andrew Johnson was born in Raleigh, North Carolina during eighteen hundred eight. He grew up in poverty, minas schooling. He became an apprentice tailor as a boy. He chose to run away to Greenville, Tennessee. Later he opened a tailor shop. After marrying Elliza McCardle he learned to speak English quite eloquently. He entered politics and began to participate in debates at the local academy. He was elected to the House of U. S. Representatives and the Senate during the eighteen forties and fifties. Tennessee ceded congress during the ceding crisis and Johnson chose not to leave. He was considered a traitor by the south and to the northern states he was a hero. He vilified the southern plantation aristocracy. However, once he became president he had numerous battles with the Republican congress violating their specific codes until the House of Representatives voted eleven articles of impeachment against him.

He was tried in the senate during eighteen sixty eight and acquitted by one vote. President Johnson supposedly was a self-trained eloquent speaker and a magnificent pretender. Extremely persuasive President Lincoln chose him for his vice president because of his philosophical traits; he could deliver the southern constituents.

Unfortunately, during his presidency, Democratic President Johnson subjected southern African Americans to the worst, grotesque, barbaric, inhumane, disastrous occurrence to ever occur in American history. By refusal to follow through on the wishes of his slain predecessor, he destroyed the enthusiasm of all southern African Americans; technically free, but still under the jurisdiction of confined slavery; due to illiteracy.

Most blacks are stigmatized today with illiteracy and incompetency because of prolong intimidation by the southern Democratic Ku Klux Klan codes of provocative, disturbed, preventative schooling for southern African Americans until Republican President Eisenhower's regime. The staggering heinous embedded results are prevalent throughout most African American society today related to genetic heritage.

When a child is conceived the brain dictates distinguishing qualities from each parent; which has numerous variances through cells; pertaining to talent which takes years to develop; beginning with parental home training and improvement through institutions for learning. President Johnson by not honoring the request of President Lincoln's proclamation to give forty acres of southern confederate plantation land and a government mule to all southern black families destroyed the human technicality and political aspirations for most African Americans eternally. Blacks has worked these plantations for shelter and the only training available was care for animals, pick, plow and harvest cotton. All people and animals inherit the philosophical traits of their ancestors. Mankind is the only organism God created with a brain that can think in a perspective of intellect pertaining to morality; which are the standard procedures of America according to the Declaration of Independence and the Constitution.

Southern African Americans were deprived of these inherent characteristics by the southern Democratic Ku Klux Klan: reading, writing, counting is a form of exchanging understanding gained through experience which is the essences of individual life. When these essentials are not acquired, the sustaining morals of people distinguishing qualities are disoriented. These are the lingering consequences that have and will continue to impede most African Americans eternally.

America is truly the most unique and remarkably diverse nation on God's earth. However, there are compulsory requirements to grasp the moral validity of sincerity; intellectual moral values and the personal to communicate with appropriate English dialogue. If you strive to accomplish these traditions, it is quite obvious you will have affection for the United States of America and occupation could be of your choosing. These creative guidelines are applicable to every ethnic race who residing in America. It is their choice to adhere and conform. Unfortunately, there are numerous people, black and white, particularly African Americans either have never been taught or have chosen not to acknowledge these American outlined policy codes of conduct. In essence, not to adhere, the consequential results can be detrimental which could consist of poverty, ghetto slum destitution or years of incarceration.

The most important philosophical distinguishing terminology is American playing fields and leveling. They are leveled by individual ambitions to succeed; as stated above, not by some grand standing speech from Jessie Jackson or Al Sharpton. They have leveled their playing field years ago by lying to their audiences, by inciting rebellious bigotry against other ethnics who have the authority and always will be in a lucrative position to assist anyone minas a misguided individual who has a bias distorted philosophical agenda of self-proclaimed selfish speech based on attentive notoriety to indoctrinate in an effort to enhance the Democratic Party.

Chronological events pertaining to history is one of the greatest American prodigies one could ever hope for because it offers an explicit explanation to what transpired pertaining to reality and also predict future occurrences. An authentic example: Democratic President Johnson arguably rejected the legislation from the Republican congress to abolish slavery for southern blacks. He vetoed their request. The Republican congress was improved through elections. It was the first time in history congress established the vetoes to override a president; vetoing ratifying the fourteenth amendment to the Constitution.

One hundred forty five years later, along came the first black president: Barack Hussein Obama, with a bias philosophical agenda parallel to President Johnson. The only difference: President Johnson was white, self-educated and an emotional speaker who fought the Republican congress like hell to maintain slavery of southern African Americans in a losing cause. President Obama is black, a graduate of Harvard University with a law degree and an emotional speaker fighting the Republican congress like hell to abolish their ratified fourteenth amendment to the Constitution in an effort to enslave all Americans to Islamic socialism. His philosophical bias agenda is to demoralize America so he may become Congo socialist monarch; exercising power and authority over the citizens of America. President Obama illustrates an explicit explanation to the mentality of most blacks. He is a graduate from Harvard University with a law degree and shamefully his thinking capacity is equivalent to a white man President Johnson who never attended institutions for learning.

There are approximately thirty eight to forty million African Americans residing in America from a total of approximately three hundred twenty million other ethnics. Unfortunately, most blacks haven't the frailest idea on how our ancestors arrived, where or when to the shores of America, or what transpired after their arrival; the reason for our arrival and the responsible individuals who established certain criteria codes and their intentions. Africans were brought to America during sixteen nineteen aboard a Dutch ship against their wishes. They arrived on the shores of British North America in Virginia. Unfortunately the captain ran out of supplies and had no funds. He negotiated with the colony representatives and traded twenty Africans for food.

After the Dutch ship departed, the colony officials realized these people are illiterate, hostile and uncivilized. They chose to house and supply their food for their farming the tobacco fields along with the white indentured servants. After a while some cared for the homes; race was not a problem, some whites and blacks were married.

By seventeen seventy the African population in the British North American colonies had grown to a million or more. However, they were not concerned about American customs. They constantly adhered to and maintained their African cultural traditions. During sixteen seventy six, a Caucasian named Nathaniel Bacon convinced poor illiterate white and black servants to wage a rebellious revolution to appropriate native American Western Virginal. Bacon forces attacked the colony and burned the colonial capital before being defeated by the militia. This was terribly disturbing to Virginians. During sixteen ninety one, South Carolina established codes for the first time and provided to British North America to sell and trade Africans into slavery over the southern states.

I have elaborated on this scenario more than once because this was the defining fiasco causing retaliation for the sale of Africans. Also, Africans chose to remain loyal to their African traditions and refused to accept the cultural traits of America. As I stated earlier, most blacks have and are still living in fantasy day dream expectancy. Most African Americans have chosen not to conform and ignore the validity codes in the stability of America formalities. Their phrase is: that it is the rich white man America and his stupid laws. Unfortunately, they will never understand for approximately three hundred thirty eight years, while our ancestors were slopping hogs, milking cows, plowing and picking cotton, Caucasians were attending learning institutions.

Republican President Dwight David Eisenhower, during his reign of nineteen fifty seven, quelled the Democratic Ku Klux Klan lynching of southern African Americans. It was the initial beginning of blacks entering bona fide integrated southern schooling. It is an established validity Caucasians taught Africans the comprehension of civilization. The young school age white children who resided on the plantations taught many to read and write.

Let's define Democratic Ku Klux Klan southern slavery and how it complicated, intimidated and are constantly destroying African American lives currently. Blacks were held in seclusion on southern plantations being illiterate for hundreds of years. They were inspired to have babies. They were held in quarters to mate like cattle because plantation owners needed additional help; some were for sale. Stop! Think what happens to an individual who has been incarcerated for thirty or forty years. His familiarity with outside changes pertaining to cities, states and the nation is extremely remote. This is what transpired with most southern blacks. They were lost in society. Once they became free to leave the plantation most older blacks remained on the plantations because of illiteracy. Many of their children wondered away. However, many returned to the plantations because of difficulty communicating in an open free society.

During eighteen ninety six, a strange demoralization turn of events occurred against southern blacks. The southern Democrats and their Ku Klux Klan revoked the fourteenth amendment to the Constitution the Republican congress had ratified: to give southern African Americans their civil and voting rights. The southern Democrats and their Ku Klux Klan used the Jim Crow Rule: separate but equal, endorsed by the U. S. Supreme Court. Many young blacks began to migrate to northern states; especially black women. They were not accustomed to city life. Many were abused by city ghetto pimps numerous times and would have several babies. When babies became old enough, they would send them south for their grandparents to raise them. This created a dilemma. Their grandparents were illiterate so they utilized their grandchildren to work the farms and not really concerned about their education. Obviously this created another generation of illiterates who proceeded into the nineteenth century.

On November 8, 1932, Democrat Franklin Delano Roosevelt was elected as the thirty second president of the United States of America. He and his wife Eleanor were two of the shrewdest politicians to ever occupy the white house in Washington, D. C. They were extremely politically crafty; very much liked by all American ethnics and foreign dignitaries. They utilized their charm to exploit the ignorant, illiteracy and incompetency of most African American. They utilized a strategic method to destroy the party that President Abraham Lincoln chose to build and reform as a part of integrity. President Roosevelt was interested in black philosophical ideology; blacks were not allowed to vote in the southern states, so he dispatched a seminar to the northern states to determine how African Americans chose their politicians. They learned with a simple accessed category they congregate behind and admire other affluent blacks and vote in a bloc and are obsessed with gratuitous agendas.

The New Deal passed consisted of relief checks for drought plagued farmers; also the implementation of social security. These were federal entitlement programs for all Americans based on qualifications. Most African Americans throughout the United States of America assumed President Roosevelt was being sensitive to their causes because their relief checks were equal to whites. Also, for the first time in Democratic history, he arranged for an African American politician from Illinois, Arthur Mitchell, to address the Democratic Convention: in essence, as denoted Mr. Mitchell gloated and praised President Roosevelt for initiating benefit programs for blacks. Roosevelt also appointed Colonel Benjamin C. Davis to the rank of General and William Hastie to the staff of War Secretary Stimson. Most African Americans then and now never realized President Roosevelt's motivations pertaining to blacks. It certainly was not their liberty. It was to eradicate the northern black block voters from the Republican Party to the Democrat Party. His mission was accomplished, but not for the well-being of blacks but for their votes only.

For the first several years of President Roosevelt's regime tragically, approximately eighteen African Americans were lynched each year. During April of nineteen thirty seven, two African Americans were burned and blow torched to death in Duck Hill, Mississippi while an applauding crowd of whites looked on and took pleasure.

Democratic southern plantation owners and their supporting Ku Klux Klansmen analyzed the philosophical distinguishing quality of most blacks approximately three hundred ninety three years ago. Their genetic heritage instincts are to assemble behind affluent self-appointed leaders monolithic particularly blacks with a philosophical agenda to distort the validity of reality in an attempt to establish erroneous recognition that is opposite to the fundamentals American was formulated on. It is one of the most astounding, apolitical, obsolete, dysfunctional, inept, illiterate and incompetent circumstances to ever exist in the United States of America.

Around the globe most African Americans have never understood or conformed to American traditions. Many have virtually excelled in every educational position available in America. Most are constantly complaining about racism. This will always be an eternal fiasco simply because of philosophical genetic heritage traits embedded from Africa. America was founded on intellectual stability predicated to individual merit based on a capitalistic referendum in conjunction with the Declaration of Independence and the Constitution. These are the stabilizing adherence codes for America; not some political bias distorting dictating ideologist who knows absolutely nothing about the Constitution or the identifying historical chronological events which have occurred within our great nation the United States of America. It is evident you can't utilize a jackass to replace a racehorse. There are many, many black jackasses all over the news media emulating racehorses. Most have identifiable affiliations to amplify name status recognition; such as Randall Kennedy, road scholar, clerk for U. S. Supreme Court Justice Thurgood Marshall, law professor at Harvard University. This gentleman, Mr. Randall Kennedy, was promoting his book having a dialogue interview with April Ryan on C-SPAN-2 on September 2, 2011; elaborating on his father's personal life during the southern Democratic Ku Klux Klan Jim Crow Rule: separate but equal, imposed on southern African Americans. Mr. Kennedy chose to elaborate on American history pertaining to blacks. He briefly commented on the fourteenth amendment in regards to Hirman Rhodes Revels being the first black U. S. Senator and some political complication he experienced. However, Herman Rhodes Revels was a Republican who served one year, during eighteen seventy, completing the term of Jefferson Davis who resigned his senate seat to become President of the Confederacy.

Most African Americans, and a segment of Caucasians, are narcissistic in regards to their successful accomplishments denoted along with their name title. Most tend to adlib based on assumptions without appropriate research. Unfortunately, because of overrated density, they assume the general public will willingly accept their premise of events because of name recognition and become mesmerized with incompetent folklore. For instance, related example: Mr. Randall Kennedy, road scholar, clerk for U. S. Supreme Court Justice Thurgood Marshall, law professor Harvard University chose to converse on American history in regards to chronological events pertaining to Republican African Americans during the eighteen hundreds and their political aspirations in an effort to accomplish recognition. These are some of the most profound American political Republican pioneers in the history of America. The southern Democratic Ku Klux Klan prohibited southern blacks from attaining education, but these persistent, brave black Republican pioneers worked diligently to establish schools to educate their children although their lives were under intense scrutiny and intimidation, including murder by the southern Democratic Ku Klux Klan. Black and white Republicans jeopardized their lives and established approximately a million schools for southern black elementary children to attend. Unfortunately many of their lives were brutally snuffed out by the southern Democratic Ku Klux Klan simply because they were black and white Republicans trying to educate little black elementary children; and for any jackass Democratic alimentary canal sucking dysfunctional, incompetent idiot to inappropriately not recognize their political status, does a grave injustice to American history and dignity of all American citizens.

Republican Pickney Benton Stewart Pinchback was the first African American to become governor of Louisiana during eighteen seventy eight. Blanche K. Bruce was the first African American to be elected as a Republican to serve a full term as a U. S. Senator from Louisiana during eighteen seventy four. As I have indicated, most African Americans live in a philosophical bias distorting, demagogic, fantasy world of indoctrination. It is terribly sad most blacks are genetically incompetent and imaginatively dysfunctional that is inevitable also eternal.

Mr. Herman Cain is an African American who has chosen to seek the presidency of the United States of America. Today is September 29, 2011 and Mr. Cain is being quoted by the news media as accusing most blacks as being brain washed, unfortunately he is absolutely right. It occurred approximately seventy eight years ago during President Franklin Delano Roosevelt's regime. He learned northern blacks could vote and voted in a bloc. They were gullible for attentiveness pertaining to socially herding together. They constantly utilized this method in regards to political agendas; advised and coaxed by affluent black and white Democratic representatives constantly reminding blacks of government control distribution of relief goods. This was a form of political brain washing and seduction President Roosevelt utilized during nineteen thirty six with the New Deal; issuing farm drought relief checks along with social security which had to be approved through congress. The Constitution demanded equality so African Americans were entitlements which southern plantation blacks had never paid into social security. However, at sixty five they were entitled to a check which created a dilemma because most southern blacks did not have a certificate of birth. Being illiterate, they formed their own tribes on southern plantations and black midwives delivered their children. Incapable of reading and writing, they could not document proof of birth. The average African American is over eighty years of age; most do not have a birth certificate to date. The only method for proof of southern black's birth was to locate the oldest white person who knew of the plantation blacks. They would testify to their assumed age. Many whites were old and senile so thousands of blacks were only forty five to fifty years old and were receiving social security.

President Roosevelt was drastically penalized for this debacle. Most southern whites switched to the Republican Party. For approximately seventy eight years most southern whites have maintained their conservative status as Republicans. The Democratic brain washed African Americans mostly monolithic nationwide has maintained their constituency support for electing Democrats simply because of political strategy. They are incapable of deciphering due to illiteracy and incompetency caused by genetic heritage; being confiscated on southern plantations for hundreds of years; utilizing tribal instincts as a way of life; victimized by southern Democratic Ku Klux Klan indoctrination; physically forced to conform to Democratic philosophical ideology. That is the genetic heritage dictating and controlling their Democratic motivations currently. Encouraged by numerous white Democratic clannish strategists and black political inept brain washed slave drivers they were required to perform on the southern plantations during slavery. Their responsibilities were to adhere to the white plantation bosses and black slave drivers.

The relative protocol to traditional effigy is constantly being displayed by numerous black slave drivers over televised and radio topics and other news outlets defending Democratic bias clannish principles that literally destroyed the fundamental values of most African Americans, synchronizing to the general aspirations coded in the chronological events of American history based on denial of philosophical individual exceptionalism predicated to capitalism. Most African Americans have never realized or understood the established standards America has to offer. If you do not understand, the capability way to approach is complex and dismal. This is why African Americans are rationalized and quantify for socialistic entitlement programs which has become a standard way of survival for many; particularly in large northern cities such as Chicago, New York, Detroit, Philadelphia, Los Angeles, Cincinnati, Newark and Washington D. C. There are a few southern major large cities polarized with black destitution, radical criminal activity and murder. However, it did not occur until decades later when mostly illiterate and incompetent blacks chose to relocate to northern states during the southern Jim Crow Rule: separate but equal; was initiated during eighteen ninety six by the southern Democratic Ku Klux Klan. Most blacks, being illiterate, were not accustomed or prepared for big city residing. Many returned to southern cities instead of the share cropping plantation. Being in northern cities for a year or two many chose to indulge in drugs. When they moved back south they chose cities comparable to cities in the north such as Birmingham, Atlanta and Memphis. Many returned to small towns all over the southern states. Most blacks attempted to utilize northern exercises in an effort to rearrange the philosophical traits of the southern states. The southern Democratic Ku Klux Klan became belligerent and retaliated with maiming, rebellious spiteful tactics including lynching.

Most African Americans have suffered dire consequences in the entire United States of America because of genetic heritage of illiteracy; beginning in Africa and brought to America; when the Republican congress ratified the fourteenth amendment to the Constitution during eighteen sixty eight to award civil and voting rights to all Americans, but specifically for southern African Americans. Two hundred forty nine years later ninety eight percent of southern African Americans were illiterate. Thousands of black and white Republican educators relocated to the southern states in an effort to teach former slaves to read and write. They were slaughtered like cattle and driven away by the southern Democratic Lu Klux Klan. For another ninety six years southern blacks were deprived of appropriate education until Republican President Dwight David Eisenhower, during nineteen fifty seven, integrated southern schools for blacks and assigned FBI Director J. Edgar Hoover to quell the lynching of southern blacks.

Not all southern whites were affiliated with the Ku Klux Klan. Many taught blacks to read and write. They assisted them to relocate north in an effort their children could receive proper education. Southern plantation owners, their white plantation supervisors and black slave drivers were the most powerful political regime in the nation. In the area cotton was the most generated commodity on the globe. Southern plantation owners were in control. They and their family counterparts had thousands, if not millions, of mulatto babies by black women. Numerous times the plantation master would have two or three house maids pregnant at the same time. Their wives were aware of these affairs and would care for the child when it was born. These children, all through their lives, were given special privileges in regards to education and responsible positions over others. Many trained themselves as specialists in certain fields. Blacks on southern plantations lived secluded lives and were immensely satisfied in their philosophical African Congo ideology; living free off the land, practicing their African culture and having babies. On many plantations they performed African ceremonies for gathering of plantation owners and other miscellaneous whites.

To understand American slavery you must dissect and delve into African genetic heritage. Their philosophical traits embedded from African; their heritage dictates being controlled by a tribal chief; hostile, uncivilized; not interested in education; no responsibility other than fathering and having babies. Their survival was from the land; hunting animals for food. These were our ancestors brought to America during sixteen nineteen. There are certain modifications God created mankind to endure controlled by genetic heritage. However, traits can be altered based on teachings, codes and systems; but only through individual determination to acknowledge through thinking and deciphering best interest. There are numerous times genetic heritage overrides best interest. Southern plantation blacks assumed living free from responsibility were in their best interest because it was compatible to their African heritage conditions. Because of illiteracy, their total philosophical functions were dedicated around farm life; growing cotton, house servants and siring babies. They had no idea there were other unifications that fortified the United States of America. They really did not care because if you are illiterate, you are isolated from modern technology and dependent on representation from society. There were thousands, if not millions, of free blacks integrated across the southern states. Ninety eight percent were mulattoes; fathered by numerous whites; rich middle class and poor illiterate white trash which created eternal black density because black women were at the mercy of the white man, also the white woman. There was an old saying in the south years ago that the only free people were the white man and the black woman because wealthy plantation owners, their male family members and white staff had their choice of white and black women.

In essence, mulatto black spear headed the prominences of most African Americans all over the nation of America because they were treated equivalent to whites. Many throughout the southern states owned slaves simply because their white heritage were elated of their accomplishments; their ability to conform to the philosophical capitalistic traits of independent comprehension. It was the white man who fathered and created intellectual moral African Americans. Southern Democratic plantation masters prestige and dominance were equivalent to monolith monarchs. They had influence around the world, especially within the political arena. They controlled the U. S. Congress for forty years to include the U. S. Courts. During eighteen fifty seven, the case Dred Scott versus Sanford, they ruled seven to two against Dred Scott having his liberties with Chief Justice Roger B. Taney reading the court opinion; declaring all African Americans had never been and could never be American citizens and that Dred Scott had no rights under the U. S. Constitution to sue in court which no white man was compelled to respect.

Also, during eighteen ninety six, the U. S. Supreme Court authorized the southern Jim Crow Rule: separate but equal, eradicating southern blacks from the fourteenth amendment to the constitution the Republican congress had ratified during eighteen sixty eight. Once the U. S. Supreme Court rules, it takes an act of congress to overrule and the Democrats controlled congress for forty years and were never enthusiastic about restoration which southern blacks were under strenuous guidelines; segregated from all public facilities, having to sit in the rear of public transportation such as busses for sixty eight years.

During this troubling, violent turmoil most southern African Americans remained loyal to their homeland in the south because most were illiterate and had no other choice. They had discovered through experience their children and other blacks returning from the northern states to sponge on their wellbeing that most blacks who remained in the southern states had no problems from whites. It was the blacks who had gone to the northern states and returned who stipulated: I am going to show these red neck hunkies how to treat us like up north. Unfortunately during this era there were no black ghetto slums originated in the south for free handouts, so the southern Democratic Ku Klux Klan delayed it as long as they could through lynching. Many returned and made the necessary adjustments to southern traditions and raised productive families. On the advice of their parents and family members as the southern states evolved into the twentieth and twenty first centuries based on constitutional guidelines for all people.

Unfortunately, there were numerous supposedly educated, road scholars and Pulitzer Prize winning blacks who utilized political bias distortion based on their philosophical agenda of assumptions and demagoguery: deceiving the general public based on ludicrous hypocrisy. Most African Americans know as much about chronological events in regards to American history, pertaining to their inception and philosophical demographics as I do about flying a jumbo jet. Most haven't the ability to differentiate between Democrat and Republican Parties.

I watched a segment on C2SPAN-2 on November 2, 2011 as Pulitzer Prize winner Isabel Wilkerson elaborated on migration. She briefly mentioned other ethnics. Her topic was mostly about African Americans and the consequences they endured under the southern Jim Crow Rule. One statement she blurted out was: the people did something President Abraham Lincoln could not do; referring to blacks migrating to the northern states. This reminded me of the statement FBI Director J. Edgar Hoover made during nineteen fifty seven about black's brains being twenty percent smaller than whites. This woman was an excellent candidate for this theory because of her exaggerated phenomenon of American history pertaining to most African Americans. The word migrate was taken out of context pertaining to blacks simply because Africans were brought to America during 1619 to Virginia aboard a Dutch war ship and twenty were sold for food supplies. For approximately seventy two years they labored on the tobacco farms along with indentured white poor servants. After seventy two years, there was a population explosion of illiterate Africans. They were brain washed by a militant Caucasian named Nathaniel Bacon to take possession of the native lands in western Virginia. They burned the capital and the governor's life was in serious doubt. However he did escape. This tragic rebellion occurred during sixteen seventy six, fifteen years later during sixteen ninety one, South Carolina initiated the first demanding codes to sell and trade Africans to other states, southern and northern. They were transported which established southern and northern slaves.

During this era America was under British jurisdiction and there were indentured white and black slaves. African American exceptionalism was throughout British America. They participated in every colonial war; including the French and Indian War which ended during seventeen sixty three. African Americans helped defend the Battle of Bunker Hill during seventeen seventy five. African American military participants were involved practically over the entire nation. Blacks from New England: Prince Whipple and Oliver Cromwell, were among the oarsmen on the boat carrying George Washington across the Delaware River to Trenton, New Jersey on Christmas night during seventeen seventy six.

Most northern states began to abolish slavery: Massachusetts— seventeen eighty three; Rhode Island, Connecticut and New Jersey— seventeen eighty four. During seventeen ninety three, Eli Whitney, a teacher educated at Yale University, travelled to South Carolina and noticed the task of separating cotton seed by hand. He chose to develop a machine with claws that could separate cotton seed at the rate of fifteen people. During eighteen twenty seven, Samuel Cornish and John Russwurm established the nation's first newspaper *The Freedoms Journal* as black editors.

Throughout the south there were comfortable relations between whites and blacks. White and black children played together on plantations. During the War of 1812, blacks were inclusive in Andrew Jackson's defeat of the British for U. S. liberty from their control. African American soldiers were instrumental in winning the Civil War against the southern confederacy. Approximately forty thousand lost their lives. Sargent William H. Carney was the first African American to receive the U. S. Congressional Medal of Honor. There were approximately nine thousand African American cavalry troops ahead of white units when the confederate capital was succumbed to surrender in Richmond.

Under the regime of Republican President Abraham Lincoln the Republican congress ratified the thirteenth amendment to the U. S. Constitution on December 6, 1865 abolishing slavery. Three years later on July 9, 1868, the Republican controlled congress ratified the fourteenth amendment to the Constitution awarding all U. S. citizens equal liberties and protection under codes. Then along came the fifteenth amendment, ratified on February 3, 1870 by the Republican congress which emphatically stipulated the right of citizens of the United States to vote shall not be denied or abridged by the United States or by any state on account of race, color or previous conditions of servitude. African American legacy is embedded in the constructive exceptionalism history of America since inception. Unfortunately, most were and are deprived and deceived with political bias distortion based on philosophical agendas of inept ingenuity demagoguery utilizing name recognition to brain wash in regards to chronological events which have occurred in American history pertaining to African Americans.

History is one of the most ideological assets in human life other than God because if you are unaware of where you came from, you sure as hell do not know where you are going. The United States of America is the greatest nation on God's earth; but if you do not understand the techniques for gaining philosophical resolutions, you might as well be living in Africa and most African Americans are in this category because of illiterate, incompetent gullibility based on herding behind self-appointed and elected black and white leaders in regards to name recognition and misguided folklore.

America is a nation of individual capitalistic compromise based on intellectual morality. Your accomplishments solely depend on your ability to perform which is established on merit of conformance to relate in a dignified prospective manner and having the ability to resolve issues based on intellectual moral values. Unfortunately, most blacks tend to exaggerate based on assumptions. For approximately three hundred years or more blacks were marred on southern plantations and deprived of educational privileges. Being illiterate they had no other choice but to remain on southern plantations which were their only stability of survival. When the Jim Crow Rule (separate but equal) was adopted most southern blacks made the necessary adjustments and carried on with their lives in regards to share cropping.

After the Civil War ended during spring of eighteen sixty five, most African Americans remained in the south because they were offered shares of crops to maintain the plantations. During eighteen sixty six, southern African Americans were allowed to attend state conventions the states had established to their constitutions which allowed blacks to vote such as South Carolina, Mississippi and Louisiana. The U. S. Congress passed the southern Homestead Act awarding blacks and poor whites who were loyal during the war approximately fifty million acres of public land in five southern states for one year. Unfortunately, the lands were not suitable for farming because of marshy swamps, boulders and trees. Many blacks utilized their funds from their military service and purchased hundreds of acres of sufficient lands for farming. Changes in human lives are inevitable. Normally it is exercised based on individual distinguishing quality. The ethnics of African Americans were unusual and unique circumstances.

Abraham Lincoln was quite a unique individual. At age nineteen, on a trip to New Orleans, he and his cousin Dennis Hanks witnessed a mulatto woman being publicly sold at an auction. This disturbed him. He stated if he ever had a chance slavery would be abolished. While serving in the Illinois State Legislature, during eighteen fifty four, he continued to denounce slavery.

Also, during eighteen fifty eight Republican candidate Abraham Lincoln challenged Democratic opponent Stephen A. Douglas for the Illinois State Senate. The topic arose concerning slavery and a debate occurred questioning its place in society. Lincoln quoted the Declaration of Independence and strongly suggested slavery was a violation of humanity because the slave holder governed the slave without his consent which the guidelines are totally different from those he laid down as a guide for himself and all men are created equal.

Democrat Stephen A. Douglas stated his beliefs: the signers of the Declaration of Independence made no reference to Negroes whatever when they declared all men created equal. During this period of time there were approximately one million free blacks in America, especially in the northern states who supported Republicans. Then came the presidential election of eighteen sixty. The Republican Party opposed slavery. They chose Lincoln as their candidate. Abraham Lincoln was inaugurated president of the United States on March 4, 1861. Southern Democrats accused him of being a black nigger loving Republican president.

Mississippi, Florida, Alabama, Georgia, Louisiana, Texas and North Carolina departed the United States to establish the Confederate States of the South. On April 12, 1861 the Civil War began when the confederate military fired on federal Fort Sumter in South Carolina. Virginia, Arkansas, Tennessee and North Carolina chose to terminate their affiliation with the United States and join the confederacy. African American soldiers from Company E Fourth U. S. Colored Infantry of over two hundred thousand fought diligently in the Civil War assuring the defeat of the southern confederate states. Their role was pivotal in the attack on Vicksburg, Mississippi. Their victory at Port Hudson and Milliken's Bend was responsible for the defeat of Vicksburg.

The fifty fourth Massachusetts colored regiment attacked and fought hand to hand combat with confederates at Fort Wagner during eighteen sixty three in South Carolina. Around the end of March or first of April, eighteen sixty five the Civil War ended with Confederate Commander Robert E. Lee surrendered to U. S. General Ulysses S. Grant. These were the most distressing, disastrous civil conflicts in American history with total of approximately seven hundred thousand Americans lost their lives, north and south. This included over forty thousand African Americans. All U. S. troops, none for the confederacy in approximately four years of combat.

President Lincoln was one of the most remarkable men God created with intellectual controllability, mostly self-taught embedded in the general aspects of guidance to clarify the human quality of mankind to control his or her destiny based on morality and comprehensive thinking formulated theory of relativity. President Lincoln was the American philosophical political Einstein of his regime. There will never be another of his comprehensibility range of action and influence. I offer an explicit explanation. He knew more about Africans one hundred fifty years ago than African Americans know about themselves today. He was totally aware Africans were sold into slavery by their own Congo tribal chiefs from the nation of Africa that was hostile, savagely illiterate from the jungles of Africa. The southern Democratic Ku Klux Klan utilized this misfortune to their advantage for two hundred forty six years.

At age nineteen, Lincoln noticed something occurring in Louisiana that was uncivilized; auctioning of a human. The brain controls the human body, mostly through the eyes which sends a message to the brain. This determines likes and dislikes which can be translated into speech. Lincoln uttered words of his dissatisfaction; if ever given the chance he would eradicate these formalities. Along with time, skillful dedication and perseverance he caused it to occur. On January 1, 1863, after his inauguration on March 4, 1861, he issued his Emancipation Proclamation; abolishing servitude for all southern plantation slaves. Most had to be advised by advancing black military personnel as to what the meaning was because of illiteracy. President Lincoln had devised a magnificent master plan for southern plantation blacks only.

Prior to his assassination, he had decided southern blacks had been held in consecration on plantations for hundreds of years. They had earned the right to own shares of those plantations. He had decided to award forty acres of plantation land and a government mule to all black families. The legislation had been processed and was waiting for congress to ratify it. After the surrender of Confederate Commander Robert E. Lee, President Lincoln addressed the nation. He spoke of southern plantation black illiteracy and the probability of their improving their skills to literate along with their children based on having their own resources. Plantation black's skills were restrained to farming or forging iron. This is why President Lincoln chose to award them southern plantation lands in an effort they could eventually become a continuity of viable in American society.

Unfortunately, John Wilkes Booth was in the audience and advised a friend he is agreeing to allow nigger citizenship and this will be his last speech. On the evening of April 14th at Ford Theater, John Wilkes Booth eradicated President Lincoln's life while he was watching a play. Booth yelled, now the south is avenged. President Lincoln passed on the next morning. He was the first presidential assassination in the history of our nation. The entire nation was stunned and infuriated. Unfortunately, President Lincoln had chosen practically an illiterate for his vice president; Andrew Johnson, a staunch Democrat from Tennessee. From the moment he was sworn in he began reconstructing the confederate Democratic Ku Klux Klan and rescinded the late President Lincoln's formulated legislation to award all southern plantation black families land and a government mule.

President Johnson immediately returned the southern plantations back to the masters during congressional vacation. Southern plantation blacks were literally brutalized by the southern Democratic Ku Klux Klan for another hundred years. They were forced to share crop. Their families were raped, molested and lynched. Being illiterate they were forced to endure. During the era of the eighteen fifties, there were additional grotesque barbaric southern Democratic atrocities against southern plantation blacks. They were literally sold and bred like animals to accumulate the physical capability of blacks to increase the selling price. Plantation masters chose special black women called breeders especially for that purpose.

Many southern Democratic whites began lucrative businesses trading and selling blacks; such as Nathan Bedford Forrest, an Illiterate from Mississippi relocated to Memphis, Tennessee. He utilized his horse trading talents to accumulate a fortune trading and selling black slaves. With his financial stability, Forrest became a general in the southern confederacy. During eighteen sixty four Confederate General Nathan Bedford Forrest's southern units under his command attacked the United States garrison in Fort Pillow, Tennessee. The confederate troops were double the U. S. troops. All U. S. troops were mostly black and many were wounded and surrendered. Confederate brigades policy was not to administer medical attention to captured injured blacks. General Forrest ordered the massacre of approximately three hundred U. S. troops. His orders were not to leave a damn one alive. It was the worst human slaughter during the entire Civil War. They clubbed the wounded to death, nailed some to walls and burned many alive. There was a river near by running red with human blood.

After the Civil War ended, white terrorist groups attempted to reinstate slavery in southern black society during the late eighteen sixties. Several of these groups were called The Knights of the White Comilla, The Pale Face

Brotherhood and The White League. There was former black slave trader also former confederate General Nathan Bedford Forrest who gave the command for his troops to slaughter injured and surrendered U. S. troops at Fort Pillow, Tennessee. This was extremely instrumental in negotiating the solidification of the white terrorist groups into accepting the identity of the Ku Klux Klan. They became the most aggressive, violent, heartless, notorious controlling group in American history. They persecuted, maimed and lynched African Americans for over ninety years in all southern states until Republican President Dwight David Eisenhower authorized FBI Director J. Edgar Hoover to infiltrate the Ku Klux Klan and quell the violence of southern Democratic Ku Klux Klan from eradicating southern African Americans. During eighteen sixty six, in Memphis, Tennessee they slaughtered a full hall of black and white Republicans. Minister Dr. Horton waved a white banner and pleaded for his life. Their answer to him was all you Republican bastards must die.

CHAPTER 26

I am beginning this chapter with a lifelong explicit exploratory tradition of most African Americans philosophical generalities pertaining to their perception of American history based on chronological events related to their ideology relating to their progress and inept dysfunctional deficiencies. If you know absolutely nothing about who you are, or where you came from; then you are wondering about America, controlled by monolithic, dysfunctional forced indoctrination, which is brain wash; most blacks are characterized with this demeanor. Progress is being capable of deciphering monologues based on comprehensive analyses to determine ethics of moral values which will distinguish human philosophical distinctive combination of traits to evaluate on individual merits.

Most African Americans over the entire nation have monolithic traditions generated through genetic heritage over thousands of years from Africa that stigmatize and dictate philosophical distinguishing quality. This is a heritage from Congo tribes controlled and advised by a chief. Also, being brought to America during sixteen nineteen and not being permitted to intermix with other ethnics or attend integrated institutions for learning, the southern black plantation dwellers adhered to their African heritage philosophy for approximately three hundred forty years.

During this extensive amount of time, they were producing mulattoes and black babies. Those are our ancestors who created approximately forty million blacks who reside in the United States of America today. Inherited genetic controllability is created from God. It is embedded in the brain cells for all God's creatures; especially mankind. Those characteristic traits are inevitable and eternal. To exchange information or opinions is the most important asset known to the human race because the brain facilitates activity based on genetic heritage that determines human traits.

Due to southern Democratic hostility; selling, trading and breeding plantation blacks, most blacks who are over eighty years old today have no idea who their great grandparents were. The southern Democratic plantation owners literally created chaos relating to African genetic heritage when southern Democratic confederate white men fathered the children of black slave women. Numerous male and female were incoherent, dense, illiterate and incompetent. The evidence of this dysfunctional impact has been displayed at the voting booth for over eighty years. African Americans are the only ethnic who reside in the United States of America who constantly vote ninety five percent for Democrats and do not have a logical explanation as to why, other than they are for us. The most important scenario in human life is competiveness based on individual ingenuity. Southern Democratic plantation owners deprived most blacks of this humanity for centuries. The results are quite evident and stigmatic in most African American's philosophical distinguishing quality today, three hundred ninety three years later.

The founding fathers utilized their unique viable special heritage talents created from God, clearly realizing God was their creator when they established the Declaration of Independence and the Constitution which has stabilized America for approximately two hundred thirty five years. Most blacks and a large segment of other ethnics are totally inept to the general principle of the Constitution and guidelines of the Declaration of Independence that protect our liberties and capitalistic adventures based on morality in the United States of America.

During my stint of employments: packaging corporation as a machinist, floor supervisor, and production control advisor for approximately fourteen years; approximately twenty three years with Chrysler and General Dynamics Corporation as a parts expediter, purchasing agent and extensive traveling consultant representative to resolve company problems during the prototype manufacture of the M1 Abrams Military Tank which is an incredible protective device for the United States of America security. During my travels over America there were favorable opportunities on numerous occasions. I would ask opinions concerning our Constitution; incidentally, these were all Caucasians in numerous paid occupation titles. All their answers were favorable to the Constitution such as: I don't understand most of it, but it is what we are governed by. If it weren't for the Constitution I would not be in business serving General Dynamics. It is the foundation America sits on that gives freedom and it's the bible to citizens of America to succeed in life.

Born a native of Alabama: as a youngster accustomed to the Jim Crow Rule (equal but separate). We as a family accepted it as a southern code and carried on with our responsibilities of survival. As a child I was taught America consisted of exceptionalism and it solely depended on individual morality how you are accepted; primarily based on communicated dialogue with others. Always, before you open your mouth to speak, think before addressing any issue in an effort to eliminate suspicions of incompetency. Growing up on a farm as an only child, I had uncles as tutors: Ben, Silas, Horace, Percy and Dowen Jones. Other than farming they had professional talents. Ben was a basket maker who was on the cover of Life Magazine during the early eighties. Silas was a cattle and hog breeder. Horace was a carpenter, barber and gunsmith. Percy was a watch and clock repairman. Dowen was a carpenter contractor. They all were instrumental in my future; especially my Uncle Horace who impacted my life the most. He and his wife Hettie had no children. He owned a truck and he or they would take me every place with them and teach me how to respond to people in general of all ethnics. One of his teachings was never distort reality and when you speak to any individual always look them in their eyes because the eyes send messages to the brain that dictate personality. Also, never expect a free ride in life. We would ride in his truck all week and early Sunday morning he would drive the truck to the creek and sit on the hill while I washed it for Sunday church. One Sunday I asked him; why should I have to wash the truck all the time. He stated, you ride free all week and whatever you need I see you get it. You really do not have to wash the truck, I will, it is your choice. However, I am going to suggest you find another truck driver who is going to give you goodies. From that day I would ask on Saturday, what time he wanted the truck washed on Sunday. Numerous times he would point to a spot I missed and his explanation was; one day when you grow up you are going to be employed and if you do not perform to expectancy according to guidelines you will be dismissed. I have never been dismissed from any place of employment during my entire range in the workforce.

I could never write anything pertaining to life unless I gave credit to my mother and grandmother. Each named Mary who constantly instilled in my mind that they were extremely proud to be Americans. When I grew up and did not appreciate the chance America gave to people to do for themselves then take my black ass to Africa and chase monkeys where white folks brought our ancestors from. They quoted: niggers will never understand America because of their stupid ass ignorance about America. That is why they are constantly being lynched; trying to change America into Africa. These writings are not about me. I would like to share a momentous experience. One occurred as a child; the other as a young adult. These experiences I have I will cherish until my demise and are largely responsible for these writings.

As a child in Alabama, my heritage dictated moral aggressiveness. This experience began during the early forties. While in grade school, there was a Caucasian gentleman named Mr. Billy Cooper. He purchased land and built a grocery, sweet and clothing store adjacent to our farm. There was another store approximately one hundred fifty yards below his, the Vices. However, many blacks accused Mr. Cooper of stealing black folks land and he was a white racist who hated blacks because of their color and stored a shotgun and bull whip behind his counter to whip blacks for no reason. I recall very vividly my mother needed Royal Crown hair dressing. She demanded I not stop at Mr. Cooper's store. It was during a weekday after school. She gave me just enough for the Royal Crown hair dressing. I rode my bike passed Mr. Cooper's store to the Vices. On my way back he was standing in his store door and signaled for me to come over. I almost fell from my bike with fear of being whipped. I stopped. He asked me my name and where did I live. I looked him directly in his eyes and stated my name and the Jones' were my people who owned the farm adjacent to his property. He asked me to come inside, which I did. This was the very beginning of my understanding courage which is one of the most important assets embedded within the human race if utilized appropriately with dignity. He asked where I was in school. I explained John Essex across Highway Eighty from my home. He asked if I saw anything I wanted. I stated yes sir but I did not have any money today, but on weekends a friend and I mucked stables for Mr. Monroe Wallace for pay. If I chose something I could pay on Saturday. I left with moon pies, jaw breakers, Brock candy and a R. C. Cola. I never told my parents.

On Saturday I returned to pay Mr. Cooper. He looked me square in my eyes, put his hand on my shoulder and stated: you are just a kid and more honest than older adult blacks. They have been using me from the time I opened this store. I let them have credit; the Vices down the road will not let blacks have credit. They refuse to pay me. When they get money they go shop at the Vices with their cash. We sat and talked. He was explaining people in general and became remorse. As he stated, I haven't the right to abuse anyone, but blacks will credit my items and lie about him being a red neck racist. He stated; most whites do not dislike blacks because of their color; it is their disposition of always trying to beat and cheat people for their wellbeing. He also stressed this is a phenomenon with most blacks. He advised me not to take his word, but as I grow up through my travels in life, just pay attention to come to my own beliefs. He then stated; not all blacks are like this, but the majority are and nothing but opportunists. They will steal and cheat their grandparents, or anyone who has more than they do and tell outrageous lies in an attempt to get pity from others.

One Saturday afternoon I stopped by Mr. Cooper's store. He called me to the backdoor and asked if I knew the person sneaking through the back woods. I said yes sir; that is Harold. We just finished cleaning Mr. Wallace's stables. He asked; do you know why he is in the woods. I had no idea. He stated; I will tell you. He owes me and now he has cash. He is sneaking through the woods down to the Vices to purchase what he wants for cash. When he spends all of his cash, he will come back to me for more credit. So, when you see him, tell him to come and talk to me. I saw Harold that afternoon and gave him the message. His answer was: fuck him, a red neck bastard. He should not credit me anyway. I never mentioned to Mr. Cooper what he said. However Harold eventually received an ass whipping inside the store. My mother heard about it and asked me what happened. I lied and pretended I knew nothing. She said lie to me once more and you are going to get your behind whipped because you have been shopping there all along because I found the hidden moon pies and candy. I then explained the entire story and suggested she meet Mr. Cooper. She did and we were friends thereafter. She jokingly accused him of stealing her son. He explained we would experience rebuff from some blacks. Later the word was out that we were white folk's niggers trying to be white because we owned our own land.

Mr. Cooper asked me one day if I was being taught anything about the Constitution in school. I asked, what is that? He refused to say, but referred me to my school teacher. The next school day I approached her desk and asked if she would explain what the Constitution was. Mrs. Worthy had a smirk look on her face. She asked me who had I been talking to about that mess; that blacks did not need to know about it because it was the white man's mess just to confuse black folks, just to keep us down. Finally

Mr. Cooper asked about if my teacher had given me an answer to the Constitution. I replied, yes sir and told him what she had said. His reply was; tell your mother to come and see me. My mother and I stopped by to visit him. His topic was; you have a bright child, please do not allow him to be indoctrinated with nigger ignorance. He needs to attend a school with teachers who have integrity. If you care about him, the responsibility is your choice because children's minds are to be improved not destroyed with nigger ignorance. When the next semester came, we had relocated to Elyria, Ohio. It was truly remarkable to be integrated with other ethnics in regards to educational competitiveness and the inspirational messages are documented in these writings sixty five years later.

My next encounter with reality in life was in Chicago, Illinois. As a young adult, I was a professional cook. I hired on with a Jewish restaurant owner, Mr. Bernard L. Sampson; a gentleman of no nonsense. He would give you the shirt from his back, but for damn sure you weren't going to take it. He horned in my human intellect beyond reproach based on human practicality; analyzing all ethnics in general related to moral decisive complex issues. His restaurant was located on the north side of Chicago. During this era, no blacks resided around Diversey Avenue. I was the only black cook. He and I traded conversations occasionally. However, his wife Marion was extremely proud of my cooking. Many times unless I prepared the recipe she would not eat. My shift was from four in the afternoon until midnight. During these times I did not have an automobile. I rode the elevator train from South to North Chicago. Diversey Avenue was the turnaround area for trains to head back south. Late nights there would be only three cars. I would be the first black to go aboard heading back south. There would be other ethnics boarding along with blacks. However, the south side of Chicago is predominately black. I was astounded to notice that either car I chose leaving the north side of Chicago, when I arrived south all blacks would be on the same car as I was. It was somewhat a mystery I had no answer for; particularly constantly occurring. I spoke with some other blacks about what was happening. Their response was; I was imagining stuff.

Mr. Sampson approached me and stated; He was going to sell the restaurant and going into the trucking business and if I wanted to come along. I asked what kind of trucking business. He answered; scavenger. I agreed. He purchased every, and anything. I had the occasion to meet his father Sam Sampson. He owned a junk yard on the west side of Chicago. He employed all blacks. He mentioned how they would steal and take advantage of his father because of his age. I mentioned the traveling experience on the elevator train from north to south side of Chicago during the time he owned the restaurant. All blacks would be congregated on the same car. His response was apparently you know absolutely nothing about your race of people. Their customs are originated from Africa embedded in tribal traits to gather around chiefs for his dictations pertaining to their responsibilities. This distinguishing character is embedded in most African Americans; not only blacks; some of the most rotten back stabbing bastards on God's earth. He insisted I not take his word, go do research; not just on blacks. You need to formalize yourself with the codes of America. He insisted I not start asking other people, because whites were not going to talk about those subjects and most blacks were to dam stupid to know anything about it.

So, I engaged in my private research. I spent the majority of my time in libraries over Chicago, denoting historical circumstances. These writings are the results of over fifty years of research delving into chronological events of American history. It has been one of the most contrasting, invigorating challenges of my life. I would not trade it if my neck was in a noose sitting on a horse because these are the real facts of reality pertaining to experience and research. However, Mr. Sampson Trucking Company expanded. He purchased three more tucks and chose me as his trucking supervisor. We needed additional employees. I hired on several to include four or five Alabama people I knew who lived in the South Chicago area. I taught them the city of Chicago, all pick up stops and how to handle the trucking equipment.

One was a Caucasian who performed maintenance on the vehicles. Unfortunately he stored a considerable amount of miscellaneous cash in his automobile trunk. Somehow one of the black employees learned of his stash and arranged to borrow his automobile. He stole his cash. I was informed about this fiasco. I called the accused to my office and questioned him. He responded; you ain't for us, you think you are white; but you ain't nothing but a white man ass licking nigger and that he knew nothing about that red neck honkey's money. At the end of conversation he was terminated. Prior to this incident, Mr. Sampson (I called him Lenny) had provided an occurrence to me that was astounding and mind boggling. Our offices were next door to each other. You could hear through the wall. We were having lunch one day. He asked me a specific question concerning the employees. It is you who is responsible for all these guys being on board here. Why don't they like you? I answered Lenny with: please allow me to enjoy my lunch. I have other things more important than joking around. He looked at me in such a manner as to say you stupid ass. We were extremely close. However, we had our disagreements and this was one. He suggested tomorrow I go sit in my office, lock the door and do not say a word. When the crew gets off and asks for you I am going to tell them you left early on personal business and will not return until tomorrow. Mr. Sampson, us been wantin to catch you alone for some time. Us want to let you know Ernie is no good for your company because when he was training us we thought he was going to wreck your trucks. You need one of us to take over his job because us will lookout for you because us know what us is doing. When he comes back don't tell him what us talked about. His statement was I am busy right now, but I appreciate the important information. They departed the office. He locked the door to the building and stated you can come out now.

We sat in his office for hours with him passing on his life experiences; being of Jewish origin, communicating with other ethnics. He began with Jews and black's lives are somewhat parallel. Adolf Hitler and his regime slaughtered over six million Jews because of their unique accountability and self-perseverance to attain philosophical prosperity through God created humanity. In essence, the southern Democratic Ku Klux Klan slaughtered thousands of blacks because of what you just witnesses today; dense dysfunctional incompetency because if anyone is embedded with these kind of heritage tendencies they are either going to kill someone or get killed and stack the correctional institutions like sardines. Their destination in life will consist of scandalous poverty because sitting judges are the sole disposition controllers of morality in the United States of America in accordance with our Constitution. My advice to you is never reveal personal advantages to anyone; not your mother or family members, and always remember herding in black society has been, and always will be, a self-destruction for most blacks, not whites. As you travel through life you will experience and learn most blacks swindle their own people and utilize racism in an effort to compensate for illiterate incompetency. He also explained why he chose me to be his first black chef; because I looked him square in his eyes and answered his questions with appropriate diction; not scratching my head and looking down on the floor as if I had lost something.

A few years later, Lenny approached me and advised he was closing shop in Chicago and relocating to Florida. We had a meeting with our crew and alerted them of his decision. They would be given plenty of time to locate other employment because he had to locate a buyer for his equipment. In privacy, he and his wife Marion asked if I would come along. I declined and we shed a few tears and departed company. That was the final exchange of our relationship. While I am on the subject, the ethnic of Jewish heritage are some of the most phenomenal people on God's earth. It is essential, repeat, essential we as a nation maintain staunch support to secure their survival in the state of Israel at any cost.

There are dire consequences if the current administration remains in power under the guidance of Dictator Barack Hussein Obama because he is a Congo ideologist who is intent on dismantling our Constitution and change America to a replica of Africa. This American dictator is a slick talking opportunist who has disdain for the state of Israel and all whites in America; particularly the wealthy. If you think this is dense incompetent propaganda, it is your choice; vote him in for another four years. My first book was entitled *Political Self-Destruction of Most African Americans*, which is on Amason.com. I predicted during the primary between Obama and Clinton that if he was fortunate enough to win, he would politically self-destruct and demoralize the Democratic Party almost to political power extinction; you be the judge.

I am a proud American with African heritage who has studied blacks all my life. All he or she has to do is open their mouth to speak and through their speech I can observe especially for quality and determine their philosophical traits.

CHAPTER 27

After Mr. and Mrs. Sampson departed Chicago, I opened a lounge on Fifty Fifth Street in South Chicago. Later, a relative I grew up with contacted me from Alabama. He served approximately fourteen years in the military. He stated he was getting out of the military and would like to come to Chicago but was broke. I asked if he had enough funds to reach Chicago, which he did with the clothes on his back. I purchased him some clothes and hygiene items, rented him a hotel room and paid his rent for a month, trained him to be a bartender and hired him for the day shift. I noticed over a period of time my stock started to dwindle. Because I worked nights and every afternoon when I would relieve him the bar would be full with women and a brief time later they would leave drunk as hell. There would be a minimum amount of cash in his check out. I was somewhat puzzled because I did not want to believe what I was thinking; all I did for him and now he is stealing from me. One of the ladies who ran a gambling house stopped for drinks during the afternoon. She accosted me and stated, you must pay your cousin a lot of money. He lost almost seven hundred dollars last Saturday night. I asked her to do me a favor; that I would be in early and if she would come and sit at the bar the next day; she agreed. When I arrived she was there. I walked behind the bar and asked my cousin about his gambling losses. He looked at the lady then turned to me and stated: it is none of your business what I do. That's what I say about niggers; because they own a little old chicken shit tavern they think they are better than everybody else. Nigger, you will never be white. I reached in the drawer pulled out my thirty eight revolver, slapped him beside his head and pulled the trigger simultaneously. He thought he was shot and screamed like a pig under a fence. I advised him to get the hell out of my place and if I ever saw him again the shot would be a reality. A few years later I closed the lounge and located employment in the private industry.

I located employment at Packaging Corporation of America; as I related earlier to being there for approximately fourteen years. When I first applied, Personnel Manager Don Scrack informed me no black had ever held a position other than catching and stacking corrugated board from the corrugating machine to manufacturing boxes. I accepted the job. He gave me a tour of the plant and introduced me to other blacks who worked with the rolling stock in back of the plant. On the way back he stated let's go back to my office. We sat. Apparently I had him scratching his head and starring at the floor because he stated; I like you style. You have a style most blacks do not have. You look people in the eye. Your verbiage is appropriate for communicating and when you are asked a question, there is no stammering gibberish. He stated; you know something? With your personality I am going to make you the first black to ever work on a machine as a helper. Curtis Lowery operates the partition slotter. You will catch and stack for him. He then walked me to the office of the Department Supervisor. Don explained where I would be working and my responsibility. There was a dismal silence. Finally he stated; what and walked me over to Curtis' machine and gave a brief introduction. The corrugating machine was in the same department; white machinist and black corrugated catchers were in a daze. Curious blacks could not wait until midnight. They gathered around the time clock waiting for me to clock out. They invited me to stop at a lounge with them, which I did. They all had questions for me; such as, man how did you do dat, us bin dare for years and day aint never did nuttin for us cose all dem honkies aint nuttin but nigger hater so you cot to no somebody up dare.

Over time I began to analyze the internal philosophical credentials of attainment, pertaining to company procedures in an effort to become an intricate part of their standards and to assist in the aggressive progressive procedures. I learned Curtis ruined lots of orders because of his inability to appropriately understand the mechanics of the machine due to part illiteracy. One day Curtis was off. The supervisory would always bring orders to be processed that day. Tony had a hot order which the setup had to be broken; run the hot order and return to the original. Different size orders were on skids taken in and out by lift truck drivers. The lift truck driver had brought the hot order and sat it by the machine. Tony approached me and stated; Ernie we are in trouble. Curt is off and I need this hot order. The PA system announced Tony had a call and he left. When he returned I had the machine running. He stated no/no we don't need any more of that old order. I stated; that is your hot order. Get me a stacker helper. It will be finished soon. He measured the order from diagram size and it was perfect. It appeared he had seen a ghost. He mumbled well kiss my behind and called one of the Caucasian women over to stack for me. That was the first time a black man had operated any machine at Packaging Corporation of America with a Caucasian helper. Later I was informed Curt had been transferred as a printing press helper up front in box print and I was the permanent slotter machine operator. I began producing partitions until it required two helpers on the belt of distribution. Most blacks quit speaking to me. However, they asked me to stop at a bar with them once again. I was interrogated; man you must be some kind of sissy for dem honkes to go and put you on dat machine as a operator day aint never did none of us like dat. I advised them this would be my last stop because insults like this will cause me jail time. I stated; you haven't seen anything yet. I am going go be in management one day. They laughed to the point of tears and called me the most stupid ass nigger they had ever seen.

Later I noticed an idle machine adjacent to my slotter. I asked my supervisor what kind of machine it was. He replied; it is a Thompson Fixed Dye Cutting Machine. He pointed along the wall base and stated those are four foot square wood dyes with razor sharp metal embedded to cut miscellaneous box patterns. You attach the wood board to the top steel plate and the bottom steel plate goes up and down to crush the corrugated board against the steel knives in order to form a selected pattern. I asked why there was no operator. He stated; a fellow's hand was cut to pieces and no one was interested any more. I asked if I came in early would he explain the operations to me. He said fine, but it is a dangerous machine. One mistake and you could lose your hand or both. I asked if he would set the machine up. He did. After analyzing the operations I asked if I could become the operator of that machine. He said he would talk to the plant manager. He returned and stated it was okay, but it was my choosing not theirs at my own risk. He would not replace my slotter position until I was sure.

I recall as a kid in Alabama, watching my uncle repair watches, wagon wheels, plows and harrows. Their theory was; never allow a machine to work you or puzzle you. You are there to work the machine because the machine does not have a brain, you do. I figured out a strategy they had never seen before as an operator on that machine. I requested a hydraulic track to be affixed to my right that would automatically adjust height to weight loss which would keep the corrugated board you were processing at same height constantly; also a rolling track to my left where an individual stood to remove excess waste from the useful box design which I coordinated a body hand synchronized motion; right in, left out; with a straight cross motion. Most people neglect to realize the important functions of their brain; it does not permit you to concentrate on two different operations simultaneously. If one wants to challenge this reality try talking on a phone to someone and have an individual speaking to you at the same time. You will have to tell one to hold on while you listen to the other. This is why numerous automobile accidents occur; due to drivers trying to dial phones and continue to drive. However over a short period of time I processed all back orders and needed two helpers to remove corrugated slag. The CEO and plant manager would come into the area or my machine and just stand and watch.

One afternoon I came in and was beginning my machine setup. I noticed one black catcher from the corrugating assembly approaching my direction. He addressed me with you black ass nigger you think you are smart then he punched me in the mouth. The other Caucasian department workers restrained each; myself and him and suggested: please do not strike back; he is only trying to get you fired. They testified to his actions and he wasn't around anymore. Quite some time later, my supervisor notified me the plant manager wanted to speak to me. While approaching his office I began to wonder what was this all about. Once I arrived he suggested I have a seat and stated: young man, I have a salary position for you; if you choose to accept. I asked what and he advised me Henry was going to retire as supervisor of the box stitching department. He would like for me to take on that responsibility. I accepted. The entire department was Caucasian. I will never forget when I was introduced as their supervisor. One lady, Helen Sipak, mumbled; what the hell does he know to manage this department he just came through the door. I have been here for over twenty years. The women who ran the stitching and box taping machines were on peace work; all over a hundred percent were theirs and they were constantly complaining of not making enough money for their efforts. Helen would never work overtime. If there was a hot order on her machine I would have to get others to stay over. I chose to check their time work sheets. None had been taught to appropriately document their time sheets.

I suggested we have a department meeting. Helen commented; what the hell does he know to tell us. I explained the fundamentals of the appropriate manner to complete their time sheets. They began to make adequate pay. Helen began working all overtime and we were a joyful department.

A lengthily time passed. Later I was summoned to the office of Bob McQuinn, the manager of plant production control. Bob stated he was on the hot seat; sales complaining about late customer orders not on time. If I would accept the responsibility for being his managing supervisor to coordinate the entire plant activity which consisted of scheduling and arranging orders to be run from the corrugating machine at specific intervals and schedule to the appropriate machine centers for processing and plant supervisors were under my guidance to carry out these responsibilities. A coordinated communicated effort must be established with the department of our sales because they are the department that accepts orders for the stability of our company.

I thought about my responsibility and determined this was one of the most unique challenges I had ever encountered. I assured upper management I would work my heart out to succeed for the best interest of the company. Over time things became worse with late processed orders. My office was at the front entrance to the plant with a sliding window. Some blacks would stop and remark; us node you wotten dat smart anyhow, us bin heir all dis time and day give you dis job, us kno moe bout dis plant dan dem bosses, just look at all dem late orders you gwing to be gone. I came to work one morning, there was a huge flexo machine out front of my office that could process over a thousand printed slotted cartons per hour. I looked at the duplicate order and it was the same that was being processed when I left that evening. I walked out along the walls of the plant and there were stacks of late orders. However, the one they were running were not due until two weeks out. This machine could process any normal size printed carton, but it was mostly used for candy company's cartons. The orders could be from ten to twenty thousand for one order. I began to realize what was happening. Across the outer front of my office there were order openings for each plant machine. I noticed machine operators were choosing what orders they wanted to process. I spoke with my manager, Bob McKuinn, and suggested we have a meeting with upper management so I could explain the cause for delinquent shipping orders and how it could be prevented.

The plan was not to allow machine operators to choose their orders to process. It should be the responsibility of their supervisor to determine what orders to process in accordance with schedule delivery dates from the aligned highlighted corrugating process because all delivery dates are on each specific order. However, one supervisor had been with packaging corporation for approximately thirty years and refused to adhere to these guidelines and was let go. In a few weeks we had every late order processed and on schedule with others. I was given a wage increase. I was employed there for approximately fourteen years until I resigned and relocated to a small city in Ohio in an effort to eliminate large city radical exposure for our young children.

Apparently it was a wise decision for the two because each are independent in life. The older has philosophical looks and traits of her mother. The younger has mostly my distinguishing quality because she is persistent and a professor of law at one of the major Ivy League universities. You guessed it. She was the first African American to teach law there. Years later I returned to Chicago on a business assignment for Chrysler Corporation. I stopped by the packaging corporation and had a conversation with my former manager, Bob McKuinn. He had located his desk to my old office. He stated; there was no one to replace me so he had no choice; also that the Thompson Dye Cut machine was still without an operator. He also said another black convinced management to give him the operator title on the slotter machine; he had enough experience to operate the machine. They gave him the job then learned he could not set the machine up. He became angry and used a hammer to break all handles from the machine so it was not operative.

These personal revelations are not for brag; but to offer an explicit explanation to people in general; particularly most African Americans and their ambiguous, dense, illiterate, incompetent, ill-gotten duplicity. Most have never incorporated the established exceptionalism of American traditions. Instead, most have created a miniature solidified replica of Africa in America. This is not a demoralizing derogatory remark. It is a fact based on chronological events of reality which have occurred in America pertaining to blacks since the inception of Africans during sixteen nineteen which is approximately three hundred ninety two years ago.

Because the philosophical inclination of most blacks are to herd, which is an embedded genetic heritage from Africa that the southern Democratic confederation compounded and expounded on based on their philosophical traits of illiterate, incompetent density and those critique ideologues are more prevalent today than ever before. The supposedly educated and successful blacks are being utilized as black plantation slave drivers as they were trained by their white plantation bosses for hundreds of years to keep plantation slaves in unison. This same tactic is being utilized today by the Democrat Party by a margin of ninety five percent constantly for over seventy five years. It is dysfunctional and despicable for an ethnic of approximately forty million African Americans not to be capable of deciphering the philosophical ideological alternative between our two party system; Democrat and Republican based on theoretical agendas of which party slaughtered blacks with blow torches, lynching, sold raped and bred black women as if they were animals and held blacks in illiterate servitude for approximately three hundred forty five years. This was a disavowal for most blacks to acquire appropriate integrated education skills and knowledge to succeed in America along with other ethnics.

America is a nation of achievements based on individual merit, not herding. Most African and African Americans have utilized this dysfunctional process for over two thousand years. The circumstantial evidence is in their bloc voting process constantly voting approximately ninety five percent for one party, the Democrats; which no other ethnic in America is committed to. I wrote about my personal accomplishments with Packaging Corporation, Chrysler and General Dynamics Corporations because large corporations are equivalent to the fundamental standards the United States of America was established on. Individuals must have relevant skills and utilize them to attain respect. Most African Americans have never had anything to offer other than dem dare white fokes is holdin us back cos us is black.

There are black dysfunctional morons on every available public broadcast network; parallel to schools of catfish all mouth and no brains; literally endorsing this theory when they rose to their pinnacle of success riding the coat tails of Caucasians for hundreds of years in America. It is unfortunately destructive these are the blacks who utilized nonsensical propaganda to seduce and brainwash other less fortunate blacks into thinking it is those old rich white racist Republicans who are responsible for you being marred in the Ghetto not being capable to read and write and speak fluent appropriate English. That is why us support Democrats; because they are for us, giving us relief checks and dat is why I am a Democrat. My mother and daddy was a Democrat, also my grandparents were Democrats cause dey look out for us.

For hundreds of years in America, blacks have utilized convoluted trickery to camouflage for being illiterate and incompetent. The main mental telepathy is to blame through indoctrinated dialect to deceive and these are the narcissistic, devious, belligerent, dysfunctional thugs who have demoralized the majority of the African American race into supporting liberal Democrats who have self-destructed themselves into slum destitution throughout every major city in America. Most blacks are habitual liars because they utilize this as a tool to distort for their illiterate incompetency in an effort to deceive for personal accommodations others will think they are intellectually marked with wit and ingenuity.

The integrity of my writings in this book is authentic and deals strictly with personal experience of over fifty years of research. I have exposed and defined the validity of each political party, Democrat and Republican. There are approximately ninety five percent of African Americans who support Democrats influenced by affluent blacks in most professions. As you read this factual, written presentation, I respectfully suggest you come to your own conclusion; either these blacks have small dysfunctional, inadequate, incompetent brains; or, they are a legitimate facsimile of accomplishment to the violent slaughter of thousands of other southern blacks by the southern Democratic established Ku Klux Klan which were our tormented ancestors. When you watch them on your television, you be the judge.

It takes years, from birth to perceive conform and attain the philosophical traits of conservatism. It is mostly passed on through genetic heritage and improved on through general consensus related to self-containment and the general principles of morality; also capable of making pertinent, individual decisions based on merit; and if incorrect, will admittedly acknowledge and yield to the appropriate correctness.

Liberalism: most liberals, especially blacks, never have any creative ideology of their own accord. However, if others create anything with substance; they will become highly belligerent if you do not allow them to instruct on operative functions. Their agenda is let the chips fall without definite aim or method; if incorrect, rely on bias distortion in an effort to convince you it was someone else's mistake. Liberals are of this distinct philosophical characterization. You can ask most a simple question; what were your chores today? They will explain the previous day's activities. They are unique professionals on the glove to distort and evade direct questions of importance pertaining to reality.

It is of the essence to concentrate on what is transpiring in our great nation, America, to date. President elect Barack Hussein Obama is a narcissistic, superficial replica of African former dictator Idi Amin Dada and Nat Turner who terrorized southern Americans during the eighteen thirties in an effort to overthrow the established civilized government and implement a socialistic Congo ideology. President Obama, I suspect, has covert intentions of eradicating our Constitution for his personal convenience to become America's first black Congo Dictator to demand resources from the financial stable and distribute among illiterate, incompetent misfits. Please take note: this is an African tradition dictators have always conquered by dividing its people. He is attempting to accomplish this mission in America by endorsing radical street demonstrators around the nation. His intent is to seduce their thinking into if he is re-elected he is going to be their philosophical creator of wealth for them.

I traveled states in America and Mexico for years on assignments for Chrysler and General Dynamics Corporations resolving problems; meeting with plant owners; presidents; and chief executive officers. My favorite question to ask before departure was: how did you start your business. Most of their answers would always be; my grandparents, parents or I began this business with a small amount of borrowed funds and have worked diligently for years to improve. Many times they would elaborate on family members who were inept and trifling and were excused from the company. Unfortunately, America was duped on planned elaborate verbiage by an individual (Barack Hussein Obama) into electing him president. He has never run a cat from kitchens.

There was a skit on national television CNN on November 19, 2011 concerning the Zulu Tribes of Africa. They dress themselves with authentic leopard skins and according to the commentator; based on their tribal beliefs, authentic leopard skins create genuine tribal controlling powers. Unfortunately, there is a genuine serious problem. According to the TV commentator, there are approximately five million Zulu tribes throughout Africa. They have eradicated the leopard into extinction. In essence the Zulu tribes of Africa and our nation the United States of America have parallel disastrous problems. The Zulus must find other than leopard skins to dress in. Our distinct choice, as a lucrative nation, must vote this nonsensical Congo dictating President Barack Hussein Obama from office in the white house or endure financial Congo tribal demoralization of extinction around the globe for the greatest nation on God's earth, the United States of America.

Please! I am not asking, I am begging, do not allow this socialist, incompetent Congo hypocritical, ideologist to destroy our nation. It is an established fact that discrimination exists in our nation and around God's world which is inevitable because God created mankind with decisive issues to think in accordance with revelations to determine fate. We have an elected president who is totally unaware of these philosophical, devastating consequences that are applicable. This is why my first book was entitled *Political Self-Destruction of Most African Americans*. If people do not compromise with the facts of reality, obviously their fate is doom. President Obama has cast this initiative on America based on total incompetency of our national heritage.

I am skeptical and pray to God we shall prevail. Stochastically we are in a quagmire based on prevarication related devious narcissism embedded in the philosophical traits of this elected president. His distinguishing quality agenda is not conforming to American traditional embedded heritage according to our Constitution but continue radical duping the American people in an effort to convince them he is concerned about their wellbeing. Trust me, all this gentleman is concerned about is being re-elected so he can maintain his efforts in sabotaging America; thinking he will become a monarch; advising all political functions in America not the congress.

In essence, Article I, Section 1 of the Constitution specifically and explicitly stipulates:

That all legislative powers herein granted shall be vested in a congress of the United States, which shall consist of a Senate and House of Representatives.

Yet, this president's intentions are to intimidate the congress and dictate to the American people that if congress does not act on his asinine proposals to desecrate the fundamental standard traditions of American he will. He is publicly advertising his intentions when he is about America. His ideology for Americans is negative with disdain and he will pursue any dimension to cause destitution with the intent to eradicate our liberties and replace with Congo socialism. There is a chance left to rectify and stabilize our nation back to moral civility during the election in two thousand twelve; unless the people of our nation allow President Obama to dup and con based on truculent, immature lies to be re-elected. Then you, the people, have politically self-destroyed our nation. However, I have tremendous confidence in most of the American people of other ethnics because most blacks are going to support him because he is black. Most blacks are inept to the philosophical distinguishing quality between Caucasians; one being a Democrat and the other a Republican. Their premise is all whites are the same, but the Democrats are on us side and have always helped us; ever since day give us our rights dat dem Republican took.

Most blacks have never qualified to think in depth to determine pertinent factions pertaining to consequences. For example: it has been approximately three hundred ninety two years since African's inception to America. Their herding after Congo ideology is more prevalent today than ever because black Congo chiefs opportunists are bulging the airways dictating narcissistic, idiosyncrasy, demagoguery in an effort to herd blacks continued constituent voting support for the Democratic Party based on their political illiterate, incompetency in regards to comprehensive privileges established standards in the United States of America. President Obama has politically self-destructed and demoralized the Democratic Party. They are aware of this fiasco and are trying desperately to maintain the African American dense support.

CHAPTER 28

During eighteen sixty eight, when the Republican Congress ratified the fourteenth amendment to the Constitution; to give southern blacks their civil and voting rights, the southern Democratic Ku Klux Klan became belligerent and extremely hostile. They emphatically stipulated and predicted blacks were illiterate, incompetent and stupid to understand political candidates in regards to voting because they were totally inept to the distinguishing quality of a candidate and could not decipher his agenda; they bloc vote based on hearsay and should continue engagement in things they are good at; such as servitude not politics.

The best guarded secret in America is how the Democrat Party has utilized African American illiterate, incompetency and deficiency to their superb advantage during servitude and now politically in an attempt to maintain elite political status within the confines of the United States of America. It is quite adequately ingenious and appropriate a black man (Barack Hussein Obama) have them totally frustrated because they assumed he would be their porch monkey yo yo on a string to solidify African American voters eternally for the Democrat Party. Unfortunately for the distinguished Democratic Party, they underestimated African black embedded philosophical distinguishing quality. Most have the ideology of a Congo tribal chief when they reach their pinnacle of success; particularly in politics. They demand notoriety attention. For instance, they format little idiosyncrasies such as President Obama has a tendency to shoulder or arm caress dignitaries which signifies I am top dog and more important than you are. This is a southern Democratic heritage facsimile of whites caressing the heads of southern blacks to insinuate authority. President hopeful Herman Cain; notice his large brim hat; that hat is a replica of southern plantation slave owners insignia that only they used for attire. However, Judas goat of the Democratic Party, President Obama has taken the advice of his minister for many years and is bringing the Democrat Party chickens home to roost. They are utilizing every calculated tactic and method to prevail; specifically the news media in an effort to maintain dominance over black voters.

Trust me, the Democratic elite are in a political panic mode simply because of Herman Cain. He is heavily supported by Caucasian voting constituency around the nation. This is the worst nightmare the Democratic Party has ever encountered in the history of their inception because it negates their hundreds of years of singing that same old broken record Republicans are racist against all Africans and are campaigning to remove Obama from office because he is black. Most African Americans are so damn politically dysfunctional inept and incompetent in regards to chronological events in regards to American history. President Obama would never have had the opportunity to vote if it were not for the Republican Party. After over seventy five years, it is a very distinct possibility the Democratic Party chickens are coming home to roost with taking African Americans vote for granted because to lose thirty or forty percent of the black vote spells doom.

Let's evaluate the circumstances. Most blacks would never vote Republican. However, they will do as older whites did during the election in two thousand eight; sit on their couch at home. This would cause atrocious political problems for Democrats. Most blacks know absolutely nothing about the guidelines of our Constitution. They assumed when Obama became president he gwing to do supin fur us; taik sum dem rich white foks mony den giv to us. Most blacks throughout the nation were of that opinion. Remember the lady's comments heard around the world; that she would not have to pay for gas or rent any more. There were calls in to talk radio boasting about how its time for the white man to sit on the back of the bus. Many were calling in suggesting President Obama should fire House Speaker Boehner for not answering his phone when the president called. This is the gossip throughout the nation of many blacks; dat main aint dun nuttin fur us, all he dun is took cear of dem white foks. Trust me! This is another serious problem for Democrats. This is the reason why President Obama is constantly screaming if congress does not act, he will in an effort to appease the Democratic black constituency.

Trust me! The elites of the Democratic Party are desperate. They have reverted back to one of President Franklin Delano Roosevelt's tactics to institute herding in the ethnic blacks. All that is necessary is to elevate another affluent black, and most of the others will adjust to demands with a process of herding support. President Roosevelt utilized this tactic over seventy years ago; to eradicate northern blacks from the Republican Party who supported President Lincoln: philosophy of conservatism which he abolished slavery from the southern Democratic confederacy plantation owner's white supremacy terrorist groups who were maiming and lynching blacks on a daily basis. President Roosevelt authorized a special task force to travel to the northern states and evaluate how blacks cast their support for political candidates. They returned with a simple answer. They vote in a bloc and congregate behind other affluent blacks. Immediately President Roosevelt promoted two blacks; Benjamin C. Davis, a military colonel was promoted to general; and William Hastie, a dean at Howard University Law School was given the title Staff of War Secretary Stinson. The rest is history. Ninety five percent of blacks switched to the Democrat Party and have continued to assist in electing Democrats to political office for over seventy years who were maiming and butchering our southern ancestors by numerous intentions such as lynching, and outright murder by shooting. During nineteen thirty seven two blacks were blow torched to death in Duck Hill, Mississippi while an applauding crowd of clannish whites were engrossed.

This is the year of two thousand eleven. President Obama has demoralized our nation along with the Democratic Party. President Obama is determined to eradicate our Constitution and establish a monarch in America. I am going to elaborate on his contrived intention. The African American block vote is absolutely necessary so he and his regime are utilizing the old President Roosevelt tactic: advance in rank black elites and they have chosen the news media to accomplish this mission. The Reverend Al Sharpton has a one hour commentary and commercial on a major national television news outlet. It takes this man at least ten seconds to formulate appropriate verbiage. In his commercial he scoffs the Republican Party by insinuating when he was a kid residing in Brooklyn, he and his siblings would rush home, eat all the blueberry pies and lie about their disappearance; but berries would be around their faces and of course he equated the Republicans of being a facsimile of that similarity; generating deliberate lies. There are others. Just to name a few who are accomplishers in securing blacks to remain on the political plantation of the Democratic Party: Eugene Robinson, Jonathan Capehart, Marc Lemont Hill, Jehmu Greene, Tara Dowdell, Charles Rangel, Elijah Cummings, Maxine Waters, Shelia Jackson Lee and James Clyburn. There are hundreds, if not thousands, but these are the magnifiers who broadcast their opinions throughout America about political injustice pertaining to our two party system (Democrat and Republican) based on utterly brainwash and hearsay and incompetency. What is so damn pathetic is they are so politically dysfunctional and incompetent they have no idea of how they are being used for political vindictiveness in an effort to eradicate our Constitution of America based on bloc herding.

The United States of America is a diverse nation of immigrants. Africans are the only ethnic who did not migrate to America by choosing American for its exceptionalism in an effort to improve their standard of living. There is a huge difference in choosing to migrate and literally coercion transported from Africa without knowing where the hell you are. However, they were integrated on tobacco farms with other indentured servants. None of the other ethnics were familiar with African heritage traditions. It continued for approximately seventy two years. Prior to being sold into slavery, their philosophical African traditional qualities consisted of isolation from other ethnics. They were never interested in British Colony formal American traditions and this crusade continued for over two hundred years after being sold into servitude through the Democratic confederate southern states. They remain loyal to their African traditions. The southern plantation owners labeled them herders because they followed leaders like cattle.

It has been approximately three hundred ninety three years since Africans were brought to America and the herding stigmatization is still in existence today. Please, I am not requesting you believe my written analysis. I am offering explicit living proof in an effort you may come to your own conclusion.

During the nineteen thirties, President Franklin Delano Roosevelt learned through his research northern African Americans who could vote constantly voted Republican. He also learned they bloc voted and could be seduced through mollifying by the promotion of other blacks. I find it to be rather extraordinary and mysterious there are black educators and professional politicians; and no one has addressed the fundamental eccentrics pertaining to each political party; Democratic and Republican; particularly when each party was established during the eighteen twenties and each party has tremendous deviations.

Let's compare the two parties.

The southern confederate Democratic Party under the guidance of Nathan Bedford Forrest consolidated other terrorist white supremacist groups under the name Ku Klux Klan during eighteen sixty six in Pulaski, Tennessee. They slaughtered southern African Americans for ninety one years as if they were cattle at a stock yard until FBI director J. Edgar Hoover quelled the slaughter and integrated southern schools for southern blacks to attend during the nineteen fifties. Republican President Abraham Lincoln abolished southern Democratic servitude in eighteen sixty five. Republican President Ulysses S. Grant ordered federal troops into the southern states; arrested and indicted Democratic Ku Klux Klansmen in mid eighteen sixties to quell the lynching of blacks. Republican congress ratified the thirteenth, fourteenth and fifteenth amendments to the Constitution which gave all African Americans in the nation their civil and voting rights. Through the late eighteen sixties and seventies, thousands of black and white Republicans poured into the southern states in an effort to each former slaves to read and write. The southern Democratic Ku Klux Klan slaughtered over three hundred in one day; mostly blacks and drove them from the southern states. They continued lynching blacks and a few years later the southern Democratic Ku Klux Klan implemented the Jim Crow Rule (separate but equal) and continued lynching blacks and forced them to sit in the back of public transportation for approximately seventy years until nineteen sixty four and five.

Most blacks have never been qualified to think in depth; to critique pertinent issues in an effort to determine consequences in regards to clarification. Most normally form opinions on hearsay and skin color. I own a business and I was listening to a conversation between two men concerning the recent baseball world series. One guy asked the other did his team win? His answer was; not really. He stated; he had been a St. Louis Cardinal fan most of his life. The other guy said, well your team won. He stated he was pulling for the Texas Rangers because they had a black manager. This was not an isolated incident. The majority of African Americans have this identical philosophical distinguishing quality and it is inevitable and eternal. This is equivalent to a contagious disease along with illiteracy and incompetency that has prohibited most blacks from becoming versed on the etiology of their density related to the United States of America.

For hundreds of years Africans, blacks, and African Americans have constantly attempted to establish a Kenya in America; separate from other ethnics to no avail. Being a native of Alabama, I was taught as a child before you begin to judge other ethnics, concentrate on the philosophical traits of yourself and others of your ethnic. For over sixty years I have and it has not been a pleasant ordeal. Most blacks can graduate from universities such as Yale, Harvard, Princeton, Cornell and others. Unfortunately, most are stigmatized with philosophical traits of dysfunctional density and incompetency. These distinguishing qualities are applicable to other ethnics, but most prevalent in African Americans because of our genetic heritage from Africa: having unique deficiencies of herding based on hearsay and assumptions passed on from three hundred forty five years of disavowal to attain appropriate integrated intellectual moral values through challenge of detail substantive dialogue with other ethnics. It is terribly unfortunate; dysfunctional, inept and incompetent that most African Americans have never deciphered the difference pertaining to numerous ethnical philosophical distinguishing qualities. Most blacks think monolith, all Caucasians are of the identical philosophical ideology unless day gwing to gimme suptin.

All African American's ancestry began in Africa. They have clung to their African heritage traditions by isolation from other ethnics. Violence has been detrimental to blacks since inception during sixteen seventy six. They chose to overthrow the government authorities in Western Virginia. They burned the colonial capital to the ground. The governor almost lost his life. This was typical black illiterate, incompetent insanity. They were going to appropriate American lands in Virginia and could not read or write. Most southern Democratic confederacy whites had terrible supremacy characteristic attitudes. Many were equivalent to blacks in regard to illiteracy.

During grade school in Alabama, my uncles were my mentors. They were farmers and extremely talented in other methods, having God given talents through the brain cells; such as a gunsmith, barber, oak split basket making, watch and clock repair, all farm equipment repair, carpentry. Ben, the basket maker, was on the cover of Life Magazine during the early eighties for his talented basket making. If you broke it they would repair it. As a kid I noticed they had a rather unusual distinguishing quality; they would get angry and fire weapons from behind trees at each other. Of course no one was every harmed. I often wondered why, because they were such wonderful people. These incidents set me off on a mission. In an effort to determine the reason for this dense activity, I recalled what Mr. Cooper, the store owner, had advised me of: first figure out and concentrate on who you are, then your ethnic and other ethnic people and compare in an effort to determine intellectual moral values based on technical category because intellectual moral values are the standard guidelines for all mankind.

I began my covert analogy research over sixty years ago. Truly, truly, one of the most remarkable adventures of my life because you venture into the brain cells that control and dictate every reflex pertaining to genetic heritage, philosophical traits embedded within the human body. Most people are totally unaware God created mankind with identical structured organs. It is genetic heritage which deviate behavioral occurrences. To clarify my theory: a woman can have three children by different fathers. Each of these children will have a split personality to correspond with each father's genetic controllability; along with the mother's traits. Let's evaluate the possible circumstances. The father of one is a gambler; the other two fathers consist of an alcoholic and a drug addict. It is a very distinct possibility she has delivered these three facsimiles later in life. It is also applicable to illiteracy. If each parent is illiterate the child will have extreme difficulty comprehending; through American history ethnics have been plagued with these deficiencies. Unfortunately, African Americans have suffered tremendously; more than any other ethnic. They are entitled with most incarcerated; most children born out of wedlock; most carriers of contagion diseases. These occurrences were programmed by the southern Democratic Ku Klux Klan due to breeding, trading and selling slaves, which created prevalent incest among blacks. For instance; if an African woman had four children and they were sold separately; each carted off to plantations in different states; once they reached their destination their names were changed. Twenty years later there is no way they could determine if they were sister and brother. After Republican President Lincoln abolished slavery, blacks began attempting to locate relatives. Trust me! The power of your God given brain cells will attract close relatives who have never seen each other before. They haven't the slightest idea why they are attracted to each other; so many blacks latched onto their sisters and brothers as lovers.

I recall very vividly, during the mid-forties in Alabama, young black women would leave the south for the bright lights of Chicago, Detroit, New York, Philadelphia and other large cities. Over time they would get connected with pimps and drug dealers; have four or five children by different fathers and send them back to Alabama for their grandparents to raise and care for. These occurrences have occurred for hundreds of years pertaining to all ethnics. However, unfortunately, it has dominated the African American race which has victimized and destroyed the generalities of conformance to attain the necessary capability to decipher the culprits who initially dispersed these atrocities on southern African Americans.

This is the year two thousand eleven. There is some dysfunctional idiot on national television with a brain compatible to an opossum. Meaning six hounds can be chasing him and there is a fifty foot oak tree alongside a corn stalk. The opossum will choose the corn stalk to climb. This individual, with a brain replica to an opossum, is literally destroying the American English; berating Republicans with such verbiage as: us combd fum schul an et toll blue bry pi dem brys wus al ovr us fase, dat dem republikns lyes. This individual, and others, have carried this malice incompetent demagoguery to the brink of disaster for most African Americans who reside in the United States of America. This is nothing more than inappropriate, incompetent forced indoctrination which has thrust most African Americans into poverty and destitution for an eternity. Most of these political black narcissistic alimentary canal sucks for the Democratic Party are incapable of deciphering the fundamental standards America was established on. Most have no idea the title and capacity of George Washington or Abraham Lincoln attained for our nation; nor knowledge of their ancestry such as grandfather, great great grandfathers and mothers. Many have no idea who their father is. However, they know one thing; us got to stick togather fur us Democrat.

In essence, this book is not written to berate African Americans; it is to offer a discrete explanation to where they came from and their introduction to America and their refusal to accept American cultural traditions. As an alternative, they remain loyal to their African Congo genetic heritage ideology which created extreme difficulty for other ethnics residing in Virginia. During sixteen seventy six, they herded together and attempted to appropriate the lands of Western Virginia. Fifteen years later, duing sixteen ninety one, South Carolina deemed it was impossible for Africans to conform in regards to American fundamental traditions. They formulated codes and presented them to the British Island Colony to sell Africans into slavery. Those were our late ancestors who were isolated exclusively from the integrated outside communicative structure of other ethnics; especially in the southern states to include the Democratic Ku Klux Klan (separate but equal) Jim Crow Rule for approximately three hundred forty six years. It is highly impossible to be isolated form other ethnics for a period of time minas education and be competitive in an intellectual moral civil society of other ethnics.

This is the year two thousand eleven. These are the philosophical genetic traits most African Americans are embedded with which cause dense dysfunctional, illiterate incompetency. It is emphatically ratified by the current President Barack Hussein Obama and his Attorney General Eric Holder when they literally forced law enforcement institutions to reduce their testing scores in an effort for African Americans to succeed. Unfortunately, this has been a constant problem for most blacks eternally. However, the necessity to clarify is warranted pertaining to the existing circumstances. There are hundreds of thousands of brilliant minded intellectual African Americans prevalent over America in numerous professional positions. Fortunately, by listening and adhering to the standards Caucasians have utilized and improving on their individual philosophical special qualities to attain prosperity based on American exceptionalism. There are large segments of African Americans who have attained the pinnacle of success. Unfortunately, they are overwhelmed with the embedded genetic ancestry heritage of illiterate, incompetency density and are in denial; or too damn stupid to realize it was their persistent talent which enhanced their stability by communicating with other ethnics to attain appropriate guidance. Yet, they will exploit their success by deliberately force indoctrinating other less fortunate blacks into thinking it is those racist Caucasians; especially Republicans who are responsible for your destitution because you are black.

My writings constantly refer to dysfunctional, density, illiterate and incompetency. These are absurdities most commonly used by affluent African Americans that is a replica of all these nomenclatures combined. These are segments of wealthy blacks prevalent throughout America that are constantly complaining about equality based on racism. There are numerous times they herd on national television having titles in miscellaneous professions such as: law enforcement chiefs, law professors, private sector attorneys, physicians, private business owners, movie actors, chief executive officers of companies; just to name a few. Unfortunately, no one has exposed this dysfunctional, inept hypocrisy because if whites were determined to demoralize African Americans to prohibit their success, how in hell could they have attained prosperity unless they were white once and their color changed to black? This charade is nothing more than an illusionary gimmick to compensate for illiterate incompetency utilizing racism in an attempt to deceive based on inadequacy passed on through heritage from generations of illiteracy.

Most African Americans are cunning improvisers to deceive based on false ingenuity in regards to hearsay. All other ethnics have and are migrating to America and are extremely proud to be integrated into American traditional culture. They utilize their foreign talents in an effort to understand and change to attain the philosophical principles of American philosophy and adhere to the standards in an effort to accomplish the American dream; owning and operating businesses throughout the United States of America. Most African Americans are just the unique opposite. They herd around behind a self-appointed black Congo ideologist leader dictating to them America should conform to their genetic traditional standards of herding socialistic propaganda: that wealthy people should share their wealth with them. The same ethnics who migrated to America utilized their talents and worked their ass off to own businesses; particularly within congregated black neighborhoods over the nation. They constantly complain; dem Arabs don took us neighborhood over.

Unfortunately, most ethnics have never realized lackadaisical and the inability embedded within the philosophical genetic heritage culture of most African Americans which is an extended trait from Africa. No one had any kind of personal responsibility pertaining to curriculum or work ethics; but dance for the tribal controlling chief. Once transported to America, the southern Democratic Ku Klux Klan subjected them to identical criteria for approximately three hundred forty six years on southern plantations. If people distort reality minas research then obviously they are a psychopathic incompetent idiot; black or white.

On December 2, 2011, I watched a television segment on MSNBC. Alex Wagner; it caught my attention because they were discussing Newt Gingrich and his comments about authentic validity pertaining to existing and past circumstances occurring in the United States of America in regards to certain secluded ecological communities. There are thousands of babies being born throughout America out of wedlock. Many young women have five to six baby by different fathers; many are illiterate. I resided in Chicago for approximately thirty years and was a witness to these occurrences. There were high-rise project buildings on south and west sides of Chicago fourteen to sixteen stories high with women twenty to thirty years old stacked in those apartments like sardines; illiterate and having babies. As Newt Gingrich stated: most of these children have no chance to facilitate an economical productive life because of their hostile stagnate environment. Their living conditions are ten times worse than southern Democratic plantation slavery. At least there was fresh air, food and a free place to live for their labor. Unfortunately, these children are born with the jail house key in their diapers. There was this small, dysfunctional brain, inept, incompetent black on now, Alex Wagner; claiming what Newt Gingrich stated was offensive and the only reason this dense idiotic black slave driver and others such; as the blueberry pie eaters and on their faces; especially because President Barack Hussein Obama has politically self-destructed and demoralized the Democratic Party.

Trust me! The Democratic elites are in a panic mode in an effort to stabilize the black herding loyalists to maintain their status quo in an attempt to re-elect Obama for a second term as president. Unfortunately, most African Americans are so engrossed in herding exclusively among themselves; sharing narcissistic rumor assumptions; they know absolutely nothing about the philosophical traits of other ethnics other than day keppin us down cos us is black.

Trust me! I have realistically studied and experienced the distinguishing quality of miscellaneous ethnics for over sixty years; particularly African Americans. Most have a unique persona of blame. Many have never accomplished any task during their entire life due to dense illiterate incompetency pronounced through genetic heritage from Africa and forced denial of education pertaining to morality established by the southern Democratic Ku Klux Klan bureaucracy for extended generations. Let's not distort and demagogue reality; no ethnic on God's earth, if subjected to these chronological events, could adequately sustain equated competitiveness as a selected nomenclature or miscellaneous ethnics nationally. Most blacks utilize distorted dialogue in an effort to explain away these genetic deficiencies. Fortunately, we reside in the greatest nation on God's earth with an established Constitution guaranteeing individual ultimate choice related to all groups of people with common customs in an effort they may choose to attain their general purpose in life.

Unfortunately, most blacks have chosen not to adhere in regard to these dignified principles. As an alternative, most have chosen to mass congregate and be advised by self-appointed black Congo chief ideologists who dictate being equal to whites is more important than being dense, illiterate, dysfunctional and incompetent because it is the whites who are responsible for their Ghetto slum destitution. They are absolutely correct. White southern Democratic confederate Ku Klux Klan are who prevented blacks from schooling, slaughtered and lynched them as a fun pastime for approximately two hundred seventy five years. As of to date, there are those radical political, inept, dysfunctional, incompetent black imbeciles, alimentary canal suckers for the Democratic Party graciously applauding the eternal destruction of our ancestors.

I am going to apologize to my readers. Unfortunately, this stupidity had to be addressed. I was born in Alabama during President Roosevelt's regime. Discipline as a child was to accept moral values and have respect for all people; especially my parents which consisted of a mother and father united in wedlock; never touch anything, particularly food, without consent. I witnessed a commercial on MSNBC national television. There was some dysfunctional, small brain, incompetent idiot utilizing gross, inappropriate verbiage insinuating he grew up in a Ghetto. He only mentioned his mother and her associates baking blueberry pies. Apparently there was no father to speak of. He addressed the fact he and his siblings would arrive home from school while their mother was at work and gobble down the blueberry pies leaving remnants about their face and lie about what transpired and utilized that occurrence as a replica to demean Republicans as liars. Stop! Think about what he is advocating over the nation to school children, young adults and all ethnics; that his philosophical distinguishing qualities consist of devour and destroy what others have assembled, without appropriate consent, having no reproof repercussions. Unfortunately, this commercial illustrates his characteristic traits that have been detrimental to many people over the years; such as the Twana Brawley fiasco; the Duke Lacrosse debacle. But mostly to African Americans who have chosen to support his nonsensical lying, radical demagoguery; most are secluded in Ghetto slums based in every large city in America waiting approximately forty six years for his promises to materialize. They never will because these kinds of people are accommodated as current day plantation black slave drivers for the Democratic Party to secure and maintain block black votes for the Democratic Party as they have for over seventy five years.

CHAPTER 29

I am nearing the end of my written commentary pertaining to the validity of chronological events that transpired in our nation, the United States of America and utilize a segment of these writings to congratulate and honor a few transparent thinking wonderful Americans.

Beginning with former Secretary of State Ms. Condolleeze Rice; U. S. Representative in Congress Mr. Allen West; TV personality Mr. Charles Payne; former U. S. Representative Mr. J. C. Watts; commentator Mrs. Angela McGlowan; Tea Party commentator Mr. David Webb; commentator Mr. Ron Christie; political analysis Mr. Joe Watkins; political analysis Mrs. Deneen Borelli; analysis Mr. Niger Innis; president contender Mr. Herman Cain; commentator Mr. Larry Elder; TV news personality Judge Mrs. Jeanine Pirro; news reporter Mrs. Arthel Neville; news reporter Mr. Kelly Wright; news reporter Mrs. Lauren Green. Mrs. Harris Faulkner, in my opinion, has extraordinary news reporting abilities. She has synchronized a method utilizing speech and body expressions simultaneously that exemplify as if she were standing at the site of the occurrence. Phoniness based on ineptness or denial has and is a lucrative asset for millions of Americans which is inevitable and eternal that is contrived to deceive and indoctrinate others for personal prosperity. I utilize the names of these few competent transparent American individuals who have chosen to reject the herding stigmatization mentality of most African Americans. These are the segmented African Americans who have utilized their individual extensive philosophical views to define established American traditions guaranteed in compliance with our Constitution which are available to all ethnics who reside in America in an effort to continue modernizing stability based on philosophical choice of an agenda adhering to their ambitions.

Most African Americans were never taught these formalities and never conformed or accepted the diverse, complex, unique renditions of individual profound capitalistic exceptionalism American was established on which is a ratified destructive great misfortune for most African Americans. Unfortunately, most backs through hundreds of years of genetic heritage have consistently been seduced by self-appointed black Congo chief ideologists and many black ministers that the American Caucasians are desperately trying to keep them in destitution because they are black. This instigated demagoguery is an inept, outrageous, fundamental, misleading lie.

Let's evaluate and define the existing circumstances. Democratic southern plantation Ku Klux Klan slave owners discovered Africans catered and herded behind leaders the same as cattle and that is why they named their slaves the herd. This has been a stigmatization of blacks for approximately three hundred ninety three years since inception to America during sixteen nineteen.

The first herding fiasco was during sixteen seventy six when they chose to follow Nathaniel Bacon in an attempt to appropriate Western Virginia.

The second rebellion was staged during seventeen thirty nine to appropriate South Carolina with an African leader named Jemmy.

The third was during seventeen seventy five with an African leader named Titus who formed a band of black guerillas (over eight hundred) (their title was the King of England Soldiers) who terrorized plantations over fifty years.

The fourth was during eighteen hundred. Gabriel and his brothers Salomon and Martin, covertly planned to capture Governor James Monroe of Virginia and slaughter all whites in the city of Richmond. Fortunately their plot was foiled. Gabriel and his brothers, along with over twenty others, were convicted for conspiracy and hanged.

The fifth rebellion was staged during eighteen eleven by an African named Charles Deslondes. They formed a military brigade of over four to five hundred black terrorists and marched to New Orleans; beating drums, burning plantations and slaughtering whites. The state militia eradicated them, severed their heads and placed them on poles along the Mississippi River.

The sixth debacle occurred during the eighteen twenties orchestrated by a free black named Denmark Vesey. He seduced other blacks into thinking they were God's chosen people. He improvised a rebellious plot to appropriate South Carolina. Their plan was to attack the Charleston City arsenal; literally murdering all the guards; burn the city and slaughter all whites. His plot was revealed and thirty to forty of Vesey's lieutenants and Vesey were hanged for conspiring and planning a revolution in South Carolina. Their bodies were dissected by surgeons and displayed as a deterrent to other attempts.

During the eighteen twenties there was an African named David Walker who instigated and made it widely known: let slave owners come and beat us from our country America because America belongs to blacks not whites. He incited for blacks to immediately rise up and take action against all whites. He insisted us blacks hate all of you and intend to destroy you. This spearheaded the seventh revolting attack against southern whites.

Those were the most brutal, astounding rebellious appropriate revolutions in the history of America between black and white. Executed during eighteen thirty one, their revolting leader named Nat Turner, an illiterate religious fanatic from South Hampton County, Virginia insisted God had chosen him to be a profit to specifically eradicate white people. He had visions of black and whites in battle with blood accumulating in surrounding streams of water due to God choosing him to control America. In essence, the sign came from the skies when the sun blackened and the thunder boomed in the heavens he could see white people's blood on corn stalks. He and his herding black following commandoes initiated a brutal attack on southern whites; raiding plantations one after the other; killing whites at will. Nat Turner and his recruits disastrously defeated the first white militia; however reinforcements prevailed. This black militant's aggressive revolution to appropriate America alarmed the white southern population from many southern states and cities such as: Virginia, South Carolina, Georgia, New Orleans, North Carolina and others. When whites retaliated it was brutal. A killing black frenzy occurred. Many were burned and shot to death from Richmond all through South Hampton County. Killing every black they could locate. Murdering approximately one hundred fifty in one day and many were innocent.

Nat Turner went into hiding. They located him weeks later; tried and found him guilty. His fate was death by hanging. Surgeons were brought in to dissect his body and purses were manufactured from his skin; trinkets from his bones. These African Americans who initially perpetrated these acts of violence to appropriate America are our late genetic heritage herding behind leaders ancestors. Most African Americans, for over three hundred ninety two years later, carry this genetic heritage controllability of not conforming to American traditions provided by our Constitution. Most are of the opinion they are God's chosen people and will control the earth one day.

I am a fixed in place believer time will revise change and chronological events in past history are repetitious. Unfortunately, most ethnics who reside in America; especially blacks; have no knowledge of American history other than distort and utilize fallacious, assumed demagoguery.

Let's equate political events which have occurred historically pertaining to past validation that is compatible to current revelations: year two thousand eleven that transpired during eighteen sixty six, one hundred forty five years ago. Democratic President Andrew Johnson, who succeeded Republican President Abraham Lincoln; President Johnson virulently opposed southern blacks having their civil rights. He demoralized and berated Republican candidates during their congressional election. He viciously attacked all programs Republicans had introduced to assist former slaves in their quest to become American citizens. The Republicans were successful in obtaining enough legislative seats to oppose President Johnson's denial of civil rights for all Americans; especially blacks. Their dedicated, strong will and persistence prevailed on July 9, 1868 when the Republican controlled congress ratified the fourteenth amendment to the Constitution which gave all southern blacks the honor of American citizenship and the right to choose candidates of their choice for political office. Unfortunately, once again, our nation is plagued with a despicable facsimile of that inhumane debacle which occurred one hundred forty five years ago: currently developing in Washington, under the current administration, under the guidance of Barack Hussein Obama as president. This is a replica of Democratic President Andrew Johnson during eighteen sixty six.

During the year two thousand ten, the Republicans seized control of the congressional house and increased their senate seats. They are being humiliated, berated and scorned on a daily basis because of their concern for America; this time not blacks, simply because political inept, stupid ass whites were carried away with enthusiasm over a black self-taught dialect of speaking appropriate English; which is contrived methodology to attract attention. Most people are totally unaware their brain cells prohibit simultaneous fixed attention on more than one subject or thing. Utilize yourself to test your ability: while speaking to someone on the telephone and someone in the room is speaking to get your attention, the brain gives only one choice: advise the individual on the phone you will call them back or tell the person in the room to hold on until you finish. This is the somber reason for the rate of accidents; while dialing or sending message over cell phones while driving. The heart and brain are the central controlling organs embedded in the human body. The heart supplies blood through the human body to the brain. The brain dictates all other reflexes and functions automatically. All individuals are accountable for it to supply nourishments such as food and water. The brain will allow reconciliations pertaining to speech dialect; meaning if one should choose to change their original genetic heritage speech dialect, the brain dictated from birth, it creates constant thinking to maintain the chosen dialect mannerism. The brain will not allow your changed choice dialect to be coordinated and mingle simultaneously with diction while addressing an audience with speeches. The citizens of America elected a president (Barack Hussein Obama) who has utilized this imposture composition to attain elite notoriety; realistically this is why he has to speak with a teleprompter.

I have studied and profiled numerous ethnics based on their philosophical distinguishing qualities for over sixty years. Never have I witnessed during certain intervals grey hair turn black unless the use of die is being applied. These acts of deceit exemplify dysfunctional, incompetency equivalent to a child sitting at the helm of the greatest nation on God's earth; playing child's games with the intentions of sabotaging and liquidating the standard traditions that have stabilized America for hundreds of years. This imposter president (Barack Hussein Obama) is a combined replica of the African Nat Turner of eighteen thirty one and President Andrew Johnson of eighteen sixty six, but worse. These two individuals were illiterate; this President Obama has assumed, because he attended Harvard, he has the wit and ingenuity to covertly carry out his pastor's wishes of God damn America and the rich controlling white men; their chickens are coming home to roost and that nine eleven was an indication.

Unfortunately, most African Americans are residing in a theological rendition and have refrained and evaded the validity of microcosm heritage America was founded on. Due to an obsession with herding behind self-appointed leaders to include most black ministers who influence their followers they are superior to whites because they are God's chosen people. The only reason they are not equal to the evil white man is because he have all the money. Our nation, America, was induced through indoctrination with a strategic covert philosophical agenda of ideology to change America to a replica of Africa by a scheming, slick talking imposter (Barack Hussein Obama) and Caucasians gulped down his alimentary canal waste like blueberry pie.

I summarized several attempts of black terrorists engaged in revolutions to eradicate the formalities of America due to herding behind black radical terrorist leaders. President Obama has intentions of emulating these philosophical agendas. The philosophical trait of herding has been detrimental and disastrous for the ethnic of most African Americans. Let's evaluate the existing circumstances. Obama is certain he is going to maintain black voting support because if there was a mule and plow waiting outside and a cotton sack inside the voting booth most blacks were advised if they voted for Barack Hussein Obama they are headed back to southern plantations. The only response you would get is: us is gwing to vot fur him becus he is one ove us, he is fur us, becus he is black lak us.

Unfortunately, most African Americans have a misconception pertaining to Caucasians; they are not obsessed and controlled by a genetic heritage of herding behind self-appointed leaders. In essence, they have utilized this heritage stigmatization to control blacks for hundreds of years. Most whites have an irresistible impulse to resolve technicalities based on their independent, intellect and a communicative diplomatic, competent dialogue with others in an effort to attain their philosophical agendas. Most African Americans are just the opposite; they rely on self-appointed black dictating leaders and their ministers to offer resolutions to their concerns and individual problems. This has been a devastating, destructive rendition of African genetic heritage that has created emphatic destitution for most blacks all over America and abroad.

There were amendments ratified to the U. S. Constitution by the controlled Republican Congress which authorized all southern blacks held in bondage be given their freedom from their owners; beginning with the thirteenth amendment December 6, 1865 that eradicated plantation slavery for blacks. The fourteenth amendment on February 3, 1870 authorized voting rights. The southern Democratic Ku Klux Klan was enraged with violent tactics against all southern plantation blacks. Most blacks had no other choice but to remain and work the plantations because of illiteracy. Many relocated to the northern states and crated Ghetto slums with a generosity of rats because on the plantations they had dogs and cats to consume their leftover food scraps. Living in cities they threw the scraps out a window to an alley. The major significance of a herding charade began during eighteen ninety six when the southern Democratic Ku Klux Klan chose to eradicate all civil and voting rights for southern plantation blacks throughout all southern states with the implementation of the Jim Crow Rule (separate but equal) through the U. S. Supreme Court ruling on the validity it was constitutional. They needed support from southern blacks to accomplish this agenda. They utilized the support of a prominent black named Booker T. Washington, the founder of Tuskegee Institute in Alabama. They convinced him to parade over the southern states; especially black populated areas, instructing blacks that separate but equal was inevitable and was in their best interest. Southern blacks applauded and herded behind Booker T. Washington with glee stipulating: he iss smatt he kno whut bes fur us, coss he is wun of us.

Their civil and voting rights were rescinded and southern blacks had to sit in the back of public transportation and enter through back doors, drink from separate public water fountains; and, technically recreated servitude for plantation blacks due to share cropping which they had to endure for sixty nine years. During this period of time, the Democratic established Ku Klux Klan slaughtered southern blacks as if they were cattle in a stockyard. They literally forced them from the Republican Party.

The next stigmatic herding blunder by most African Americans occurred during the early thirties under then President Franklin Delano Roosevelt's regime. He earned northern blacks could vote and herded behind prominent blacks and bloc voted in unison. During nineteen thirty six, for the first time in American history President Roosevelt chose a black man, Arthur Mitchell, a congressman from Illinois to address the Democratic convention. He congratulated the president for his social programs awarded to southern black farmers. The political indoctrinating extended further to stimulate African American herding for their bloc votes.

He also promoted Colonel Benjamin C. Davis, a military black to General and William Hastie to War Secretary Stimson. This was a political calculated strategic success based only on black genetic heritage of herding. Ninety five percent of the northern black voters switched their political party affiliations from Republican to Democratic. The Democrats founded the Ku Klux Klan during eighteen sixty six in Pulaski, Tennessee. They literally slaughtered our southern ancestors for approximately ninety one years by every possible cruel way possible such as during nineteen thirty seven in the town of Duck Hill, Mississippi. Two blacks were burned to death with blow torches while a crowd of insensitive people applauded.

Since the inception of Africans to America during sixteen nineteen, Democrats exclusively and some Republicans and other elite blacks have and are utilizing the genetic herding African instincts of most blacks to their advantage in regards to political agendas: the most significant being their seduction into applauding the implementation of the Democratic southern Jim Crow Rule (separate but equal) during eighteen ninety six. The most absurd political debacle occurred during the early nineteen thirties when northern blacks bloc voters chose to vacate the Republican Party and change to Democrats simply because President Roosevelt chose a black to speak at the Democratic Convention and promoted two other blacks. This was over seventy five years ago. Blacks are the only ethnic who reside in the United States of America to support one political party, the Democratic, constantly in all elections by a margin of approximately ninety eight percent. This assisted in their controlling congress for forty years. The election of Barack Hussein Obama, a black president, solidified the genetic African heritage tradition. Most all ethnics who reside in America, particularly blacks, are totally unfamiliar with African genetic cultural heritage. For thousands of years Africans are extremely narcissistic of themselves to attain demanding control of others. They also have a negative compassion for anyone based on consideration, other than to accomplish their philosophical agenda. Africa is a continent in the eastern hemisphere. It has a unique traditional heritage, dating back thousands of years. African kings authorized the raiding of internal jungle tribal villages; slaughtering their tribal chiefs; capturing their tribes and selling them into slavery for copper, gold and brass trinkets which became a global commodity.

In essence, we as African Americans are culturally embedded and carry this specific genetic heritage. In an effort to clarify my psychoanalysis: during eighteen seventy one, Republican President Ulysses S. Grant suspended the Writ of Habeas Corpus in southern states. He used federal troops to quell the violent lynching and slaughter of southern blacks by the Democratic Ku Klux Klan who emphatically predicted and stipulated all blacks were illiterate, stupid and incompetent and could never understand American politics. To comment on their prediction is extremely difficult for me. However, they were absolutely correct because during eighteen seventy one, ninety five percent of southern plantation blacks were illiterate. Unfortunately historically, African Americans constantly utilize accusations; the dominant reason for racist discrimination is because they are black. This is total fallacy, inept nonsense because the appropriate evidential validity is documented beginning during sixteen nineteen with the initial inception of Africans to the British Colonies in Virginia, America. They were integrated along with white indentured servants for seventy two years prior to being sold into servitude. The authentic validity for being auctioned off into slavery: they violently refused to conform and adhere to American codes of traditions and constantly segregated themselves from other ethnics and practiced their African genetic heritage of Congo ideology for approximately two hundred fifty years. The prime authentic reason why southern whites eagerly rebelled and denounced school integration was simply because they did not want their children exposed to Congo ideology voodooism. This is not something I researched. I am an example of personal experience. As I described in my writing earlier, I began grade school in Alabama during the early forties. It was an all-black faculty with approximately nine or ten teachers to include the principal. I was advised to enquire about the Constitution because I had no idea of the meaning. When I inquired about the definition from teachers the answer I was given was: whu bin tellin yu bout dat mes, dat is whit man mes, it aint fur us, al it do is kep us doun.

These philosophical sensibilities are embedded in African American culture based on genetic heritage. Most blacks are totally unaware of why they are plagued with dense incompetency pertaining to the fundamentals American was founded on and constantly utilizing racism as a standard solution to camouflage for incompetency. Most blacks constantly complain about racism for hundreds of years. God created humans with identical organ body structures. However, it is genetic heritage that determines philosophical distinguishing qualities. I have constantly analyzed my reactions to all circumstances over sixty years pertaining to personal involvement on all decided participations. If you understand who you are, you can tentatively analyze the philosophical traits of others. We, as humans, have millions of brain cells that determine our reactions through dialogue with others or self-consequences. Genetic heritage controllability determines reactions when individuals are concentrating on identical subjects. They are utilizing identical cells from each of their brain to resolve. What causes differences in opinions is genetic heritage based on intellectual moral values. These values are taught to a child by parents and improved on through self-quick and ready insight by adhering to established coded guidelines and utilizing edifications appropriate to your genetic skills to resolve simplistic and technical problematic individual involvements with diplomatic concepts pertaining to unique formalities that ethnics have. Most African Americans were never interested or allowed to indulge in these competitive formalities due to their adherence to African Congo ideology for hundreds of years. Unfortunately, some of these African traditions still exist today. Through genetic heritage, blacks have lost their ambitions to sharpen their spear to hunt monkeys, but the Congo chief herding process technically still exists in a unique disguise relative to the southern Democratic Ku Klux Klan tradition during slavery.

Let's establish the chain of command during slavery and equate it to modern day existence. During slavery the chain of command consists of the plantation owner, white plantation supervisors and chosen black slave drivers who reported to the supervisors. The slave driver's responsibility was to keep all plantation blacks herded together in an effort for them to adequately perform their chores. This, disguised, criteria is currently effective and more prevalent than ever. Fortunately, over time, Republican presidents, Republican controlled congresses and modern technology has eliminated southern Democratic Ku Klux Klan plantation chores. Unfortunately, most African Americans are still on the plantation supporting the Democratic regime with their ninety five percent bloc voting; herding behind self-appointed vote hustling black slave drivers.

Let's define the criteria and expose current day Democratic strategic specialty in maintaining their superiority over most African Americans for their political bloc voting traditional capacity. The Democrat Party has controlled blacks since inception during sixteen nineteen (three hundred ninety two years). Three hundred forty six of these years were for plantation slavery. They were literally forced to perform plantation chores until nineteen sixty four and five when their southern voting and civil rights were restored from the Jim Crow Rule (separate but equal). The southern plantation owners were highly disturbed and intolerant to the disposition of southern blacks. Fortunately, Republican President Dwight David Eisenhower had quelled Democratic Ku Klux Klan lynching of southern plantation blacks during nineteen fifty seven. So inevitability southern whites conceded to integration; but it was only a formality, because blacks continued to herd to themselves; equivalent to tribes in Africa. Many would not allow their children to attend schools with whites. I was there to witness this exercise and constantly returned after departure because my relatives remained in Alabama. John Essex High School was three hundred yards from where I was born. Our homestead land that my great grandfather purchased during eighteen eighty three is still there and was passed on to me through heritage. Prior to my mother's passing, I would visit annually and periodically now. I always visit the school and have a dialogue with the faculty and some of the attending students and older blacks in the area. I always inquire about segregation; most of the answers I get are: us don't bother dem and day don't bother us, us kep to us selvs and us tec us chulens to sty awy frum whit foks becus day all is alak. Unfortunately, this is the stigmatization aggregated blacks to be sold into slavery because they literally refused to conform to the philosophical standards established in America.

There has been minimum change with most African Americans. Due to this insane, inept distinguishing quality, the Democrat Party has utilized this herding process to their advantage only for their bloc herding votes to assist in maintaining political dominance in America. With the political self-destruction of President Barack Hussein Obama, he has demoralized the Democrat Party. The Democratic Party regime is struggling with passion to maintain political superiority over their political, alimentary, canal blowing, political inept, plantation block vote herding blacks. If they lose fifteen or twenty percent of the African American's who recover sanity and realize what is transpiring, the Democrat Party liberal spokesmen distorting, demagoguery asses are grass and the Republican's spokesmen are the lawn mowers.

Because Democrats are utilizing every political tactic possible to dupe and seduce blacks into cohering as usual for their votes; they have reverted back to the old President Franklin Delano Roosevelt political tactical scheme of catering to elite blacks and awarding lucrative promotions which caused most other herding, stupid blacks to assume this was a will of good intentions for the ethnic blacks; when it was only for their votes to support the Democratic superiority political power structure. This identical procedure is being utilized currently through most of the major news networks; especially MSNBC, being the authoritative magnetizing network. This is a replica of southern plantation slavery in regards to literally indoctrinating by utilizing political and history inept blacks as surrogates replicating political southern plantation slavery by utilizing stupid ass black slave drivers to get their message to the nation's Democratic Party black loyalists. They are begging, please remain with the Democratic Party although they founded the Ku Klux Klan that literally butchered, raped black women, and bred them as if they were animals, and sold blacks through auctions as they were personal property.

Chronological past events that have transpired is truly invaluable to the human race because it substantiates the validity of reality that will determine inappropriate, dysfunctional, illiterate and incompetency. Most African Americans I rightfully accredit with being the most political and historical dysfunctional, inept, incompetent ethnic on God's earth. There is circumstantial convictions illustrated on national television; however let's begin during eighteen sixty eight when the Democratic founded southern Ku Klux Klan literally murdered over three hundred Republicans in one day; mostly blacks, and forced the remaining who were illiterate and had no place to go to become Democrats. They have remained loyal Democrats for one hundred forty three years and never chose to research history to determine and decipher the distinguishability between the two political party system; Democrat and Republican which were established during the eighteen twenties, one hundred ninety one years ago.

It is terribly saddening a productive ethnic of black people can live in fictitious fantasy pertaining to transpiring events that occurred in the United States of America related to black heritage and never investigate the true validity of reality. Most blacks have and area living according to passed on assumed demagoguery that has denigrated their status currently in America to political indentured servants for the Democratic Party: based on their political self-destructive choice related to political, dysfunctional, incompetency; being incapable to distinguish the philosophical parameters of American history pertaining to genetic ancestry legacy and define the validity of reality to substantiate past events and relate to current political agendas. Or, how self-appointed black leaders still have most African Americans technically replicating picking cotton and slopping hogs by constantly surrendering their liberties to the Democrat Party's process; inevitably block herding with their votes and not being interested in the philosophical traits of the individual who is seeking political office. Most blacks are going to vote for them as long as they are Democrat. These insidious indulgent bloc voters exemplify illiterate, dysfunctional, incompetency based on herding behind elite self-appointed black leaders and many ministers.

Let's evaluate the validity of the circumstances. MSNBC has solicited more black slave drivers than any other national news network only to impress bloc voting blacks to continue supporting the Democratic Party because a black Republican, Herman Cain seeking to become president sent exploding shivers up their spine. They were of the opinion a few backs could stray away from their slobbering Democratic plantation and complicate the re-election of Barack Hussein Obama. In essence, the outreach to solidify Democratic black voters has reached a peak of ludicrous desperation when MSNBC, a national news network, awarded Al Sharpton and hour long talk show and commercial. This individual hasn't the ability to paraphrase an appropriate dialectal sentence in English. His commercial is relegated to the slum Ghetto establishment. I was born in Alabama during the thirties and I cannot recall any sane intellectual, moral valued individual who would openly exploit disrespect for their own mother on national television to the nation and the entire globe; implying when he was a youngster attending school in Brooklyn, New York his mother and her associates would bake blueberry pies. When they were at their place of employment, he and others would literally gobble down the pies and lie about the disappearance. Apparently there was no other adult around to chastise them, because any child who is taught moral obedience would never attempt such a savage, egregious act of disrespect; especially on their mother. Unfortunately, this is typical genetic heritage of Ghetto slums. This is the impact that has obliterated most blacks nationwide; no respect for others or themselves.

However, I must congratulate MSNBC because they are constantly recruiting black analysts along with their regular political black house indentured servants. I have to admit they are the supreme best because they have solicited blacks who have given names that correspond with a facsimile of what most blacks have practiced on Democrats for hundreds of years; blow their alimentary canals.

CHAPTER 30

I begin this chapter with God Please Bless America!!!!

As I begin this chapter it is December 25, 2011, Christmas Day. These writings are my legacy. The knowledge will be absorbed by many; especially designated inclusive pertaining to my immediate family.

As I sit in my home staring across open farm lands, concentrating on what a great nation America is and how we are blessed with having independent liberty, I contemplate my thoughts are of concern for my grandchildren and great grandchildren; will they have the same freedom of choice as my entire ancestry family has had? My great grandfather, Dowen Jones, was born during eighteen forty seven. As I have stated numerous times before, he trained himself to be a carpenter and built the first cotton gin in Marengo County, Alabama; purchased land during eighteen eighty three and recorded the deed in the court house of Linden, Alabama. #z/330.

America is the greatest nation on God's earth because my great grandfather, Dowen Jones, established that perception one hundred twenty eight years ago. Based on his ability of conformance to the principles of American exceptionalism and understand the necessary requirements and adhering to American codes and utilizing his philosophical traits to exceed. These are the distinguishing qualities most African Americans have never adhered to because of negativity; waiting for someone to advise and do something for them.

Then, along came this crafty imposter; Barack Hussein Obama. People dribble saliva over his alimentary canal because of how he trained himself to speak in delivering speeches is all that voted him into the white house. He is a narcissistic speaker along with a teleprompter. He is gloating over his making an ass out of most Americans with nothing more to offer than redundant speeches.

Trust me! Our nation is in peril because most blacks know absolutely nothing about the formalities of the Constitution. Most assumed once Obama became president he would be at liberty to exercise all authority. The voice heard around the globe, the lady at a service station stating she would not have to pay for gas anymore and her rent would be paid.

The people of our nation know absolutely nothing about this President Obama. I have studied the philosophical distinguishing qualities of humans for over sixty years; the moment he spoke I could analyze his thinking pertaining to agenda. If you do not fully understand something, then the element of surprise can be shocking. President Obama was caught completely by surprise during two thousand ten when the Republicans were voted in control of the House of Representatives; and he has not recovered. Most blacks are embedded with a dense genetic heritage when attempting to resolve complex issues. During the election of two thousand ten, Obama was forced inside a space capsule in regards to his planning on how to eradicate the Constitutional codes of America. At this time he has lifted off heading into space; totally frustrated.

Trust me! He does not understand the American people. He assumed all ethnics were a faction of herders equated to blacks. This president is so incompetent pertaining to people in general until it is pathetic. He is constantly harping about Republicans and it is Democrats lying camouflage in the weeds. Literally they can't go after him for fear of losing block herding black voters. The Democrats are totally aware of how he has demoralized their party; during Jim Crow Rule (separate but equal) they lynched blacks for less.

If African Americans cannot determine which party founded the Ku Klux Klan during eighteen sixty six, and literally slaughtered southern blacks (which was the Democrat Party they support with their bloc voting by a margin of ninety five percent); there is absolutely no way in hell they can determine the strategic implementation currently.

What most people do not understand about the political sphere of activity is: covertly Democrats and Republicans will unify. Example: during nineteen fifty seven, Republican President Dwight David Eisenhower created legislation for the first civil rights bill for southern blacks in over ninety years. Lyndon Baines Johnson was the majority senate leader and the bill was defeated because twelve Republicans decided with Democrats.

President Obama has a mental deficiency based on philosophical traits related to genetic heritage. Most African Americans have arrogated calculated expectations of what America should be and for hundreds of years have been trying to modify to their satisfaction claiming racism. Being politically inept to the Constitution, most blacks assumed when Obama became president he was God sent to take charge of America. Ravish Caucasians resources, distribute to them because they are being subjected to racism. Most whites have never understood the philosophical mind contemplating of most African Americans. Their idiosyncrasies pertaining to the fundamentals of reality are mythical distorted with extreme demagoguery.

Basically the elected President Obama is of the identical philosophical characteristic distinguishing quality. His intent is to sabotage the greatest nation on God's earth, the United States of America through developing skills to evade segments of the Constitution; utilizing executive orders in hopes of being re-elected because his initial strategic self-plotted scheme was delayed due to Republicans being elected in control of congressional representation. However, to be brief, his entire philosophical ideological concept is to eradicate our Constitution.

He has no compassion for America. All he does is travel about the nation utilizing phony charm in an effort to mesmerize young, political inept Caucasians because most blacks are going to support him if while he was giving a speech he stopped to light a crack pipe. The entire approximately three years he has been president, he has been grooming and seducing constituents for re-election in an effort to accomplish one thing; to rescind the liberties of American citizens as the southern Democrats illustrated during eighteen ninety six; revoking their civil and voting rights for sixty nine years.

President Obama's intentions are to divide the nation with incendiary remarks about the rich not paying their fair share; there have been rich people in the private sector and in politics beginning with our first president and his wealth: George Washington. This rich spectacle is nothing more than Congo ploy to incite white dysfunctional, political inept, idiots that can be smelled ten yards away. President Obama is attempting to get them to herd and bloc vote the same as most blacks; deliberately lying about spreading wealth.

I have literally personally accessed and evaluated the philosophical traits of numerous ethnics through either reporting to them, their reporting to me, or mutual dialogue pertaining to millions of substance subjects, for over sixty years covertly; dealing in business transactions, listening to their frustrations and their motives pertaining to millions of other situations and their intentions on how to effectively resolve in their best or worst interest.

The reason for this intensive study: we live every day of our lives communicating with numerous ethnics. As a society of diverse people, we must adhere to the philosophical standard guidelines pertaining to intellectual morality: compliance with the Declaration of Independence and the Constitution. President Abraham Lincoln abolished slavery based on those unique principles. He interceded into a Civil War with southern confederate Democrats because they did not believe in liberty and justice for all mankind, as the Declaration of Independence emphatically stipulates. This historic, unique, diplomatic, diplomacy martyr, President Lincoln, was eradicated because of his ideology and compassion for liberty pertaining to all people; especially blacks. Prior to his being assassinated, his intentions were to unite America in an effort that every ethnic could adjust and settle to the stipulated comprehending traditions embedded in American culture. That is the realistic reason why he chose to give southern plantation black slaves forty acres of southern Democratic plantation owner's land. He knew most plantation blacks were illiterate and with them owning their homeland could have changed their philosophical extensive view to educate themselves and their children and to also conform to American traditions instead of adhering to African culture.

Our nation has endured numerous tragedies. However none can be equated to current circumstances. We have had devious, cantankerous presidents who have made unscrupulous attempts to succeed with their philosophical agenda. But, not any have attempted to sabotage the diplomatic integrity of America catering to foreign nations. This current president, Barack Hussein Obama, can and will be a sudden great misfortune for our great nation if people keep slobbering over his self-trained, phony verbiage dialect. His intentions are to divide our nation with incendiary remarks about the rich not paying their fair share in taxes is nothing more than a Congo ploy to incite white political dysfunctional, inept idiots that can be smelled fifty yards away. His agenda is nothing more than deception in an effort to attain their voting constituency. This president is playing child's mental deficiency games with the greatest nation ever established on God's globe.

During my personal experience in formulating motives of numerous ethnics pertaining to past and current events for over sixty years, I came to the conclusion regards to this current president he utilized many years of his young life analyzing people; black and white; but mostly whites. According to the news media he was mostly reared by his Caucasian grandparents. In essence, he was persuaded by their perceptions and became a community organizer for blacks in Chicago. He was clever enough to combine the philosophical distinguishing qualities of each ethnic based on each ethnic's strengths and weaknesses in regards to manipulation, while constantly improving on his correlation simultaneous speech dialect and body motions. This is how he verbalized himself into the presidency. The initial speech at the Democratic convention was a lure, because if Jessie Jackson or Al Sharpton could speak fluent, appropriate English American would have had a black president years ago. This is why Jessie Jackson wanted to cut his balls off. In essence, to speak appropriate English with a charismatic dialect synchronized with eye contact and body motions with moral intellect is the road to stability in the United States of America eternally.

All ethnics would like to understand a method of detail message. Unfortunately, if you are speaking with an informal nonstandard vocabulary, they do not understand what the hell you are trying to convey. This has been a distinguishing quality, inferiority complex embedded in most African American's genetic heritage for hundreds of years; more stigmatic prevalent today than ever. Vocabulary diction can be corrected and improved, but most blacks are taught from children that to speak fluent appropriate English he or she is trying to be white. When they seek to become an employee of whites, speaking informal, nonstandard vocabulary and not accepted for employment they leave claiming racism. Day dun dis to us becuz us is blak.

Most African Americans are a stubborn ethnic who are adverse to change. Once a self-appointed leader or their minister dictates to them adherence, Jesus Christ could catapult from the heavens and could not change their gullible opinions. They are never at fault for anything, it is always someone else causing problems for them because they are black. To substantiate the validity of my claim; it is exercised and portrayed by none other than President Barack Hussein Obama and his Attorney General, Eric Holder. President Obama has accused and blamed the Republican Congress for impeding his progress in sabotaging and eradicating the Constitution of America. Attorney General Holder has given egregious and suspect of lying to congress under oath in regards to fast and furious his sincere claim is: congress is investigating and questioning him is because he and the president are black.

In essence, the year two thousand twelve is one of the most important election years in the history of America. It is to salvage our nation from becoming a replica of African Congo socialist ideology. If you watch or listen to any form of news, you can expect to be hazed with those old skits of the nineteen sixties with the Democratic Ku Klux Klan water hosing and maiming blacks; also, those old documentaries Dr. Martin Luther King marching for southern black's civil rights. And, of course, it never would have occurred if the southern Democratic Ku Klux Klan had not nullified civil rights for southern plantation blacks during eighteen ninety six with the Jim Crow Rule (separate but equal).

Please, never forget the Rev. Al Sharpton with his hour program televised on MSNBC along with his commercial, suggesting he and his siblings had no respect for their mother, because these are his remarks. His mother and her associates would bake blueberry pies prior to being off to their place of employment. Al and his siblings would return from school, gobble up the blueberry pies and lie about their disappearance.

Trust me! We, as sane Americans, are going to be plagued with this kind of insidious, inept, demagoguery over every news outlet available all year long portrayed by herding black political idiots. This is an old Democratic strategic ploy utilized for the control over blacks which began during slavery with their maintaining the southern plantations, herding behind chosen black slave drivers in an effort to produce major crops. The identical scenario is being implemented today in an effort to produce major black votes for the Democratic Party; herding behind black political slave drivers; particularly congregated being televised on MSNBC.

The elite Democratic regime is totally aware there is no problem with black voters herding behind President Obama with their constituency support. They are also aware blacks alone cannot elect a president; they absolutely need a large segment of white constituency. This is why we, as a nation, are going to witness and suffer through those old southern Democratic Ku Klux Klan documentaries of the sixties, advertising water hosing, dragging, maiming and arresting blacks with dogs barking.

Current day blacks, all over every news outlet, are screaming racism and what savage acts those were. Most are so damn politically dense, stupid, and inept they will never comprehend it was the Democratic Party and their established Ku Klux Klan most black constituents support today by a margin of ninety five percent, who committed all those barbaric atrocities against southern plantation blacks.

As of today, January 2, 2012, Democrats are attempting to use black political ignorance in an effort to re-elect Barack Hussein Obama as president by utilizing these old southern adventures over and over of blacks being tortured by the Democratic Ku Klux Klan; the late Governor of Alabama, George C. Wallace repenting for his racist activities; and elite blacks over every network available, screaming and yelling like schools of catfish (all mouth and no brains) that it is white racism in America against blacks; that is the only reason they are not equal to whites.

Trust me! This is a Democrat Caucasian political regime staged scenario in an effort to maintain black loyalty to the Democratic Party. Most blacks are totally inept to this agenda. For instance: Rev. Al Sharpton was given an hour long television talk show and commercial. This entire episode of political bias distortion is based on Democratic philosophical agendas in an effort to seduce a segment of Caucasians into thinking they are being racist against blacks; should feel guilty; have compassion for blacks; vote to re-elect this mental deficiency, socialistic, imposter of a president Obama.

This vindictive president has intentions of sabotaging America in an effort to distribute the rich white people's wealth; as his pastor for twenty years and his tutor insinuated; the rich white men control America. This is why I label him as being mentally deficient pertaining to the American people; especially whites. He created one of the most devastating errors of his entire political, professional career by underestimating the mental thinking capacity of the American people; especially Caucasians. He has equated the distinguishing qualities of blacks as being equivalent to most other ethnics in determining, grasping and adhering to the fundamental codes America was established on.

Most African American's mental philosophical distinguishing qualities are infiltrated with a servitude mentality and have assumed President Obama was going to be their modern day Robin Hood. Most blacks have a prefix genetic heritage from Africa that has consistently exemplified their philosophical traits throughout slavery which is being concurred and adhered to currently because of their constantly complaining about the rich whites. When are they going to do something to help the poor blacks instead of constantly helping other rich whites? These are minds of thinking capacities that are equivalent to the initial twenty Africans brought to Virginia, America.

Most African Americans have never understood the United States of America consists of exceptionalism and a capitalistic society of ethnics who migrated to America and utilized these traditional standards to their advantage in an effort to attain their wealth. Most African Americans have never chosen to acknowledge or adhere to these standards due to their irresistible impulse to convert the United States of America into a replica of African cultural traditions of herding behind a Congo tribal chief; which most blacks in America assumed President Obama would accomplish.

Trust me! I have fixed my attention for over sixty years. I am of the opinion there is going to be one hellish disappointing experience during November of two thousand twelve for most blacks who reside in America. Simply because most chose not to adhere and accept the dignified appropriate constitutional codes that were established; to offer all ethnics equality based on individual choice in regards to their qualifications and ability to perform based on intellectual moral values.

The United States of America is a unique, dynamic, sophisticated, diverse nation. Most blacks have never engaged in the philosophical necessary obligatory standards in an effort to improve. Their cynical demagogic topic has been; day wont do nuttin fur us coz us is black.

CHAPTER 31

On January 2, 2012, late during the night, I was constipated. I awoke early morning January 4, 2012 thinking of a laxative. I tuned my television to C-SPAN Washington Journal, six o'clock a. m. Their subject was: Romney wins Iowa caucuses. I listened to portions of their calls. Several blacks called in and I did not need a laxative any more. My stomach began to growl and I had to rush to the toilet. Their topic did not address the subject. They called to give expression about their same old nonsensical political inept dysfunctional demagoguery about what the white man haven't did for them and should do because of slavery and how they built America for the white man and they are indebted to blacks. This is a philosophical genetic heritage distinguishing quality embedded in the basic traditions of most African Americans inherited from the tribes of Africa; being controlled and advised by a socialistic Congo tribal chief.

Many blacks are going to assume these remarks to be demoralizing pertaining to our African heritage, but God created these philosophical traits embedded in Africans, which being African Americans, we inherited these distinguishing qualities through genetic controllability which is inevitable and eternal in regards to socialistic chieftain monarch propaganda. This is being instigated by certain elite blacks in the United States. Currently the ambitions of most African Americans has always been to change America to their satisfaction in regards to being controlled by a monarch; opposed to *WE THE PEOPLE* politically electing official delegates in adherence to our Constitution.

Most elite blacks are constantly complaining and utilizing racism as an excuse to distort for dysfunctional density; but the emphatic validity is; most African Americans have never conformed to American philosophical constitutional established standards. As of to date, there are those (Nat Turner): surrogates such as: Carl Dix; along with Cornell West on national television January 5, 2012 C-SPAN (2). Their logo: race, inequality and student activism revolution; advocating the abolishment of our current capitalistic American standards along with our Constitution and replace with socialism; which is the philosophical, political agenda of President Barack Hussein Obama.

Africans began their initial wishful rampage of appropriation in Western Virginia during sixteen seventy six. They were soundly defeated by the Virginia militia for this dense dysfunctional revolution. All southern blacks were devastated by this tragedy because hundreds lost their lives. During sixteen ninety one, South Carolina authorized codes to sell blacks into slavery which placed southern blacks on southern plantations for two hundred seventy four years.

There are some repetitive comments pertaining to numerous occurrences. However, they are being utilized to extrapolate on different scenarios related to alternate subjects; such as: chronological events that occurred hundreds of years ago at different intervals that have revolved into current American society; particularly African Americans because of density related to the American system; also denial. Most haven't the necessary concept ability to accept and adjust to the fundaments of reality that has existed in America prior to our ancestor's handover from a hostile, uncivilized, illiterate Africana environment that had to be taught civilized activities by none other than American Caucasians.

Most blacks who reside in America who have attended institutions of higher learning are numerous and have reached their pinnacle of success in manufacturing enterprises, law enforcement, and many other enterprise entities throughout the United States of America. However, most elite blacks will never detail or reveal their emblematic protégé after they become young adults and become eligible to pursue gainful employment. The avoided, hidden, philosophical agenda of most blacks is never to discuss their Caucasian motivating mentors. It is simply because of their African embedded genetic heritage instincts to herd behind self-appointed black leaders and constantly lie on whites as being the racist culprits who are responsible for the destitute failure of other blacks.

The United States of America consists of ratified codes that are embedded in our Declaration of Independence and the Constitution. There are major, dire, drastic, consequences that can be determined and applied to any American or foreign individual for plotting and attempting a rebellious insurrection against America. John Brown was put to death on December 2, 1859 for such activities; also there are dire consequences for lying to judges, congress and the Supreme Court under oath. Political bias distortion is based on philosophical agendas to sabotage with malice after being chosen by a voting constituency to serve in their best interest.

Trust me! Most Caucasians do not herd; they strategically resolve problems on individual comprehension retaliation at the very next voting cycle outcome overwhelmingly. The year two thousand twelve is going to be the most unique important presidential election in the history of our great nation, the United States of America. Our Constitution entrusted the authority to *WE THE PEOPLE* to determine political elected officials particularly presidents; not monarchs. Unfortunately, this is exactly what occurred during two thousand eight with Barack Hussein Obama. His philosophical agenda is to become the supreme ruler of America. These distinguishing qualities are embedded in his genetic heritage because he is a direct descendent of Africa and heritage dictates the philosophical ideology of all humans. It is utterly impossible to utilize a jackass and develop a racehorse.

Most African Americans haven't the slightest idea of how their African genetic heritage has caused dire devastations and hindering in the United States of America based on self-destructive activities; accusing everyone but themselves for their illiterate, incompetent and dysfunctional failure; particularly Caucasians. This has been a continuous lying debacle since the inception of Africans to Western Virginia simply because of a genetic heritage herding process behind self-appointed black advisors. This is a facsimile of an African Congo tribal chief speaking Ebonics. Significantly, most blacks assume and equate other ethnics to their philosophical ideology because most do not know who they are, or where they came from; because most blacks in America over eighty years old haven't the slightest idea who their great grandfathers were. A large segment of all ages can't identify with their grandparents; which is quite obvious if one cannot identify with their genetic heritage ancestors they are living in a hypothetical fantasy universe; inept to the realistic circumstances that being an African American has absolutely nothing to do with intellectual, moral values. Without question, it is demeanor that determines functional or dysfunctional characterization relating to all races. There are ratified stabilizing constitutional standards that all ethnics residing in America should tolerate and endure for individual best interest.

In an effort to attain communicative, dignified benevolence with others this is a standard procedure that is a creative method to exchange opinions through appropriate English dialogue with all ethnics. In an effort to determine philosophical distinguishing qualities pertaining to particular ideology with the appropriate capabilities to decipher decisions or opinions given by others that solely depends on the ability to characterize based on merit and morality. These are the inevitable, established standards that are embedded within the system of American philosophy. Most African Americans have not and never will conform to these dignified, diverse, cohesive American principles because of their herding to the advice of self-appointed black leaders who have utilized divisive tactical methods of vile racism to reach their pinnacle; and to remain in their private black monarch compatible to an African Congo tribal chief. They rely on constant malicious, erroneous gossip in an effort to seduce blacks to remain on the Democratic Party plantation.

Most blacks are habitual complainers; constantly lying and distorting reality; and are constantly seeking circumstances that they are not qualified to perform. However, there are numerous of times they convince others they are capable. Once they are chosen for a position; and it is proven through their performance they are not qualified, or caught abusing their position; it is never their fault. These are some of their excuses: if caught stealing from their place of employment—racist remarks from whites that work there caused their behavior; and if removed from a position because of deficiency it occurred because they are black; the prime example talked himself in to becoming president of the greatest country on God's earth, Barack Hussein Obama, with his choice of attorney general: Eric Holder.

There has never been an explicit documental written pertaining to chronological events of Africans being brought to Virginia, America and their philosophical, genetic heritage, distinguishing qualities, being capable of relenting to American ratified customs initiated during sixteen nineteen. The stigmatic rebellious illusion still exists; they as an ethnic should control the economic process in America utilizing other ethnic's assets that are willing to comprehend and compromise intellectually and take advantage of lucrative opportunities while African blacks were engaged in slopping hogs and herding cattle on southern Democratic Ku

Klux Klan plantations adhering to and practicing their African heritage culture.

Now current society three hundred ninety three years later blacks are supposedly intellectually educated. Unfortunately, that small brain dysfunctional factor still exists that FBI Director J. Edgar Hoover accused blacks of having during nineteen fifty seven. Most blacks in current society are advocating give us the wagon reins. Years ago it was loaded with cotton; now times have changed us; ben to schul so u wlety ric white foks lodd yawl mony on wagon us gwing to driv dis country to what us bin trin to do fur hunded yers. Cheng dis cunty to sam as africur so us kan hudee to guather, danc and ete bobcu hog an chekin weng des us is hapi, cos us got evin wit u whit foks. This terminology could be misconstrued as derogatory, demagoguery; but I am a proud American with African heritage who has concentrated on the philosophical integrity of people in general. I am going to offer substantial validity to my authentic personal experienced expertise.

CHAPTER 32

The majority of ethnics residing in the United States of America are Caucasians. There is a segment who are inept to herding black philosophical agenda to change America to their standard of African socialism when they attempted to appropriate American lands in Western Virginia beginning in sixteen seventy six.

There were other deadly altercations after that. Three hundred thirty six years later there was a black president at the helm of America: Barack Hussein Obama. There is an all-out effort, with blacks herding behind him, to eradicate our Declaration of Independence and the Constitution and implement African socialism.

Let's deal with the authentic, explicit facts of reality. Prior to Obama being elected, his minister for twenty years, as reported, went publicly ballistic with rebellious statements; such as: God damn America being controlled by rich white folks; their chickens are coming home to roost; and, nine eleven was an indication.

After Obama won the presidential election, Mrs. Obama publically stipulated this was the first time she was proud of being an American; Carl Dix, along with Cornel West on national television, C-SPAN 2 on January 5, 2012, with their logo; race inequality and student activism, revolution, socialism.

The incomparable, narcissistic Rev. Al Sharpton, MSNBC television commercial: are we going to let them at the top take this country, or are we going to make this country work for everybody? This is a blatant instigation of socialism.

January 11, 2012: Hannity FOX news; Cornel West; the Republicans are not doing enough for our brown sisters and brothers; racism is holding black people back. This is one of the most recent incompetent small brain dysfunctional statements; because Cornel West is recognized as a Princeton University professor. Maybe if he would release his best guarded secret to his brown brothers and sisters on how he became a professor at Princeton it could very well nullify the accusation of racism holding his other brothers and sisters back.

These writings are to expose the elite black hypocrisy portrayed in the United States of America. There are successful, choice select groups of blacks all over America, and many chose to herd together and hold town hall meetings, and constantly distort reality to other less fortunate blacks with insinuations it is white racism that is holding blacks back. I have researched the philosophical, dignified distinguishing quality of people in general for over sixty years. I do not ever recall any elite blacks, or self-appointed black leaders holding town hall meetings to offer an explicit explanation on how they attained success to the general public.

Racism has been a free pass for most blacks for decades; especially those who attend institutions of higher learning. Unfortunately, density is an African American genetic heritage because of southern plantation Democratic Ku Klux Klan owners prohibiting schooling for slaves. Most of our ancestors in southern states were illiterate for three hundred forty six years. This genetic heritage of density is prevalent throughout all African American society currently.

There are segments of blacks not influenced by this philosophical genetic trait by having the common intellect not to herd and utilizing their God given brain power to over-ride dysfunctions and decipher the elements of moralistic reality. In essence, all ethnics are plagued with this dysfunctional disorder. Unfortunately, it has effected most blacks into oblivion because of their being held in servitude by southern Democratic plantation owners who prohibited association for common purpose with all other ethnics. Once communicative integration was awarded to blacks, particularly southern plantation blacks, it was utterly impossible for most blacks to decipher the contrasting philosophy of Caucasians because of the enormous difference in philosophical genetic heritage traits that dictate remarkable diplomatic comprehension related to association with the pursuit of economic engineering to attain certain goals in America.

Beginning from the bottom up; these proceedings were being composed by whites, while blacks were slopping hogs on southern Democratic plantations controlled by their Ku Klux Klan. Most blacks will never perceive the intellectual integrity persona of Caucasians and make the necessary appropriate regulative bonding simply because of herding behind self-appointed black bigots lying about racism. Racism is eternal, globally; but not to the degree in America that rebellious blacks constantly lie about for personal narcissistic enthusiasm in an effort to camouflage no skill dense incompetency by utilizing racism.

I am writing from living participant experience. I was born in the Alabama during the early thirties and am quite familiar with the Jim Crow Rule (separate but equal). I will take this testimony to my grave; whites couldn't give a damn about keeping blacks down.

During the Civil War, Sergeant William H. Carney was the first African American to receive the Medal of Honor during 1863. Booker T. Washington was the founder of Tuskegee Institute in Alabama during the eighteen nineties. Frederic Douglas was the most noted black author during eighteen forty five. Eli Whitney the inventor of the southern cotton gin, during eighteen fifteen. George Washington Carver, born eighteen sixty four, was a noted outstanding botanist and chemist. His remarkable discoveries assisted in stabilizing America.

America was established on individual intellectual talented skills. Most blacks have never had any; so they have chosen to utilize malice bigotry demagoguery as a parity to compensate for illiterate, dysfunctional incompetency.

The United States of America is a nation consisting of extraordinary talent; based on performance. Unfortunately, if you have no talent, you cannot perform. This was always conclusive circumstances with most blacks for hundreds of years; predicated to population explosion under the illustration of illiteracy and dysfunctional incompetency. Due to these circumstances of illiterate population explosion during sixteen ninety one; Africans were initially sold into slavery. The slave for sale code provided by South Carolina in an effort to reduce rebellious revolutions; particularly in Virginia, where they had burned the governor's state capital down in an effort to appropriate Western Virginia.

Chronological events of history are repetitious. Unfortunately three hundred twenty one years later with the election of the first black president, Barack Hussein Obama, and a population explosion of political inept, illiterate and dysfunctional, incompetent people black and white. During sixteen seventy six, a Caucasian named Nathaniel Bacon recruited illiterate blacks in an effort to revolutionize and appropriate Western Virginia.

The year is two thousand twelve and blacks are stimulating whites along with the endorsement of President Barack Hussein Obama once again to sabotage America to their satisfaction of socialism. It is prevalently smoldering nationwide with militant black and white activists herding together in an effort to appropriate their philosophical agenda in regards to eradicating our Constitution.

To name a few of these mentally unstable wishful thinkers: Cronel West, Carl Dix, Rev. Al Sharpton, Van Jones, Roland Martin, Russell Simmons, Jehmu Green, Ben Jealous, Tara Dowdell, Karen Finney, Eugene Robinson, Soledad Obrien, Marc Lemont Hill, Keith Olbermann, Ed Schultz, Lawrence Odonnell, Alan Colmes, Rachel Maddow, Chris Matthews, Cynthia Tucker, Dylan Ratigan, Joe Watkins, Jams Clyburn, Maxine Waters, John Lewis, Elijah Cummings, Michael Moore, Jonathan Capehart, Shelia Jackson Lee, Tamron Hall, Michael Eric Dyson, Carl Jeffers and Mary Anne Marsh. Lastly we have an elected president, Barack Hussein Obama who has characteristic principles theoretically that is in conjunction with their philosophical agenda; to deliberately eradicate the fundamental philosophical established standards they have utilized to attain their principle elaborate agendas.

I grew up on our farm my great grandfather purchased in eighteen eighty three in Marengo County, Alabama. As a youngster, being an only child, I was taught very early in an effort to sustain in life you must utilize your brain not brawn. As you care for the animals, constantly concentrate on their behavior patterns although they can't think. If humans would view their instincts, it would be beneficial to decipher.

I recall very vividly my Uncle Horace Jones built me a bird house. I sat and observed those black martin birds shared the house with wrens. It was a two story house with eight holes on each level; martins on the top level, wrens on the bottom. I watched these bird's pairs, male and female, work together from dawn to dusk building their nests to raise their young. Once the eggs hatched, male and female worked around the clock feeding them. Once they became eligible to fly, they were trained the philosophical traits of survival and the adults went about their business.

As a youngster I observed and patented the instinctive traits of many animals; horses, mules, goats, cattle, cats and dogs; plowed mules; chopped cotton; picked cotton; mucked horse stables. You can section any ten to fifteen male animals together on God's earth. They will never have sex with each other. I elaborate on these subjects because I learned at six years old animals are more intelligent than some people. For over sixty years

I have analyzed the motivations and the perceiving abilities of people in general.

Trust me! I would never trade these remarkable experiences under any circumstances simply because understanding people offers an explicit explanation as to the way the Constitution begins with: *WE THE PEOPLE*. It's quite obvious the founding fathers understood and related to people: that is why the United States of America and the people have the greatest democracy on God's earth.

There was a plaguing, horrific, disastrous devastation error put into place during two thousand eight with the election of Barack Hussein Obama as president of our great nation: the process of him being re-elected. Our nation is going to revert back to the southern Democratic Jim Crow Ku Klux Klan rule (separate but equal) during the sixties. The Democratic demagogic lying radicals are going to have a field day with their black slave driving Rottweiler if a Republican purchases a black pair of shoes; he is going to be labeled a racist. Most blacks who are citizens in America should be given a Medal of Honor for being the most political ignorant, stupid, inept, dysfunctional, illiterate and incompetent ethnic on God's earth.

It was the southern Democrats who initially sold black Africans into slavery; recommended and coded by South Carolina during sixteen ninety one. It was the southern Democrat plantation owners who held blacks in slavery until eighteen sixty five. It was the Republican controlled congress that ratified the thirteenth amendment to the Constitution on December 6, 1865 that abolished slavery. It was the Republican controlled congress that ratified the fourteenth amendment to the Constitution July 9, 1868 giving southern plantation blacks their civil and voting rights. It was the Republican controlled congress that ratified the fifteenth amendment to the Constitution February 3, 1870 specifically demanding the right of citizens of the United State to vote shall not be denied or abridged by the United States or by any state on account of race, color or previous conditions servitude.

It was the southern Democratic Ku Klux Klan that rescinded all three of these constitutional amendments during eighteen ninety six when the U. S. Supreme Court ruled the Jim Crow Rule (separate but equal) was constitutionally based on compatible assets which subjected southern plantation owned blacks to remain tentatively enslaved because being illiterate they had no other choice but share cropping and remain on southern plantations. This was the reason Dr. Martin Luther King's life was taken; because southern Democratic Ku Klux Klan guidelines denying southern plantation blacks their liberties.

During nineteen sixty four and five, the southern black plantation farmer's civil and voting rights were restored simply because Republican congress people rose to the occasion to over-ride Democratic Senator Robert Byrd's seventeen hour filibuster and restored civil and voting rights for southern plantation black sharecroppers. Republican President Richard R. Nixon authorized affirmative action.

It is utterly appalling and a disgrace to humanity that there are approximately thirty eight million ethnic blacks who reside in American citizenry and there are thousands who are supposedly intellectual in numerous professions of knowledge. Unfortunately, they are totally inept to the transformation that has occurred in America pertaining to our African heritage ancestors and what political party helped or hindered the progress of African Americans. The Democrat Party founded the Ku Klux Klan during eighteen sixty six in Pulaski, Tennessee. During the early fifties they were lynching and slaughtering southern blacks as a hobby. Republican President Dwight David Eisenhower authorized FBI Director J. Edgar Hoover to quell this disaster. He was successful.

Then President Eisenhower formulated the first civil and voting rights bill for southern black plantation workers in ninety years. He presented the bill to the Democratic controlled congress. It was rejected without their even reading the bill by none other than Senate Majority Leader Lyndon Baines Johnson.

It is a very distinct possibility some of my writings are redundant. However, if so, it is to clarify different scenarios. In essence, at this time I am going to elaborate on the unique solidarity embedded in the genetic heritage philosophical distinguishing quality of most African Americans. Beginning with: they are monolithic; are of the opinion all Caucasians are of the same characteristic distinguishing ideologue and label them all as being white and against blacks. This is the reason most blacks haven't the ability to differentiate between numerous ethnics who reside in America; such as Jewish, Italian, German, Spanish, Russian, Canadian, Irish, Australian, Danish, Swedish, Japanese, Chinese and Chilean; just to name a few.

Most African Americans have never given consideration to the established fact that all miscellaneous ethnics have philosophical traits of genetic heritage from their native homeland. Most blacks are of the opinion all ethnics who are not of their characteristic distinguishing qualities scorn them because they are black.

Ladies and gentlemen of our great nation, the United States of America, these writings are to offer an explicit philosophical chronological validity of events that have determined African Americans consequences in America. Our genetic heritage originated from Africa; mostly uncivilized with characteristic traits of distinctive narcissistic exclusive herding among themselves. When brought to America during sixteen nineteen, for seventy two years they chose to seclude from other ethnics. During sixteen ninety one South Carolina drafted codes to sell Africans into slavery based on that particularly instinctive monolithic trait. This was a trend practiced all through slavery and is currently prevalent throughout America pertaining to most blacks.

America is a nation consisting of competitive symbolic logic utilizing ideas in an effort to compete with other ethnics to attain and share individual knowledge in an effort to improve on intellectual moral values. Because of self-exclusiveness and slavery most blacks had and have absolutely nothing to present for acceptance. Currently, hundreds of years later, all they have to offer is infringement on others and constantly promote racism in an effort to compensate for dysfunctional, dense, inept, incompetency; lying tactic to convince others they are just as compatible to perform, but are denied because they are black.

Most blacks are enormous lying emulators. That vindictive black imposter, brain-washed the American people into electing him president of the greatest nation on God's earth, the United States of America. He is attempting to demoralize and sabotage to his philosophical ideologue of socialist agenda along with his inappropriate mental deficiencies excluding the American people. He never understood their philosophical principle of traits. As I have stated throughout my writings, I have concentrated on the philosophical tendencies of people for over sixty years. America has some of the greatest intellectual moral ethnics on God's earth to share and receive opinions. America became the greatest nation on earth because of this cohesive philosophy.

This is an election year. We must salvage, and maintain, these strategic established standards. There is going to be one of the most philosophical radical, distorting, demagogic all out accusations of racism in American history. There are strategic worked out actions to mobilize thousands of blacks over the United States of America; on radio, television, town hall meetings and churches; grinning like jackasses eating thorny briars; herding together like schools of catfish; all mouth and no brains; screaming racism against blacks. It is those old rich Republicans who are keeping us down. This is a planned covert carefully worked out Democratic agenda in an attempt to seduce political inept, dysfunctional, stupid whites to have sympathy for blacks and vote this devout radical Muslim socialist President Barack Hussein Obama back for re-election.

During eighteen seventy one, the southern Democratic Ku Klux Klan made an inherent prediction about blacks delving into politics. They accused blacks of being ignorant and incompetent people; attempting to rise above their natural place of servitude in society. I often thought about that remark as I observed the political future of many blacks over the years; most recently; presidential candidate Herman Cain. I came to the conclusion their accessed opinion was valid. The political involvement of blacks began in the southern states during eighteen sixty eight after the Republican congress ratified the fourteenth amendment to the Constitution. Prior to this no one had any ancestor heritage background. Most had no idea who their fathers were and certainly not their grandfathers.

In essence, being black and familiar with politics is an assumption. One hundred forty four years later it still is because this is what our nation has as president in Barack Hussein Obama; a great pretender with no intention of understanding the fundamentals of American standards and taking people for granted. He is chasing around the world utilizing the status of being an American president; gloating with self-satisfaction; hey mam look at me I am in charge; and is totally incompetent to the responsibilities the people elected him to perform. This is a genetic heritage that is standard with most blacks. Once they are advanced in rank, or an elected official, they are narcissistic; everything is about him or her, and not about the obligations they were chosen to fulfill.

There is an explicit explanation for this kind of overall mannerism. It originated from the tribes of Africa with the Congo chief being in control of his tribe; genetic heritage was transported to America during sixteen nineteen and adhered to all through slavery on the southern plantations when blacks were chose to be slave drivers over other blacks. They were extremely narcissistic and dominant. Numerous times they would maim other slaves; a genetic heritage currently in existence with most African Americans; it is inevitable and eternal; particularly if they are chosen for the guidance of Caucasians. When consequences prevail for their ill-advised ruthless incompetent behavior, their ready, devised ingenuity will be they are being reproofed or discharged because they are black. Our nation is going to be inundated with this kind of dense, dysfunctional, radical, demagoguery until November with small brain dysfunctional, liberal whites promoting and blacks claiming they are being targeted because they are black. This has already begun to be instigated by Attorney General Eric Holder; claiming he, and the president, are being alienated against because they are black.

In closing, I appeal to you, the American people; which our Constitution has given the responsibility to *WE THE PEOPLE*; to be held accountable for the outcome of our nation.

I am certain we shall prevail in attaining the standard liberty and dignity our founding fathers entrusted to the people to determine destiny for the greatest nation on God's earth, the United States of America.

I pray God continues to bless America and our way of life eternally.

www.ingramcontent.com/pod-product-compliance
Lightning Source LLC
Chambersburg PA
CBHW061348280526
45784CB00001B/186

* 9 7 8 1 4 6 6 9 2 9 0 3 6 *